JUST WAR
AGAINST TERROR

Books by Jean Bethke Elshtain

PUBLIC MAN, PRIVATE WOMAN:
WOMEN IN SOCIAL AND POLITICAL THOUGHT

EDITOR, *THE FAMILY IN POLITICAL THOUGHT*

MEDITATIONS ON MODERN POLITICAL THOUGHT

WOMEN AND WAR

CO-EDITOR, *WOMEN, MILITARISM, AND WAR*

EDITOR, *JUST WAR THEORY*

POWER TRIPS AND OTHER JOURNEYS

CO-AUTHOR, *BUT WAS IT JUST?:
REFLECTIONS ON THE PERSIAN GULF WAR*

DEMOCRACY ON TRIAL

CO-EDITOR, *POLITICS AND THE HUMAN BODY*

REAL POLITICS: AT THE CENTER OF EVERYDAY LIFE

AUGUSTINE AND THE LIMITS OF POLITICS

WHO ARE WE?: CRITICAL
REFLECTIONS, HOPEFUL POSSIBILITIES

NEW WINE AND OLD BOTTLES:
INTERNATIONAL POLITICS AND ETHICAL DISCOURSE

CO-AUTHOR, *RELIGION AND AMERICAN PUBLIC LIFE*

JANE ADDAMS AND THE DREAM OF AMERICAN DEMOCRACY

EDITOR, *THE JANE ADDAMS READER*

JUST WAR AGAINST TERROR

The Burden of American Power in a Violent World

JEAN BETHKE ELSHTAIN

BASIC BOOKS

A Member of the
Perseus Books Group

Copyright © 2003 by Jean Bethke Elshtain

Published by Basic Books,

A Member of the Perseus Books Group

Designed by Lisa Kreinbrink

Set in 11-point Garamond MT by the Perseus Books Group

Library of Congress Cataloging-in-Publication Data

Elshtain, Jean Bethke, 1941-

Just war against terror : the burden of American power in a violent world / Jean
Bethke Elshtain.

p.   cm.

Includes bibliographical references and index.

ISBN 0–465–01910–2 (alk. paper)

1. Terrorism—United States.   2. War on Terrorism, 2001- .   I. Title

HV6432.E427 2003

363.3'2—dc21

2002154549

03   04   05 / 10   9   8   7   6   5   4   3   2   1

Once again

for

JoAnn, Christopher, Bobby

It is essential to condemn what must be condemned, but swiftly and firmly. On the other hand, one should praise at length what still deserves to be praised. After all, that is why I am an artist, because even work that negates still affirms something and does homage to the wretched and magnificent life that is ours.

—ALBERT CAMUS, *RESISTANCE,
REBELLION, AND DEATH*

Now when victory goes to those who were fighting for the juster cause, can anyone doubt that the victory is a matter for rejoicing and the resulting peace is something to be desired?

—ST. AUGUSTINE, *THE CITY OF GOD*

. . . It is hard for those who live near a Bank
To doubt the security of their money.
It is hard for those who live near a Police Station
To believe in the triumph of violence.
Do you think that the Faith has conquered the World
And that Lions no longer need keepers? . . .

—T. S. ELIOT,
CHORUSES FROM "THE ROCK"

CONTENTS

ACKNOWLEDGMENTS

PORTIONS OF THIS MANUSCRIPT were sent to friends and acquaintances, some of whom responded with specific and detailed commentary and criticism. Because I do not wish to associate anyone else with my argument in whole or in part—they did not sign on to take the heat, as I did when I proposed writing this book—I am not going to single them out. But they know who they are, and I appreciate the criticism and the encouragement. Thanks also to my meticulous editor, Jo Ann Miller, and my agent, Glen Hartley. My family, by this time, looks upon the writing of books as routine, not exceptional, so the household flows on around the process. I doubt that this book is any better as a result, but it is certainly none the worse.

JUST WAR
AGAINST TERROR

INTRODUCTION

"Politics Is Not the Nursery"

IN ALBERT CAMUS'S NOVEL *The Plague,* an allegory on the coming of totalitarian terror, one of the protagonists comments acerbically on the naive reactions in a time of crisis of those he calls the "humanists," people who see themselves as living in a reasonable world in which everything is up for negotiation. They believe there is a utilitarian calculus by which to gauge all human purposes and actions. Walking down the streets of Oran (the city in which the novel is set), "humanists" may smash underfoot a rat carrying the plague bacillus but claim, "There are no rats in Oran." Why? *Because there cannot be.* That sort of thing does not happen anymore. In modernity, it simply must be the case that all human purposes and the means deployed to achieve them are open to adjudication and argument. Just get the aggrieved parties to really *talk* to one another, because that is the way *reasonable* people do things. The thinking of the "reasonable," Camus's narrator suggests, is dominated by their own internal preferences, rather than the concrete realities of the situation.

Camus's "humanists" are unwilling or unable to peer into the heart of darkness. They have banished the word *evil* from their vocabularies. Evil refers to something so unreasonable, after all! Therefore, it cannot really exist. Confronted by people who mean to kill them and to destroy their society, these well-meaning persons deny the enormity of what is going on.

To such arguments the late political theorist Hannah Arendt would have had a sharp retort. "Politics is not the nursery," she liked to say. Practicing a reasonableness based on the calculations of the "humanist" world of infinite negotiation and "logical" explanation is often of little use in helping us to face harsh evidence unfolding before our eyes. Moreover, naivete—including the conviction that horrific events are momentary setbacks and will surely be brought to heel by "reasonable" persons (who shrink from speaking of evil)—can get thousands of innocents killed.

Certain critical events in the past remind us of this mordant fact. Looking back on twentieth-century fascism, we do not wring our hands and blame everyone but the Nazis for their murderous policies. Of course, it is important for historians and political analysts to take account of the political, social, and economic milieu out of which National Socialism emerged. But the difficulty and desperation of post–World War I conditions—runaway inflation, a war-torn economy, and war reparations, all of which Germany faced—do not add up to the inevitability of the evil that was Nazism. To claim such is to set in motion an exculpatory strategy that, whether intentionally or inadvertently, rationalizes political pathology. The overriding truth and most salient fact of National Socialism is simply stated: A group of people took over state power, aimed to expand an Aryan Empire through ruthless force, and, as dictated by their ideology of biological racism, murdered whole categories of people not because of anything they had done but because of who they were.

Why, then, in the context of America's war against terrorism, do so many tick off a list of American "failures" or even insist that America brought the horrors of September 11, 2001, on herself? Let me be clear that I exempt from this mode of argument the ludicrous claims that have arisen since that day, such as the slander that Israel carried out the attacks after having first warned Jews who worked in New York's World Trade Center towers to stay home that day, or the preposterous charge that American officials, up to and including the president of the United States, engineered the attacks to bolster their popularity. This sort of inflammatory madness exists outside the boundary of political debate and festers instead in the fever swamps of conspiracy theory.

Conducted within the boundary of reasonable political debate, however, are those arguments that an international "war on poverty and despair," or a change in the direction of U.S. Middle Eastern policy, or a different U.S. policy toward Iraq will stay the hands of murderous terrorists in the future. Certainly these arguments deserve a hearing. Pushing more programs that deal with poverty and despair or rethinking American foreign policy, including our approach to Iraq, may have desirable outcomes. But no such change, either singly or together, will deter Osama bin Laden and those like him. To believe such is to plunge headfirst into the strategy of denial characteristic of the citizens of Oran in Camus's novel. We could do everything demanded of us by those who are critical of America, both inside and outside our boundaries, but Islamist fundamentalism and the threat it poses would not be deterred.

As do most contemporary commentators, I reserve the terms "Islamist fundamentalism" and "Islamicism" for those who believe in a literal understanding of the Qur'an and condemn all who disagree, Muslim and non-Muslim alike; who have hijacked Islam, in the view of many devout Muslims here and abroad, for their own intolerant purposes; who advocate militant theocracy; and who insist that there can be no distinction between civil law and the strict, fundamentalist Shari'a law, the ancient Islamic holy law.

When I claim that changes in our policies would not satisfy Islamists, the reason is quite basic: They loathe us because of who we are and what our society represents. Of course, these radicals indict specific U.S. actions, both now and in the past. For example, in his 1998 declaration of war against America, "Jihad Against Jews and Crusaders," Osama bin Laden denounces our occupation of the "lands of Islam . . . in the Arabian peninsula." However, we are also "pagans" in his eyes, finally and irrevocably, and that is why he calls "on every Muslim who believes in Allah and wishes to be rewarded to comply with Allah's order to kill the Americans and plunder their money wherever and whenever they find it."[1] We are so unused to such language that we have a hard time taking it at face value.

We had better get used to it, however, because bin Laden and his followers mean it when they call us "infidels." To Islamists, infidels are those who believe in separation of church and state. Infidels profess the wrong religion, or the wrong version of a religion, or no religion at all. Infidels believe in civic and personal freedom. Infidels educate women and give them a public presence and role. Infidels intermarry across lines of religion. Infidels believe that all people have human rights. Whatever else the United States might do on the world scene to allay the concerns of its opponents, it cannot repeal its founding constitutional principles, which condemn it in the eyes of such fundamentalists.

Osama bin Laden insists that the mere presence of infidels in the land of Saudi Arabia is a blight on the holiest of places for the Islamic faithful: Mecca and Medina. The United States could remove all military personnel from the Arabian Peninsula—something our Arab allies do not want us to do—but American civilians would still live and work there. Suppose we went a step further and violated our own norms of personal freedom by compelling all Americans, including those married to Saudis, to leave the Arabian Peninsula. Can anyone seriously believe that the radical Islamists would then be appeased? Their hatred of America runs much too deep to be assuaged by any such policy change.

There are those in the academy who respond with the charge of "essentialism" to my claim that we are hated because of who we are and what our society represents. To this I have two replies. First, in bin Laden's 1998 fatwa, he invoked the Prophet Muhammad: "I have been sent with the sword between my hands to ensure that no one but Allah is worshiped, Allah who put my livelihood under the shadow of my spear and who inflicts humiliation and scorn on those who disobey my orders."[2] Bin Laden's gloating about the deaths of three thousand people whose only crime was to go to work on September 11, 2001, is understandable as the vindication of a violent interpretation of a prophetic stance. Those killed were infidels and deserved to perish— hence his joy when both towers of the World Trade Center collapsed, for this represented maximum destruction of "the enemy."[3]

Every civilian death is a tragedy, but not every civilian death is a crime. The deaths on September 11 in New York City, Washington, D.C., and Pennsylvania were both tragic and criminal. Contrast the gleeful reaction of bin Laden and his cohorts to the collapse of the twin towers with the widely broadcast apologies of America's top military leaders, including, on occasion, the chairman of the Joint Chiefs of

Staff, for errant American bombs, whether in Afghanistan or else-where, and for any and all unintended civilian deaths. These military men understand that civilian deaths are to be avoided if at all possible and that each and every civilian death is an occasion for moral regret and a reexamination of strategy and tactics.

Second, to those who believe that if we change our policies the terror will cease, the answer is straightforward: We can change, through the political process, what we do and how we do it in the realm of domestic and foreign politics, but we cannot repeal our commitment to personal freedom. We cannot negate the First Amendment to the U.S. Constitu-tion, which guarantees the free exercise of religion—any religion. It is an official religion that radical Islamists want, and they would impose that official religion everywhere they can, through terror if necessary. Free people argue about the meaning of freedom, but they can do this only because freedom is part of the air they breathe. Those who despise our freedom as the mark of wickedness are not interested in our own ongoing debate about the good and ill uses of freedom. It is freedom it-self that they despise.

An irony of our post–September 11 world is that some icons of the popular culture whose perceptions many of our own moralists would disdain appear to understand full well what is at stake in this struggle—for example, Neil Young with his song "Let's Roll," or Bruce Springsteen with his haunting, elegiac songs on *The Rising*. Written in solidarity with America and in sympathy with the victims of 9/11, Paul McCartney's anthem "Freedom" appreciates that those who believe in freedom must sometimes "fight for the right to live in freedom."[4] This recognition from so many in popular culture adds piquancy to the disappointing words from many of our intellectuals, academics, and religious leaders: like Camus's "humanists," they fail to take the measure of the terrible and difficult threats our society faces.

In bin Laden's declaration of war against America, he disdains any distinction between Americans in uniform and those going about daily civilian life. His claim is that to "kill the Americans and their allies—civilians and military—is an individual duty for every Muslim who can do it in any country in which it is possible to do it, in order to liberate the al-Aqsa Mosque and the holy mosque [Mecca] from their grip, and in order for their armies to move out of all the lands of Islam, defeated and unable to threaten any Muslim." "God willing," he tells us, "America's end is near."[5]

To some, as I have already indicated, bin Laden's demands suggest that if America withdrew all Americans, civilian and military, from the Arabian Peninsula, terrorist attacks against us would cease. This possibility was put forth in a letter signed by 120 Saudi intellectuals and published in May 2002. It was written in response to a statement, "What We're Fighting For," of which I was one of the principal authors as well as one of sixty signatories. In their response, the Saudis argued not only that "there was a causative relationship . . . between American policy" and the terrorist attacks of September 11, but that only "if the United States sought to withdraw from the world outside its borders, and removed its hand from inflammatory issues" would Muslims "not be bothered whether or not it is a progressive, democratic, or secular nation."[6] In other words, if the United States becomes isolationist, then what the Saudis call "the Muslim world" (assuming that they, or bin Laden, speak for all Muslims everywhere) will stop being "bothered" by American freedom. If we do not withdraw, we are fair game.

This, of course, we cannot do. The fight against German fascism and Japanese militarism put us in the world to stay. With our great power comes an even greater responsibility. One of our ongoing responsibilities is to respond to the cries of the aggrieved. Victims of genocide, for example, have a reasonable expectation that powerful nations devoted to human rights will attempt to stay the hands of their murderers. We have sometimes responded to such legitimate cries for help in the past, but sadly, we have failed to respond as often as we might have. This wider understanding of America's role in the world, and of why we cannot withdraw from the world simply because the terrorists would have it so, is a necessary feature of any analysis of the war against terrorism.

The burden of the argument in the pages to follow is that we must and will fight—not in order to conquer any countries or to destroy peoples or religions, but to defend who we are and what we, at our best, represent. We are not obliged to defend everything we have done, or are doing, as a country. But we do bear an obligation to defend the ideal of free citizens in a polity whose ordering principles make civic freedom and the free exercise of religion available to all. Moreover, international civic peace vitally depends on America's ability to stay true to its own principles, for without American power and resolve, the international civic stability necessary to forestall the spread of terrorism can be neither attained nor sustained.

I wrote this book because I have been provoked by much of what has been written and said about terrorism and our response to it; because September 11, 2001, reminded me of what it means to be an American citizen; because I come from a small people, Volga Germans, who would have been murdered or exiled to the Soviet Union's farthest provinces by Joseph Stalin had they remained in Russia rather than making the wrenching journey to America in the waning years of the nineteenth century; because I am a woman who believes women must have scope to exercise their educated powers to the fullest; because I have grandchildren who deserve to grow up in a world of civic peace, as do all of the world's children; because I am a believer who believes that other believers have the same rights I do because we are all equal before God; because I also believe that with our rights come responsibilities, including the responsibility to reflect on the use of force and whether it can ever be used to promote justice; and because I share the commitment of my late friend, Christopher Lasch, to a robust culture of democratic argument.

As I pen these words, September 11 is a year behind us. By the time this book appears in print, the second anniversary of the attacks will be approaching and we may be embarked upon the perilous course of a war against Iraq in order to force a murderous regime to disarm. Other events may have crowded out our memories of that horrible day in 2001, and the waters may have started to close over. Some of us may be forgetting what it was really like. We shouldn't. It was just as bad as we remember it. Our emotions at the time were not extreme: They were appropriate to the horror. Anger remains an appropriate feeling.

Looking back, what I find remarkable is how few cries for vengeance one heard among the American people. Mostly there was sorrow and a desire for justice to be done. The critics who claim that America the cowboy nation immediately went on a rampage are proven wrong by the facts. America did no such thing. America waited and considered carefully what a measured response would be. As the war against terrorism continues, we should recall all those walls lined with handmade signs imploring, "Has anyone seen . . . ," and the people on television describing sons, daughters, mothers, fathers, sisters, brothers, children, grandchildren, fiancés, colleagues—the gallery of grief.

An image that crowds out many others in my mind is that of tens of thousands fleeing New York City by foot. As I watched and wept, I recalled something I had said many times in my classes on war: "Americans don't have living memories of what it means to flee a city in flames. Americans have not been horrified by refugees fleeing burning cities."

No more. Now we know.

1   WHAT HAPPENED
ON SEPTEMBER 11?

MANY RECALL A MEMORABLE line associated with Sergeant Joe Friday of the classic television series *Dragnet*. At some point in his interrogation of a witness or a suspect, the stony-faced Friday would stare the person in the eye and intone flatly: "Only the facts, ma'am," or, "Just give us the facts, sir." There is no substitute for the facts. If we get our descriptions of events wrong, our analyses and our ethics will be wrong too. The words we use and our evaluations of events are imbedded with important moral principles. Even though ethicists and moral philosophers engage in heated debate about this and related matters, most of us intuitively understand what is at stake. When Pope John Paul II described the attacks of September 11, 2001, as an "unspeakable horror," we nodded our heads: Yes, that seemed right.

Those attacks would have been an "unspeakable horror" whether they happened in New York City or Moscow or Tokyo or Delhi or Karachi or Riyadh. But they happened here, and we bear a special burden to pay attention and get the facts about them right. Our depiction of the event carries our moral evaluation of it. "Unspeakable horror" is not a neutral description of September 11. The pontiff's words convey the ghastly, almost unimaginable viciousness of the perpetrators and the miserable fruits of their labor.

By contrast, the ideological fanatic who sees the events of September 11 as a "glorious deed" begins by misdescribing what happened. His words aim to draw our attention away from the desperate office workers plunging like birds with broken wings to their deaths, trying to escape a more horrible death by fire or from buildings imploding and shattering thousands of human beings into minute bits of rubble and dust. The fanatic does not represent the innocent civilians as what they were on September 11: workers from more than eighty-six countries doing their jobs in the World Trade Center towers and at the Pentagon, four planeloads of businesspeople and retirees, children and grandparents, traveling coast to coast. Instead, he represents these civilians as "infidels" and delights in their destruction. He strips them of their status as noncombatants and denies them the protection against intentional targeting and assault afforded anyone of that status by the laws of war.

One description condemns an intentional attack using instruments of peaceful travel—commercial airliners—against buildings in which commerce was conducted and people worked to support their families, and the other revels in it. Labeling their victims—calling them "infidels," the Islamist term for non-Muslims or Muslims who do not share their hatred; "bacilli," a Nazi term for Jews; or "bourgeois reactionaries," a Communist term for any who opposed their violent revolution—is but one way in which some human beings strip others of their protected status as noncombatants or, even more radically, of their very humanness. Such rhetoric is endemic to terror that knows no limit and traffics in strategies of exculpation and denial. Islamist fanatics tell themselves that the infidel is a lower order of being and a menace, and they are doing a good deed by eliminating a threat to the purity of their faith and all the faithful.

How we describe the attack is closely related to how we speak about the attackers. How should we describe the hijackers? Were they martyrs to their faith, as some claim? A martyr is generally recognized as one who dies for his or her faith. Even if he kills himself in the process, however, *a person who murders is not a martyr but a murderer.* To glorify as martyrs those whose primary aim is to murder civilians because they deem the end glorious is to perpetuate a distorted view of the world. The *Oxford English*

Dictionary provides the original definition of a martyr as one who "voluntarily undergoes the penalty of death for refusing to renounce the Christian faith or any article of it." A martyr, it follows, is one who suffers death "in behalf of any religious or other belief or cause." Nowhere is a martyr defined as one who "tries to kill as many unarmed civilians as possible and, in the process, meets his or her own end."

Why should we accept a radical redefinition of an old and noble term? When we think of a martyr, we picture an unarmed individual who meets death bravely because he or she refuses to recant the faith. If we extend this idea of unearned suffering to encompass perpetrators of mass murder, we traffic in distortions of language that lead to contortions of moral meaning. Muslim scholars have pointed out that Islam looks upon suicide as an "unpardonable sin," not a glorious deed. As was true of the early Christians, an Islamic martyr is also a witness for the faith. But naming a martyr is the business of Allah, the scholar Amir Taheri reminds us, not of those "in pursuit of political goals. . . . Muslims who implicitly condone terror know they cannot smuggle a new concept into Islamic ethics." Taheri argues that "not a single reputable theologian anywhere" endorses the new trick word that has been added to the Islamic lexicon by those who are trying to get around restrictions against suicide bombing.[1] In other words, those who describe suicide bombers and other mass murderers as "martyrs" knowingly get the description wrong in order to justify and glorify what cannot be justified and should not be glorified.

POLITICS AND THE CAPACITY FOR JUDGMENT

In a talk at Columbia University in 1946, Albert Camus characterized the crisis "in human consciousness" that had been forced upon humanity by World War II. He illustrated that crisis through four vignettes, spare descriptions of events, one of which went like this:

> In Greece, after an action by the underground forces, a German officer is preparing to shoot three brothers he has taken as hostages. The old mother of the three begs for mercy and he consents to spare one of

her sons, but on the condition that she herself designate which one. When she is unable to decide, the soldiers get ready to fire. At last she chooses the eldest, because he has a family dependent on him, but by the same token she condemns the two other sons, as the German officer intends.[2]

In a story that displays with admirable economy an act of despicable cruelty, Camus locates us in the heart of darkness. This is not an abstract "discursive experience" that we can treat as something removed from the real world. No, this heart of darkness is an ever-present possibility.

Camus laid the responsibility for the crisis he described on the doorstep of an unchecked will to power. From an urge to dominate flows the notion that one can remake the world in precisely the way one wants, purging it of all that is undesirable in one's own eyes, cleansing it and reconstituting it. Camus forces us to look evil in the eye and not to deflect our gaze. Given his deep and abiding moral concerns, Camus would have resisted with all his might any description of this World War II event that would attempt to make the horror look good, or exemplary, or a fine day's work. He would have gone further and said that we *cannot* make such an event, a mother being forced to make so terrible a choice, look good.

There are those who disagree, claiming that no one can ever get it right because all of us all of the time are simply expressing our own subjective opinions when we claim to be stating the truth of the matter. It follows that John Paul II's "unspeakable horror" and Osama bin Laden's "glorious deed" are both descriptions of what happened on September 11. We just happen to agree with the former and to repudiate the latter. The pope and bin Laden are describing September 11 from their respective points of view, according to this argument, and there is no compelling way to distinguish between them, no ground of truth on which to stand in such matters.

Thus, the philosopher Richard Rorty, a leader of a dominant strain in contemporary thought that claims that our descriptions are arbitrary acts of self-justification, insists that one can describe the German officer in Camus's vignette in ways that make his brutal actions look not only acceptable but heroic. Rorty imagines that the German officer and his friends were college students before the war who had learned to "rise above slave morality" and to "outdo each other in scorn for the weak" and who shared "a concomitant contempt for everything stemming from Platonism and Christianity. Home on leave, the officer tells his friends the story of how he broke a Greek mother's heart. . . . His friends, hearing his story, are envious of the robustness of his moral stance. . . . They swear to themselves that, when they return to their posts, they will imitate the good example their friend has set." Everybody, Rorty continues, "tries to whip up a story according to which he or she did the right thing," and nobody "knowingly does evil" (a bit of truth derived, Rorty says, from Socrates, with whom he otherwise disagrees).[3]

Let's grant Rorty one of his points: Many people do try to "whip up" stories according to which they did the right thing. But surely we are obliged to call them on it when they do; otherwise, we are in a world in which nothing can be definitively distinguished from anything else. Let's take this one step further and ask: What are the implications when we say that Camus's description of that horrid event from World War II and the imagined postscript in which a German officer tells friends that he did a noble day's work are but two different descriptions of the same event?

This claim treats a Nazi fanatic and Albert Camus as equally reliable describers of the world. Each is self-interested, whipping up stories to make himself or a cause look good. It assumes further that we have no nonarbitrary way to distinguish between competing descriptions with their attendant evaluations. So which way of telling the story will prevail? Not the version that is most apt and least distorted, Rorty and his cohorts would argue, but the version told by whoever has the biggest guns or the most clout. There is no way to get the story right, for all of us arbitrarily pick and choose details as we see fit in order to make ourselves or our cause look good. The literary scholar and academic gadfly Stanley Fish illustrates this point nicely, if chillingly: "The moral vision of Hitler is a moral vision. We have to distinguish between moralities we approve and moralities we despise. A morality simply means that someone who has one has a world view in which certain kinds of outcomes are desired and certain kinds of strategies are necessary."[4]

As the legal scholar Stephen Carter put it in asking whether African Americans can blame "white racism" for everything that goes wrong in the black community, "a pile of garbage" lies at the end of this line of thinking:

We must never lose the capacity for judgment, especially the capacity to judge ourselves and our people. . . . Standards of morality matter no less than standards of excellence. There are black people who commit heinous crimes, and not all of them are driven by hunger and neglect. Not all of them turn to crime because they are victims of racist social policy. . . . To understand all may indeed be to forgive all, but no civilization can survive when the capacity for understanding is allowed to supersede the capacity for judgment. Otherwise, at the end of the line lies a pile of garbage: Hitler wasn't evil, just insane.[5]

The exculpatory strategy that Rorty suggests for the German officer and that Carter criticizes so sternly was taken to a preposterous extreme by Robert Fisk, a British journalist in Afghanistan who was badly beaten by an Afghan mob shouting "Infidel!" as they attacked him. He writes:

A small boy tried to grab my bag. Then another. Then someone punched me in the back. Then young men broke my glasses, began smashing stones into my face and head. I couldn't see for the blood pouring down my forehead and swamping my eyes. And even then, I understood. I couldn't blame them for what they were doing. In fact, if I were the Afghan refugees of Kila Abdullah, close to the Afghan-Pakistan border, I would have done just the same to Robert Fisk. Or any other Westerner I could find.[6]

The journalist Andrew Sullivan comments that there is a word for Fisk's casual claim: racism. For Fisk "believes that the color of a person's skin condemns him automatically and justifies violence against him," that his own skin color and ethnicity exonerated or at least nullified the responsibility of the mob who beat him up, leaving him smashed and bleeding. "Alleged victimization," Sullivan concludes, "sanctifies any evil perpetrated by the oppressed race."[7]

The important point here is that the cynical but very common notion that all of us arbitrarily describe events to our self-advantage and then decide which, if any, morality applies, is invalid. Not only is a moral evaluation imbedded in the description itself, but any description of an evil act as good is *false to the facts*. Think of how we would react to an attempt to make a death camp or a gulag look good. Telling it straight, on the other hand, evokes the horror. As the theologian Robin Lovin puts it:

> To say that a person or a state of affairs is morally good, to conclude that an action is the right thing to do, to identify a goal as better than the existing conditions—all these moral statements express our understanding that a particular constellation of facts links aspirations and limitations in that peculiarly satisfying way that wc call "good." *If we get the facts wrong, we will be wrong about the ethics, too;* for the reality to which moral realism refers is not a separate realm of moral ideas, independent of the facts. Moral realities are facts about the world, properties that we judge persons, actions, and situations to have precisely because they have identifiable factual characteristics that link up in appropriate ways with other sets of facts and possibilities. (emphasis mine)[8]

Let me offer one final example to clarify the moral nature of the factual world before we turn to the hotly contested question of what it means to call someone a terrorist. Imagine that a group of people have gathered to listen to a description of an event in which young children were tortured systematically by sadistic adults. The account is replete with details of the desperate pleas of the children and the imperious cruelty of their torturers. One listener, who believes there is no relationship between a descriptions of events and our evaluation of them, insists, when the speaker is finished, that he tell the group whether he is sympathetic to the plight of the children or to the actions of the torturers.

Does this demand make any sense? The speaker has already characterized the situation on the basis of those features that are most relevant. These include the details of the suffering of the children at the hands of torturers, and the listeners know from the simple recounting of what happened that these persons were remorseless, brutal, and sadistic. Imbedded in the description of events is a moral claim. A person devoid of a moral compass would have described the torture of the children in another, and wildly incorrect, way. Or, enchanted perhaps by the supposed arbitrariness of our descriptions, he would have said, "Of course, I don't want children to be tortured. But a sadist would describe this differently, so we can't go by my description." Again, would this caveat make sense? As in Rorty's imagined outcome to the tale of the Nazi forcing a mother to consign two of her sons to death, this narrator makes a sadist an interlocutor of equivalent moral weight. *Why would one do that?*

Our evaluations of what is going on depend on the testimony of others. We cannot be everywhere and see everything for ourselves. That is why a person's past deeds and characteristics, if we have knowledge of such, enter into our determination as to whether we find a description trustworthy. I am going to discount a good portion of what is said by a friend who specializes in hyperbole. I am going to discount everything said by an acquaintance who is an inveterate liar. Whose description of September 11 am I going to trust? That of a person who disdains any distinction between combatants and non-combatants and who believes Americans are infidels who deserve to be killed, or that of John Paul II, an ecumenist who has opened up a dialogue between Christianity and Islam and a near-pacifist who has often criticized U.S. military action? The pope calls September 11 an "unspeakable horror"—based on the facts of the case—and when I add to that description what I witnessed with my own eyes, heard with my own ears, and read in dozens of magazines and newspapers, here and abroad, an unspeakable horror it is.

THE CORROSIVE EFFECTS OF MISDESCRIPTION

Why belabor our attempts to get our description of September 11 right? These efforts are important for the simple reason that there are many among us who resist calling things by their right names and who systematically misdescribe moral and political reality in the interest of furthering an ideology. Ideology, by which I mean a totalizing and closed system that discounts or dismisses whatever does not "fit" within it, has very little use for accurate descriptions of what is going on.

For example, during the Cold War some commentators proclaimed a moral equivalence between the United States and the Soviet Union, based on wildly inaccurate characterizations of the two systems. This sentiment was not shared by the brave dissidents in the Soviet Union and the occupied satellite states of Central Europe. On my pre-1989 trips to the region, I was struck by the fact that none of the dissidents I spoke with had a problem with President Ronald Reagan's characterization of the Soviet Union as an "evil empire." Of course, they knew about America's racial problems and the debacle in Vietnam. They also knew that democratic protest against Jim Crow had led to the 1964 Civil Rights Act and a profoundly altered American social and political system. They knew that American political leaders had to take the language of rights seriously because that is the lingua franca of American political culture. Seeing that Americans had a way to put things right, these dissidents were astonished at the vitriol that visiting Americans frequently expressed about their own country.

In a 1985 essay, "Anatomy of a Reticence," Václav Havel, the Czech dissident, playwright, and first post–1989 president of the Czech Republic, noted how ironic it was that representatives of Western peace groups who visited his part of the world were often suspicious of dissidents like himself. Havel and other dissidents and human rights advocates had paid the price for their protests against an authoritarian regime through jail sentences, beatings, or worse. But they found themselves being viewed as "suspiciously prejudiced against the realities of socialism, insufficiently critical of Western democracy and perhaps even sympathizing . . . with those detested Western armaments. In short, for [the peace group representatives] the dissidents tend to appear as a fifth column of Western establishments east of the Yalta line."[9]

The Western visitors were unmoved when Havel tried to explain that even the word *peace* had been drained of its meaning given its overuse in empty, official slogans like "the struggle for peace" against "Western imperialists." The dissident, "unable to protect himself or his children, suspicious of an ideological mentality, and knowing firsthand where appeasement can lead," had positioned himself against "the loss of meaning," including a diminution in the meaning and power of words. Draining words of meaning is a mark of what Havel calls "pseudoideological thinking," which separates the words we use from the realities they purport to describe.[10] What Havel calls "evasive language" has "separated thought from its immediate contact with reality," as I noted in a 1993 article, citing Havel, "and crippled its capacity to intervene in that reality effectively."[11]

WHAT IS A TERRORIST?

This line of reasoning pertains directly to how we talk about *terror* and *terrorists*. Just as the words *martyr* and *martyrdom* are distorted, whether in the Western or the Islamic tradition, when applied not to those prepared to die as witnesses to their faith but instead to those who commit suicide while killing as many civilians as possible, so *terrorist* is twisted beyond recognition if it is used to designate anyone anywhere fighting for a cause.

Terrorists are those who kill people they consider their "objective enemy," no matter what those people may or may not have done. *Terrorist* and *terrorism* entered ordinary language to designate a specific phenomenon: killing directed against all ideological enemies indiscriminately and outside the context of a war between combatants. According to the logic of terrorism, enemies can legitimately be killed no matter what they are doing, where they are, or how old they are.

The word *terror* first entered the political vocabulary of the West during the French Revolution. Those who guillotined thousands in the Place de la Concorde in Paris were pleased to speak of revolutionary terror as a form of justice.[12] Since the era of the French Revolution, a complex, subtle, and generally accepted international language has emerged to make critical distinctions between different kinds of violent acts. Combatants are distinguished from noncombatants. A massacre is different from a battle. An ambush is different from a firefight. When Americans look back with sadness and even shame at the Vietnam War, it is horrors like the My Lai *massacre* they have in mind. Those who called the slaughter of more than four hundred unarmed men, women, and children a *battle* were regarded as having taken leave of their senses, perhaps because they were so determined to justify anything that Americans did in the Vietnam War that they had lost their moral moorings.[13]

A terrorist is one who sows terror. Terror subjects its victims or would-be victims to paralyzing fear. In the words of the political theorist Michael Walzer, terrorism's "purpose is to destroy the morale of a nation or a class, to undercut its solidarity; its method is the random murder of innocent people. Randomness is the crucial feature of terrorist activity. If one wishes fear to spread and intensify over time, it is not desirable to kill specific people identified in some particular way with a regime, a party, or a policy. Death must come by chance."[14] Terrorism is "the random murder of innocent people." The reference is not to moral innocence, for none among us are innocent in that way, but to our inability to defend ourselves from murderous attacks as we go to work, take a trip, shop, or ride a bus. In other words, civilians are not combatants.

Terrorists are not interested in the subtleties of diplomacy or in compromise solutions. They have taken leave of politics. Sometimes elements of movements that resort to terrorism—say, the Irish Republican Army—may also develop a political arm and begin negotiating a political solution. No political solution is possible, however, when the terrorism is aimed at the destruction of innocent civilians—when that itself is the goal.

THE IMPORTANCE OF
MAKING THE RIGHT DISTINCTIONS

The designation of terrorism becomes contested because terrorists and their apologists would prefer not to be depicted accurately. It is important to distinguish between two cases here. In some hotly contested political situations, it may be in the interest of one side to try to label its opponents as "terrorists" rather than "combatants" or "soldiers" or "fighters." We must ask who such men (and women) are attacking. Do they target soldiers at outposts or in the field? Do they try to disable military equipment, killing soldiers in the process? As they carry out such operations, are they open to negotiation and diplomacy at the same time? If so, it seems reasonable to resist any blanket label of "terrorism" for what they are up to.

In a situation in which noncombatants are *deliberately* targeted and the murder of the maximum number of noncombatants is the *explicit* aim, using terms like "fighter" or "soldier" or "noble warrior" is not only beside the point but pernicious. Such language collapses the distance between those who plant bombs in cafés or fly civilian aircraft into office buildings and those who fight other combatants, taking the risks attendant upon military forms of fighting. There is a nihilistic edge to terrorism: It aims to destroy, most often in the service of wild and utopian goals that make no sense at all in the usual political ways.

The distinction between terrorism, domestic criminality, and what we might call "normal" or "legitimate" war is vital to observe. It helps us to assess what is happening when force is used. This distinction, marked in historic moral and political discourses about war and in the norms of international law, seems lost on those who call the attacks of September 11 acts of "mass murder" rather than terrorism and an act of war under international law, and who go on to claim that the United States has also engaged in "mass murder" in its legally authorized counteroffensive that removed the Taliban and disrupted the Al Qaeda network and its terrorist training camps in Afghanistan. This argument perpetrates a moral equivalence that amounts to the "pile of garbage" that Stephen Carter noted.[15] If we could not distinguish between an accidental death resulting from a car accident and an intentional murder, our criminal justice system would fall apart.

And if we cannot distinguish the killing of combatants from the intended targeting of peaceable civilians and the deliberate and indiscriminate sowing of terror among civilians, we live in a world of moral nihilism. In such a world, everything reduces to the same shade of gray and we cannot make distinctions that help us take our political and moral bearings. The victims of September 11 deserve more from us.

THE IMPORTANCE OF
DISTINCTIONS TO DEMOCRATIC ARGUMENT

A robust politics of democratic argument turns on making the right distinctions. America's war against terrorism would collapse into a horror were we to fail to distinguish between combatants and noncombatants in our response. It is thus both strange and disheartening to read the words of those distinction-obliterators for whom, crudely, a dead body is a dead body and never mind how it got that way. Many of these same individuals would, of course, protest vehemently, and correctly, were commentators, critics, and political actors to fail to distinguish between the great world religion that is Islam and the terrorists who perpetrated the events of September 11. One cannot have it both ways, however, by insisting on the distinctions one likes and heaping scorn on those that put pressure on one's own ideological and political commitments.

For example, those of us who locate ourselves within a tradition that insists on critically assessing the policies of our own government, past and present, by deploying criteria that help us to determine whether a resort to war is or is not justified, cannot simply abandon those criteria when we feel like it. This tradition—called "just war"— requires that we apply distinctions and limitations to our own side as well as to the other side in any conflict. I will unpack the just war tradition in detail in chapter 3, but for now it is important to emphasize that if the United States was training its combatants to be terrorists rather than soldiers fighting under strict rules of engagement, the just war analyst would have to say so and in no uncertain terms. Those of us who have studied this matter in detail, however, know that a basic norm of U.S. military training is the combatant-noncombatant distinction—the principle of discrimination. We know that American soldiers are trained to refuse to obey illegal orders under the code of restraints called the "laws of war," derived in large measure from the historic evolution of the just war tradition and its spin-offs as encoded in international conventions and arrangements.

U.S. military training films include generous helpings of "what went wrong" in various operations. "Wrong" refers not only to U.S. military losses but also to operations that led to the unintentional loss of civilian life. These films ask: How can such losses be prevented in the future in a theater of war? No one is encouraged, or even allowed, to call the killing of civilians "God's will" or, even worse, an act carried out in God's name.

Consider, by contrast, a training video now being used to recruit Islamist radicals. An analyst for the British newspaper *The Observer*, which obtained a copy of this training video, found it "worse than anything expected." It emanated from the Groupe Salafiste pour Predication et Combat (Salafist Group for Preaching and Fighting, or GSPC), "the most radical of Islamic terrorist groups who have been fighting the Algerian government for more than ten years."[16] This film has been screened in various sites but is routine fare in a particular mosque in Finsbury Park, North London, where young men who come for spiritual guidance are subjected to a course in radical terror instead. (This is the mosque through which Richard Reed, the would-be "shoe-bomber," passed and where Zacarias Moussaoui, the so-called twentieth hijacker, used to worship.)

The video shows enemies being decapitated with knives after they are disarmed—something strictly forbidden by the laws of war. The film's narrator intones: "You have to kill in the name of Allah until you are killed. Then you will win your place forever in Paradise. The whole Islamic world should rise up to fight all the sick unbelievers. The flag of Jihad will be forever held high. Our enemies are fighting in the name of Satan. You are fighting in the name of God."

The viewer is subjected to "excited shouting as the militants notice that one soldier is still alive. 'He is moving, he is moving,' calls out a fighter. A militant calmly bends down and runs a knife across the wounded conscript's throat. The image of the blood pumping from his severed carotid artery is shown five times during the video." Another scene shows "ordinary young men doing their national service" being killed. These Algerian soldiers are tarred with the same brush as all "enemies of Islam," including the "Jews and the Christians."[17] Some, reading this description, will say, "But this is extreme." Yes, it is. That is the point. Terrorism is extremism. And Islamist fundamentalism is an extreme repudiation of modernity itself—another reason why it is impossible to negotiate and split the differences between its adherents and those immersed in the Western politics of negotiation and compromise.

Without in any way claiming that there is something intrinsic to Islam that "makes it hostile to modernity," Francis Fukayama, writing in *Newsweek,* takes note of the basic facts as gleaned from the first-person accounts, the reports, the fatwas, and the manuals of Islamist extremists:

These groups celebrated September 11 because it humbled a society that they believed was at its base corrupt. This corruption was not just a matter of sexual permissiveness, homosexuality and women's rights as they exist in the West, but stemmed in their view from secularism itself. What they hate is that the state in Western societies should be dedicated to religious tolerance and pluralism, rather than trying to serve religious truth. . . . So this is not simply a "war" against terrorists, as the American government understandably portrays it. Nor, as many Muslims argue, is the real issue American foreign policy in Palestine or toward Iraq. Unfortunately, the basic conflict we face is much broader.[18]

This brand of Islamist ideology is promoted in textbooks, "including one mandated for use in Saudi tenth-grade classes" that declares it compulsory for Muslims "to consider the infidels their enemies."[19] That is why I argue that such persons hate us for *what we are and what we represent and not for anything in particular that we have done.* How could we respond to their demands? By refusing to educate girls and women? By repealing the franchise? By establishing a theocracy run by radicals? As an editorial in *The Economist* insists, "Militant Islam despises the West not for what it does but for what it is."[20]

To be sure, there are those who oppose U.S. foreign policy in specific ways and say so, often vehemently. That is different from promoting indiscriminate slaughter. One can argue with such critics. One may even come to agree with them on some points. But one fights back against those who have declared you a mortal enemy unfit to share our beautiful earth. The terrorist commits himself to violence *without limits.* Those fighting under a set of established restraints fight back by observing limits, most importantly between combatants and noncombatants. It is reasonable to argue that certain changes in U.S. foreign policy *might* reduce the attraction of radical Islamism to many young men. It is unreasonable to assume that changes in U.S. foreign policy would disarm radical Islamism.

JUSTICE, NOT REVENGE

One final distinction is vital to this discussion: the distinction between *justice* and *revenge.* They are not the same, and any attempt to equate them only adds to the disastrous line of reasoning of which Stephen Carter writes. In President George W. Bush's speech to the nation on September 20, 2001, announcing the war against terrorism, there was not a word, a phrase, or a paragraph that could be reasonably characterized as a call for revenge. He distinguished carefully between Islam as a great world religion and terrorists who are "trying, in effect, to hijack Islam itself." He pointed out, rightly, that we are hated because of our freedoms and our rights. The fight would be engaged in behalf of "all who believe in progress and pluralism, tolerance and freedom."[21] One could argue that the president's call for a war against terrorism and those who harbor terrorism does not articulate sufficiently the limits to be observed in such an effort, although these were imbedded, at least in part, in the care he took to distinguish combatants from noncombatants as legitimate targets.

The distinction between revenge and justice is as clear as the distinction between the actions of a lynch mob and a conviction by a jury in a first-degree murder case arrived at after a fair trial and hours of careful deliberation. If a trial for murder is not fair, it may result in revenge by default, if not intent. But an open and fair verdict rendered under the best judgment of fellow citizens cannot be equated to a group of inflamed persons running amok and stringing someone up without a trial. With this distinction in mind, I find that there is no justification for calling President Bush's speech a cry for revenge.

Revenge stems from a desire to inflict harm for a real or imagined harm one has sustained. Revenge does not involve deliberation or care, and it often recognizes no limits. The vengeful spirit knows no rest until harm has been exacted to the ultimate degree. The protagonist William Munney, at the conclusion of Clint Eastwood's great film *Unforgiven,* promises to return and to kill all of the "sons of bitches" in the town of Big Whiskey should they leave his best friend, who has been murdered and put on display, unburied. That is vengeance and revenge.

Justice, by contrast, is measured. Iconographically represented as a blindfolded figure holding balanced scales, justice has to do with equity, with putting things right when an injustice has been committed. We contrast justice to injustice and ask what might be done to right the balance and restore the scales of justice. But what is the contrast to revenge? It is hard to think of one. Perhaps one reason revenge tends to run riot is that it is not framed by a recognition of some alternative. Revenge attaches to no scale of political concepts, values, or virtues.

Can justice slide over into revenge? Yes, it can, and that is why caution is always in order. But to do nothing as people are slaughtered makes one complicit in injustice. The anti-Nazi theologian and martyr Dietrich Bonhoeffer, for example, writing as one dedicated to overthrowing Hitler, judged harshly those who retreated into the "sanctuary of private *virtuousness*" when confronted with hideous injustice. "Anyone who does this must shut his mouth and his eyes to the injustice around him," Bonhoeffer writes. "Responsible action" involves contamination—one cannot altogether avoid getting "dirty hands" when acting in the political world in a responsible way.[22] Bonhoeffer also criticized a "naive lack of realism" on the part of the "reasonable" people whose failure, he argued, "is obvious," since they believe, with "the best of intentions . . . that with a little reason they can bend back into position the framework that has got out of joint."[23]

Bonhoeffer charted a course between corrupt inaction and action motivated by revenge rather than a call to responsibility, a distinction that reminds us again of the difference between justice and revenge. No one speaks of responsible revenge. That would be a ludicrous oxymoron, for the definition of the word *revenge* precludes the modifying word *responsible*. But the responsible enactor of justice makes a great deal of sense. Justice implies responsibility.

What is our responsibility when we have sustained a violent attack and egregious harm? What is at stake? How do we assess the central issues in a measured way? That is the subject to which I now turn.

2   WHAT IS AT STAKE?

On February 3, 1943, President Franklin Delano Roosevelt issued a wartime proclamation assaying the difference between the United States and those we were fighting. "Americanism," he said, "is not, and never was, a matter of race or ancestry. . . . The principle on which the country was founded and by which it has been governed is that Americanism is a matter of the mind and heart."[1] FDR, a student of history, knew of course about slavery and racial discrimination and the decades of controversy leading up to women gaining the right to vote. But he appreciated the critical distinction between a *practice* and a *principle,* and it was foundational principles to which FDR referred in his proclamation.

MORAL EQUALITY

Several of these principles are critical to appreciating what is at stake between us and those who regard the United States as a godless society fit only for destruction. The first American foundational principle is moral equality: All human beings are created equal and are endowed by their Creator with certain inalienable rights. To be sure, the Declaration of Independence referred to "men," not "human beings," but "men" was the universal "we" in that time and place, and women were by no means considered exempt from moral equality. Those who would later press the cause of women did not have to argue that the Declaration of Independence should be abandoned or ignored but rather that it should be honored: They used a founding *principle* to defeat *practices* that violated that principle.[2]

Although it is disparate views of women's place in society that most dramatically separate us from radical Islamism, some among our critics point to America's checkered racial history and argue that we have no right to criticize others for their inegalitarianism. This claim is tendentious. The critical question is not whether Americans behaved badly on the basis of race in the past. Instead, we should ask: What was it in the Western (and American) tradition that permitted or even required its citizens over time to examine their practices in light of basic founding principles and beliefs? In the West it has long been a basic view, at least since the inception of Christianity, that all human beings are created in God's image and possess thereby a dignity that states do not confer and that states cannot withdraw. Commitment to this view took shape over time in the language of natural law, natural rights, and moral equality. The principle of moral equality was secured in revealed and natural theology and philosophy alike. The American founders, including the author of the Declaration, Thomas Jefferson, certainly knew that slavery could not be squared with the principle of moral equality, but they believed that it was politically expedient to do nothing to dislodge slavery at the inception of the republic in order to gain the support of representatives from the slave-holding states for the Constitution.

But, as Abraham Lincoln was to put it later, no nation can long exist half slave and half free. Lincoln deployed the Declaration of Independence, with its commitment to moral equality, to argue *against* the *Dred Scott* case, which, in 1857, had upheld the notorious Fugitive Slave Act.[3] The Supreme Court, Lincoln claimed, was "blowing out the moral lights among us." There was a higher law by which statutory law could be judged and found wanting. This higher law was not extraconstitutional but basic to "a new nation conceived in liberty and dedicated to the proposition that all men are created equal." Lincoln could not have made such a claim if he had lacked the principles from which to challenge the abhorrent practice he condemned. Slavery was not a founding American principle. It was a repulsive practice that clashed with our principles and was therefore doomed.

As we fought against racially based totalitarianism during World War II, our commitment to the universal principle that defined our particular polity—that all persons are created equal—set in motion developments that helped bring about the end of the Jim Crow system of racial segregation after the war. The first American institution to be desegregated was the U.S. military. The ability of the American polity to use its own tradition's commitments to eliminate abhorrent practices tells us something basic: In a decent polity, our prejudices should be *challenged* rather than *reinforced* by our principles.

Most American citizens understand this. No one could criticize a practice using American constitutional and ethical norms and precepts if such norms and precepts did not exist. The history of American politics is unintelligible without an account of ongoing attempts to bring our practices and our principles closer together. Of course, not all American citizens agree on what that means, or on what it is that they and their polity are required to do. There is deep disagreement about a range of issues between people who agree on basic principles but disagree on how best to realize them in practice. Democracy is defined by such contests. Thinking *politically* requires looking at both principles and practices and considering how they do, or do not, conform to one another.

THE SEPARATION OF CHURCH AND STATE

It is also necessary to think *historically* in order to evaluate what is at stake in the current struggle between us and radical Islamism. This brings us to another feature of our political culture that separates the American polity from those who have declared war on it, namely, the separation of church and state. Article 1 of the Bill of Rights prohibits the establishment of religion and guarantees the free exercise of religion. Between those who believe they are under divine command to set up theocracies and those who begin with that fateful moment when Jesus of Nazareth picked up a coin, examined it, and told his followers to "render unto Caesar that which is Caesar's and unto God that which is God's" (Luke 20:24–25), there is a gulf as wide as any political, legal, or religious gulf can be. Is it *two* (church *and* state) or *one* (no distinction as church and state are fused into a powerful monistic structure)?

When those who have declared themselves our enemies call Americans "infidels," they are condemning us on at least two counts. First, most Americans are condemned a priori in the eyes of Osama bin Laden and his followers for following a religion that is not Islamist fundamentalism. And second, Americans accept on principle a constitutional order that keeps church and state separate even as, on the level of political culture and civil society, religion and politics commingle in many and diverse ways. Thus, our opponents disdain our principles, not simply our practices. They are not telling us to live up to our own principles but rather to abandon them—or, better yet, to convert to a theocratic doctrine.

Despite a history of official state religions in certain times and places, the West has not been hospitable to theocracy. The offices of pope and emperor, of bishop and king, have always been kept separate, even when, at particular historic moments, throne and altar were closely allied. What we now call "church" and "state" were never fused in such a way that no distinction between them could be made. Indeed, Western politics and culture have been formed in large part by the centuries-long struggle demarcating the appropriate and legitimate realms of religious and political authority. Civil law and canon law have also been kept distinct in the historical struggles to determine which law should be applied to different areas of human life and activity and to different offices and persons.

Christianity, not being a law-based religion, never presented a comprehensive, all-encompassing law good for all societies and covering every aspect of human existence. Islam, by contrast, is a law-based faith. In extreme forms, as in Taliban-dominated Afghanistan, all aspects of life were governed by a theocracy based on one law, a severe version of Shari'a, the traditional Islamic holy law. The debate within Islam on the fanatical, literalist application of Shari'a goes forward, and some traditions of legal interpretation within Islam offer alternatives to Taliban-type oppression and repression. At the same time, however, the history of Islam shows an affinity for theocracy that never took root in the West.

Why are there no theocracies in the modern West? The distinguished historian and student of Islam Bernard Lewis posits that "secularism in the modern political meaning—the idea that religion and political authority, church and state are different, and can or should be separated—is, in a profound sense, Christian." The origins of the separation of church and state, he continues, "may be traced to the teachings of Christ, confirmed by the experience of the first Christians; its later development was shaped and, in a sense, imposed by the subsequent history of Christendom."[4]

What are those Christian teachings that have sprouted the seeds of secularism in Western society? The Christian Savior proclaims that his Kingdom is not of this world. He eschews earthly dominion when it is offered to him as a temptation by the devil. Most important, Jesus tells his followers to render unto Caesar only that which is Caesar's and unto God what is God's. What is Caesar's is limited: One does not owe Caesar or any earthly power one's life or one's uncritical loyalty. And one does not owe Caesar worship: That would be idolatry. If the demands of Caesar and the worship of the true God conflict, it is Caesar who must be rejected, even if the price is martyrdom—dying for one's faith, not killing for it.

The progress of Christian pilgrims has been measured in their perseverance against sin and temptation and their commitment to living out their lives within the framework of a community that cares for its neighbors and lives in hope of eternal life. The Christian community is not territorial, that is, it is not tied to a specific place and space. From the beginning, Christians have been a pilgrim people, living within historic time and moving across earthly space. As pilgrims, they are not defined by their territorial location or identity. God is not confined to a geographic place. Peter Brown, one of the most distinguished historians of the late antique world, writes:

> Christianity emerged as an unusually democratic and potentially wide-reaching movement. It takes some leap of the modern imagination (saturated as it is by later centuries of Christian language) to under-

stand the novelty of seeing every human being as subject to the same
universal law of God and as equally capable of salvation through the
triumphant or the studious conquest of sin, brought about through
permanent and exclusive membership of a unique religious group. . . .
[A] commitment to truth and moral improvement were held to be
binding on all believers, irrespective of their class or level of culture.[5]

Even as Jesus preached that he came to fulfill the law and the
prophets, he challenged the strictures of traditional Jewish law, with its
detailed regulations: He harvested grain and healed the sick on the Sab-
bath; he ate with publicans and sinners; he told a parable about a *good*
Samaritan whose act of mercy saved a Jew, despite the fact that Samari-
tans and Jews at the time disdained one another; he stopped a crowd
from stoning to death a woman taken in adultery. Repeatedly, Jesus challenged ancient notions of taboo, impurity, and taint. The Apostle Paul
stretched the boundaries even further with his famous sermon proclaiming that in the *kerygma,* the good news of this new faith, there is
neither Jew nor Greek, male nor female, free nor slave, but all are one.
Old distinctions were downplayed; new identities were forged.

HOW THE CHURCH-STATE
DISTINCTION FARED IN THE WEST

For two centuries Christians were persecuted by the great empire of the
ancient world, Rome. With the collapse of the Roman Empire and its
subsequent "Christianization," tight alliances between throne and altar
emerged, beginning with the fourth-century conversion of the Emperor
Constantine. Christianity was proclaimed the official religion of the empire, but the Caesar-God distinction continued to haunt Christianity. Centuries of tension and open struggle between *regnum* (political dominion or
rule) and *sacerdotium* (sacred authority) lay ahead. Emperors might be
Christian, but they were not the final de jure authority in the Church. Following several centuries of wrestling with the remnants of Roman rule,
the barbarian incursions, and the complexities of East-West relationships,

the bishop of Rome emerged as the key figure, in tandem with various configurations of bishops and church councils.[6] The head of the church, or a singularly powerful bishop, could—and sometimes did—take the head of the state to task.

When the imperial capital was shifted to Byzantium, the so-called Theodosian settlement became official imperial law. The Emperor Theodosius II (408–50) issued edicts against heretics under the Theodosian Code, promulgated in 425 A.D. as one part of a grand reorganization of empire and restoration of political stability. East and West drifted apart. In the East, later known as the Byzantine Empire, the rise of Caesaro-papism would consolidate political and ecclesiastical power in the emperor. As a result of this fusion of political dominion and sacramental function, the patriarch of Constantinople never played an autonomous authoritative role in the East in the manner the bishop of Rome did in the West.

Although most Western churchmen had no problem with the Theodosian settlement, the greatest among them did. The bishop of Hippo, known to us as St. Augustine (354–430), rejected the notion of an official Christian empire. To him, this violated the message of Jesus of Nazareth and the story of a pilgrim people wending their way along the pathways of the earth's various political configurations. The Augustine scholar Robert Markus writes that Augustine regarded the "Christianization of the empire as illusory"; having initially succumbed to the notion, he "managed to break the spell."[7] Earthly institutions have a real claim on us, Augustine insisted, but that claim is not and cannot legitimately aspire to the absolute. Centuries of fruitful struggle would follow as the West debated the relative positions and power of what we routinely call church and state.

The church-state distinction and the struggle between them was represented by the so-called two swords doctrine, articulated by Pope Gelasius I, who occupied the throne of Peter from 492 to 496. This doctrine held that the Church received the spiritual sword directly from God and was superior within its own sphere. The emperor received the secular sword from God, but the spiritual sword was of a higher dignity than the secular sword. The upshot was a blurring of the lines between church and state; there was no tidy separation of the two in either reality or theory. But the distinction was never lost. At times the papacy claimed supremacy for the spiritual sword; at other times the emperor proclaimed the dominance of the temporal sword.

By the late eleventh and early twelfth centuries, the West was transfixed by the investiture struggle, a contest over the symbols of spiritual and secular authority as well as an actual test of the relative power of church and empire to intervene regularly in one another's spheres. Pope Gregory VII, who was known as Gregory the Great and whose papacy was from 590 to 604, deposed and excommunicated the Holy Roman Emperor Henry IV. Henry journeyed to Canossa, where Gregory VII was staying, and offered himself as a penitent, kneeling in the snow for three days until his repentance was accepted. This drama unfolded in 1077 and is usually considered one of the high-water marks of papal intervention in imperial politics.

It is important to note that, although Gregory VII claimed he could judge monarchs, he did *not* claim supremacy in temporal as well as spiritual affairs. Instead, he argued that, because of his spiritual position, he could intervene in secular affairs when matters of sin and spiritual doctrine were involved. Even so, Pope Gregory, one of the most powerful of medieval popes, seems to have been singularly ambivalent about his authority; hence, his deposition of Henry IV was circumscribed to mean that Henry could no longer claim to be a Christian king. Ecclesiastical sanctions were removed from his exercise of power, but he was not removed from the temporal throne: Henry remained legitimate where the secular sword was concerned. Such distinctions do not exist in theocracies.

The Emperor Frederick Barbarossa, in 1157, fought back by declaring that kingdom and empire received power directly from God and the intermediary of the Church was not required. He still acknowledged that there were two swords but insisted that the temporal sword was conferred directly on the empire, not proffered to him by the bishop of Rome. Powerful popes would resist such strong assertions of complete temporal independence. A "plenitude" of declared papal power in temporal affairs is associated with the pontificate of Pope Boniface VIII (1294–1303), who issued a spate of bulls on papal supremacy over the secular realm in which he asserted that the two swords were to be wielded by one person: the bishop of Rome. Ironically, however, this articulation of a doctrine that blurred a fundamental distinction central to

Western history coincided with an actual decline in papal power and authority. Soon national monarchs would challenge imperial unity, and the Reformation would challenge church unity.

WHOSE LAW GOVERNS WHAT?

Church-state struggles in Western Christendom often centered on the law. What law governed what institutions and relationships? How far did the writ of the emperor—or later, the king—run? Did Church law extend beyond Church matters? Indeed, how did one determine what was a church matter as opposed to a civil matter in an epoch in which religion saturated all institutions, relationships, and cultural habits? Christianity never offered up a comprehensive holy law to reign over all aspects of life, both sacral and civil. A few of the legal struggles sorting out which law prevailed, when, and where, took on emblematic and symbolic status.

Thomas à Becket, Archbishop of Canterbury, claimed that clerics could not be tried and sentenced in secular courts but fell instead under the writ of church law or canon law exclusively. King Henry II parried with the Constitutions of Clarendon, his 1164 proclamation that the "king's justice shall send to the court of the holy church to see in what manner the matter [of a charge against a cleric] will be treated there. And if the cleric shall be convicted or shall confess, the church ought not to examine him as for the remainder." He warned that "if the archbishop fails to deliver justice, they must come finally to the lord king, in order that by his command the argument may be ended in the court of the archbishop, thus it must not proceed further without the assent of the lord king."[8]

The importance of what might at first glance appear to be a musty, even arcane, twelfth-century dispute is that no territory save those directly under the control of the papacy was governed solely, strictly, and exclusively by canon law in the centuries we call Christendom in the West. Throughout the twelfth century in England, for example, justices were regularly appointed, juries existed, and some regularity in legal norms and punishments was established. The king might have had the final say in many matters (an appeal to Rome could always be thrown down as a trump card), but imperial arbitrariness was slowly stripped away. Also, the institutionalization of the Church contributed to the relative autonomy not only of the Church but of the state. Because the Church was not the seat of ultimate authority, it was compelled to develop a coherent stance toward the secular realm. The same necessity pertained in the other direction. A patchwork set of laws emerged with no single holy law (or any other law) triumphing over all.

Perhaps most important, earthly rule was limited in a variety of ways. There was always the counterpressure of the institutionalized Church. Notions of a higher law—a law not reducible to the statutory laws of any particular kingdom—took hold and eventually yielded a heritage of principles of natural law and natural right that would play a central role in the founding of the American republic. The same principles were central to the most significant American political struggles, from the fight for women's suffrage to the civil rights movement. In this natural law or higher law tradition, aggrieved persons can "appeal to heaven," in John Locke's phrase, even up to the point of revolution, in order to overturn an oppressive regime that is destroying natural law and rights.

As early as the twelfth century, John of Salisbury, in his treatise *Policraticus,* articulated a distinction between the *tyrant* and the *king* that was to play a role in Western notions of legitimate rule and the limits of temporal power. The king must himself obey the law. He is not above the law and superior to it. He should see himself as a servant of his people. The good prince loves justice and prefers the good of the whole, refusing to submerge that good to his own private will. Such a prince desires "to be loved rather than feared, and [to] show himself to them [his people] as such a man that they will out of devotion prefer his life to their own." The tyrant, by contrast, "oppresses the people by rulership based upon force, while he who rules in accordance with the law is a prince. . . . The origin of tyranny is iniquity, and springing from a poisonous root, it is a tree which grows and sprouts into a baleful pestilent growth, and to which the axe must by all means be laid."[9] Indeed, the tyrant may even be killed. These radical notions set in motion the ideal of principled revolt against tyranny as not an anarchic activity but a commitment to law and justice. As discussed in chapter 3, justice-based norms also came to prevail in the long tradition of Western thinking on war and peace.

The ability to challenge kings, tyrants, and popes, depending on the nature of the issue involved, was made possible in part by the interpretive freedom central to Western Christianity. St. Augustine, writing in the fourth century, consistently offers allegorical interpretations of scriptural passages. At times he even throws up his hands and says, in effect, "I'm not sure what this means. There are a number of possible coherent meanings. Take your pick." We must always distinguish between literal, allegorical, and figurative meanings when we read and interpret texts. Truth may be singular, Augustine argues, but meaning is multiple. How can it possibly bring harm "if I understand the writer's meaning in a different sense from that in which another understands it? All of us who read his words do our best to discover and understand what he had in mind, and since we believe that he wrote the truth, we are not so rash as to suppose that he wrote anything which we know or think to be false."[10]

The text in question is scripture, so the principle of interpretive freedom is particularly exigent. Augustine acknowledges that two sorts of disagreements may arise where interpretation is concerned: disagreement concerning the truth of the message, and disagreement concerning the meaning of the message. We can never know exactly and with absolute certainty what was in an author's mind. The realm of immutable truth gives birth to many meanings, and these multiple meanings may all be acceptable. Professing to God, Augustine writes, "I see nothing to prevent me from interpreting the words of your Scriptures in this figurative sense."[11] This interpretive flexibility is fundamental. It helps to underwrite an elasticity to law and governance that exists, not in opposition to truth and justice, but as part and parcel of it, something that hard-line theocrats of any stripe must fail to understand.

RELIGION AND
POLITICS IN AMERICAN CULTURE

How did the distinction between church and state, between the temporal and spiritual realms, fare on America's shores? The answer to this question reveals the fault line between us and those who have declared themselves our enemies. Declaring our religious freedom anathema, they want to establish regimes that fuse political and official religious power. How do we negotiate with ideological extremists taking that position? The answer, of course, is that we do not. Religious freedom or no religious freedom is a distinction that is fundamental to disparate ways of life, not a set of alternative positions that two parties can negotiate about and yet retain their way of life. It must also be observed that a struggle against radical Islamist theocracy goes on *within* the Islamic world as well as *between* Islamicism and the nontheocratic West, although the historic and textual resources drawn upon to make the antitheocratic case within Islam are quite different from the resources used by the West, and not nearly so foundational to the faith as they are in Christianity.

Those who have declared themselves our enemies assume that a secular state necessarily equates to a secular society, hostile or indifferent to religion. This is wrong. It is odd for an American to hear our country depicted as "godless." We are the most religious among the Western democracies. Americans speak "God talk" at least as much as "rights talk," and American politics is indecipherable if severed from the panoply and interplay of America's religions. Much of our political ferment, both now and in the past, flows from religious commitments. The majority of Americans have long believed that our history of religious liberty—free exercise coupled with disestablishment — is what distinguishes America from so many other polities. Currently over 90 percent of Americans claim to believe in God, and fully 70 percent claim membership in a church, synagogue, or mosque. What these figures signify is in need of interpretation, but it can certainly be said that our embrace of faith as a grounding of human meaning, purpose, and identity and as a distinguishing feature of our culture builds a variety of tensions and conflicts into the tissue of American life.[12]

That tension is our variation on the God and Caesar themes assayed earlier. The history of the postmedieval West is the story of the various unions and subsequent separations of church and state. But religion and politics in the United States have interacted in another important way: Religion has played a central role in the cultivation of what the great French observer of the American democracy, Alexis de Tocqueville, called the "habits of the heart" that are the true core of any political culture. In his classic *Democracy in America,* Tocqueville argues that the great movement toward equality was unintelligible without the Christian insistence that all human beings are equal in the eyes of God.

Ideas about the dignity of the human person are central to American democracy because they flow directly from the religiously shaped commitments of Americans. These ideas engender energetic debates in our politics about whether this fundamental dignity is or is not compatible with abortion on demand, or capital punishment, or many other practices. We can have such debates only because *we are committed to the principle*. Otherwise, there would be nothing to debate about. If separation of church and state distinguishes us from Islamist fundamentalism, so too does a whole range of practices related to gender that are drawn from the principle of moral equality. These differences are deep and striking, as we shall learn.

GENDER PRACTICES:
POLITICAL EQUALITY OR PURDAH

It is not just the free exercise and nonestablishment of religion in the West that contrasts strikingly with Islamist theocracy. There is also a huge gulf between American culture and radical Islamicism in gender practices. We underestimate the centrality of the gender question at our peril.

The political equality of women in the West, deriving from a commitment to moral equality, contrasts sharply with traditional purdah, the confinement of women, as resurrected by the Taliban and advocated by Islamist radicals, for whom women (in the words of the hijacker Mohammed Atta) are "unclean." Most Americans learned about purdah during the coverage of the Taliban regime in Afghanistan. There are no contemporary Western analogues to this practice. Neither is purdah similar to the historic civic disenfranchisement of women in Western constitutional regimes—a practice that did not prevent women from playing central and very public social roles in culture. Women's suffrage, of course, was not in practice anywhere when the American republic was established. It took time for the argument to prevail that the practice of women's suffrage flows directly from our basic constitutional principles, and that, indeed, refusing to grant women the vote was a practice in opposition to these principles. As the American experiment in self-government went forward, women asked: What about us?

The great Jane Addams, founder of Hull-House in Chicago, is just one of many examples of American women who played a major public role in America long before they could vote. Addams received a college education, chose not to marry, and was followed everywhere she went by controversy, but she was not barred from taking an active role in political life or forced to remove herself from the glare of public scrutiny. She was what purdah does not allow women to be: a public woman.

In the early centuries of Christianity, there were churchmen, including St. Augustine and Martin Luther, who condemned contempt for women—including the contempt sometimes voiced by other churchmen. Augustine insisted that women are fully human, rational beings with immortal souls, although there might, he averred, be certain physical weaknesses associated with the sex. This presumption of moral equality yielded political fruit over the centuries. There is no doubt that theologians and philosophers in the West often acquiesced in the practices of their respective eras that militated against equal dignity for women, or even articulated views that justified such practices. But St. Augustine in the fourth century criticized men who cherish their own manhood, as he put it, and want everyone in the household at their beck and call. He chided men who despise women and attacked an imperial law that forbade the appointment of a woman, even an only daughter, as an heir: "I cannot cite, or even imagine, a more inequitable law."[13] He often took aim against the false pride of the Roman Empire that dictated as a cultural norm that it was honorable for women who were raped in war to kill themselves from shame. The shame, Augustine insisted, was that of their attackers, not the women, the victims.

Within radical Islamism, women are unclean persons who must be kept hidden, covered entirely, and made subordinate. Whatever the Qur'an and subsequent Islamic teaching requires or claims where women are concerned—and certainly Islam is compatible with a variety of gender practices—there is no doubt that where Islamist fundamentalism prevails, the status and well-being of women plummet. Under the Taliban, women were executed for alleged infidelity. They could be beaten on the streets for displaying a limb or going out of doors unsupervised. Although pre-Taliban Afghanistan, a Muslim society, had included a significant number of professional women, women were forced under Taliban rule to with-draw from law, government, and teaching. These practices show us that gender practices are not a sidebar to the war against terrorism as a cultural struggle, but a central issue.

Bernard Lewis writes:

> The emancipation of women, more than any other single issue, is the touchstone of difference between modernization and Westernization. . . . The emancipation of women is Westernization; both for traditional conservatives and radical fundamentalists it is neither necessary nor use-ful, but noxious, a betrayal of true Islamic values. It must be kept from entering the body of Islam, and where it has already entered, it must be ruthlessly excised.[14]

Harsh abuse of women was characteristic of the Taliban from the be-ginning. Secretary of State Madeleine Albright declared in 1997: "I think it is very clear we are opposed to the Taliban because of their despicable treatment of women and children, and their general lack of respect for human dignity."[15] Among the most startling scenes that Americans wit-nessed were covertly filmed incidents in Taliban-controlled Afghanistan showing men—any man could do so—using special sticks and rods sup-plied for the purpose to beat women who were in alleged violation of any one of the minute laws regulating their behavior. This was done under the auspices of the Ministry for the Promotion of Virtue and the Preven-tion of Vice. As Peter Bergen notes, "Such policies reached their apogee of absurdity in an ordinance ordering homeowners to paint their win-dows black so that no one might accidentally see the faces of women in-side."[16] This practice was in line with a proverb common among one ethnic group, the Pathan, who formed the top leadership of the Taliban movement: "Women belong in the house or the grave."[17]

The words and regulations of the Taliban were part and parcel of a rigid interpretation of purdah, the practice of covering and isolating women, refusing them a role in public life, and, in its most extreme forms, keeping them illiterate and making them subject to arbitrary male brutal-ity. The *New York Times* reported on the horror of so-called honor killings—in this case in Pakistan—in which women who have "shamed" their families are killed by outraged male relatives, whether fathers or brothers, and on the almost impossible situation faced by women who are raped in a society governed by strict Shari'a regulations. The entire culture discourages women from accusing men of rape when they have been attacked because of the value put on "woman's honor and chastity," which evaporates "as soon as she accuses someone of rape. Moreover, some 60 percent of women who lodge complaints of rape—which requires two witnesses for a conviction—are later charged themselves under Pakistan's Islamic-based laws, with having had sex outside of marriage."[18]

We want to blame such practices on ignorance, and there is something to this notion. Illiteracy is an enormous problem in overwhelmingly Muslim Arab countries. According to a warning issued in a report of the Arab League, an estimated 68 million people in the twenty-two member countries are illiterate, or more than one-fifth of their total population.[19] (The Afghanis are not Arabs, of course, but the years of Taliban rule give an indication not only of how women—and indeed all persons where alarming rates of illiteracy are concerned—fared in those years but of the fate that lay in store had the Taliban not been displaced.) Nevertheless, the sad social fact of illiteracy is not adequate to account for an officially sanctioned mandate that women are to remain uneducated as a *norm,* not an *aberration.*

It is unfair to moderate Muslims and to the brave Muslim women fighting for democratic reform to refuse to criticize radical Islamicism's severe gender practices by burying them under the label "cultural diversity." Such "tolerance" is wrongheaded at best. It is not diversity we are talking about but systematic, legally mandated cruelty that goes so far as to threaten the lives of women and even to destroy their lives capriciously should they violate a draconian directive about the consequences of their "sinful" behavior.

Some sins are most assuredly crimes and rightfully fall under the censure and punishment of civil authority. But others are not. One mark of modern constitutional orders is that this distinction is fundamental, and one mark of religions that gave up centuries ago the aspiration to a monolithic fusion of church and state is that they agree. When Jesus confronted the crowd and the terrified woman, "taken in adultery," he recognized her sin. A sin, surely, he said, but who among us is without sin? The crowd quietly put down their stones and withdrew.

In a theocratic order there is no distinction between a sin and a crime. The fusion of the two invites an all-encompassing, punitive order. Most persons with religious convictions agree that infidelity in marriage is a sin. But we are horrified at the thought that a woman caught in adultery should be shot in the back of the head in a stadium or stoned to death.

There are many signs of what happens when the heavy hand of a wicked regime is removed. In post-Taliban Afghanistan, girls are flocking back to school and women are openly teaching again. One young woman, twenty-year-old Tuiba Habib Rasolle, "who wants to follow her father into the practice of medicine," commented that "if the Taliban had not come here, I would be in my third year of college." She is returning to school as an eleventh-grader, the grade level she was in when the Taliban took over Afghanistan in 1996. Her school was once a "thriving academic center for 4,800 girls. Under the Taliban, it became a place of strict religious instruction for a dwindling number of boys befuddled by the radical curriculum." The vice principal of the school, a determined woman who continued to educate women underground (and would have paid severely if discovered), states: "I can't say how happy I am. . . . The Taliban thought they would be here forever. But now they are gone."[20] These Afghani girls and women can go to school and teach because of the use of force by America and its allies to roll back the Taliban and rout Al Qaeda from its hiding places.

The rough road faced by Afghan women, now and in the future, is clear. They live in a land decimated by six years of brutality and the destruction of the civic infrastructure. Although some women continue to wear the burqa out of conviction, many women do so out of fear of showing their faces in public because men, addicted to their lust to dominate, may threaten unofficial punishment even without official legal sanction. As report after report has noted, the journey of women from isolation to public life will be difficult. The return of many educated Afghan women from exile should help.

Evidence continues to mount concerning Taliban cruelty and excesses in enforcing the draconian regulations allegedly instituted out of respect for women and for their protection. The actual behavior of the Taliban, Tim McGirk and Shomali Plain reported in *Time*,

> made a mockery of that claim. . . . Now it is clear from the testimony of witnesses and officials of the new government that the ruling clerics systematically abducted women from the Tajik, Uzbek, Hazara, and

other ethnic minorities they defeated. Stolen women were a reward for a victorious battle. And in the cities of Kabul, Mazar-I-Sharif, Jalalbad and Khost, women victims tell of being forced to wed Taliban soldiers and Pakistani and Arab fighters of Osama bin Laden's Al Qaeda network, who later abandoned them. These marriages were tantamount to legalized rape.[21]

Hundreds of women simply disappeared in the wake of Taliban offenses, having been used as "comfort women" for Taliban and Al Qaeda fighters and then discarded. Some committed suicide from shame. British Prime Minister Tony Blair did not mince words: "Women are treated in a way almost too revolting to be credible. First driven out of university, girls are not allowed to go to school; no legal rights; unable to go out of doors without a man. Those that disobey are stoned. There is now no contact permitted with Western agencies, even those delivering food."[22]

Lest any reader harbor the lingering conviction that Taliban practices were somehow an aberration violating legal principles rather than enforcing them, consider a few of the decrees relating to women. The decrees inhibiting health care for women were directly life-threatening. Women had to remain veiled during a medical examination. They were enjoined to see female physicians only. Women were allowed to remain in medicine for the express purpose of dealing with female patients, who were not permitted a male physician unless dire necessity dictated such. If a woman had to see a male physician, he was hampered in his ability to give adequate medical care because he was not allowed to "touch or see the other parts of female patients except for the affected part." Sitting and speaking "between male and female doctors are not allowed." And "the Religious Police are allowed to go for control at any time and nobody can prevent them."[23]

And yet, in a rather salacious depiction of paradise—this common feature in popular Islamist cultural lore was referred to in testaments by the September 11 hijackers—the martyr who kills for the faith and perishes in the process is given seventy-two black-eyed women to serve him. His reward will come ten minutes after his "martyrdom." This simplistic picture is challenged by many experts on Islam, including Georgetown University Professor Yvonne Haddad, who has stated that such concepts are "nowhere to be found in Islamic writings."[24]

It takes a seriously distorted imagination to see respect for women or anyone else in these measures. Indeed, there seems little doubt that many classical Islamic jurists are appalled by Taliban excesses. The fact that the new Afghan government moved immediately to rescind Taliban measures without in any way labeling postwar Afghanistan as anything other than a Muslim country and culture is evidence that the abuse of women and their harsh treatment are not necessary concomitants of an Islamic culture and governance. The question of women's political and social equality, however, remains an issue. In *Time* magazine, Lisa Beyer wrote that

> nowhere in the Muslim world are women treated as equals. . . . Part of the problem dates to Muhammad. Even as he proclaimed new rights for women, he enshrined their inequality in immutable law, passed down as God's commandments and eventually recorded in Scripture. The Qur'an allots daughters half the inheritance of sons. [A Roman practice, even disallowing daughters to inherit at all, that Augustine blasted as inequitous in the fourth century!] . . . Under Shari'a, or Muslim law, compensation for the murder of a woman is half the going rate for men. In many Muslim countries, these directives are incorporated into contemporary law.[25]

This presents enormous challenges to reformers.

THE CRISIS WITHIN ISLAM

What are the sources within the Qur'an that support or sustain moral equality between men and women? How have these been drawn upon to support more equitable practices? Or do equitable practices emerge in some Muslim countries despite rather than from Islamic principles? These questions need clarifying in light of the long-standing and quite dramatic differences between Western culture and Islam in the matter of gender. That cultural dialogue can go forward, however, only if Islamist extremism is defeated, for its ideological rigidity prevents cultural dialogue even as it seeks to quash internal cultural debates.

There is a "crisis within Islam," as one scholar of Islam after another has put it in the wake of September 11. Who speaks in the name of Islam? Who governs in the name of Islam? It is no exaggeration to say that the future of humanity turns importantly on the answers to these questions, particularly in light of the fact that, in "an Islamic state, there is in principle no law other than the *shari'a,* the Holy Law of Islam." Women's rights have suffered "the most serious reverses in countries where fundamentalists of various types have influence or where . . . they rule. Indeed, . . . the emancipation of women by modernizing rulers was one of the main grievances of the radical fundamentalists, and the reversal of this trend is in the forefront of their agenda."[26] We cannot treat the violation of women's rights as a minor peccadillo when respect for women's rights is a key reason America is number one on the enemies list of radical Islamists.

Authentic cultural dialogue can go forward only when the threat of terror is removed. Much of this dialogue will clarify our differences. Perhaps we will also come to see our commonalities. In the meantime, those who use their religion to underwrite the brutal treatment of women as a mandated cultural practice and who despise the free exercise of religion cannot as a matter of principle find common ground with those who abhor abuse and second-class citizenship (or no citizenship at all) based on gender and who embrace religious and political liberty. It is naive folly to assume that rational grievances in reaction to American policy or even American perfidy lie at the root of the terrorist threat. Whatever America's sins and shortcomings, Islamist fundamentalism requires none of these to turn people into ideological fundamentalists with whom dialogue is impossible—as a matter of principle, not merely prudence—and who are not content to "live and let live."

There is a great deal at stake in the current struggle, and there are worthy values worth defending. But the matter of *how* we choose to defend these values is all important, for in fighting terror that knows no limits, there are limits we ourselves must observe.

3   WHAT IS A JUST WAR?

IN THE IMMEDIATE AFTERMATH of September 11, I said to a friend, "Now we are reminded of what governments are for." The primary responsibility of government is to provide basic security—ordinary civic peace. St. Augustine calls this form of earthly peace *tranquillitas ordinis*. This is not the perfect peace promised to believers in the Kingdom of God, the one in which the lion lies down with the lamb. On this earth, if the lion lies down with the lamb, the lamb must be replaced frequently, as Martin Luther opined with his characteristic mordant wit.[1] Portions of the U.S. Constitution refer specifically to security and public safety. "To ensure domestic tranquillity" was central to what the new order being created after the American Revolution was all about. None of the goods that human beings cherish, including the free exercise of religion, can flourish without a measure of civic peace and security.

What good or goods do I have in mind? Mothers and fathers raising their children; men and women going to work; citizens of a great city making their way on streets and subways; ordinary people flying to California to visit the grandchildren or to transact business with colleagues—all of these actions are simple but profound goods made possible by civic peace. They include the faithful attending their churches, synagogues, and mosques without fear, and citizens—men and women, young and old, black, brown, and white—lining up to vote on Election Day.

This civic peace is not the kingdom promised by scripture that awaits the end time. The vision of beating swords into plowshares and spears into pruning hooks, of creating a world in which "nation shall not lift up sword against nation, neither shall they learn war anymore," is connected with certain conditions that will always elude us. That vision presupposes that all persons are under one law. But our condition of pluralism and religious diversity alone precludes the rule of one law. Moreover, our condition of fallibility and imperfection precludes a world in which discontents never erupt.

That said, the civic peace that violence disrupts does offer intimations of the peaceable kingdom. If we live from day to day in fear of deadly attack, the goods we cherish become elusive. Human beings are fragile creatures. We cannot reveal the fullness of our being, including our deep sociality, if airplanes are flying into buildings or snipers are shooting at us randomly or deadly spores are being sent through the mail. As we have learned so shockingly, we can neither take this civic peace for granted nor shake off our responsibility to respect and promote the norms and rules that sustain civic peace.

We know what happens to people who live in pervasive fear. The condition of fearfulness leads to severe isolation as the desire to protect oneself and one's family becomes overwhelming. It encourages harsh measures because, as the political theorist Thomas Hobbes wrote in his 1651 work *Leviathan*, if we live in constant fear of violent death we are likely to seek guarantees to prevent such. Chapter 13 of Hobbes's great work is justly renowned for its vivid depiction of the horrors of a "state of nature," Hobbes's description of a world in which there is no ordered civic peace of any kind. In that horrible circumstance, all persons have the strength to kill each other, "either by secret machination, or by confederacy with others." The overriding emotion in this nightmarish world is overwhelming, paralyzing *fear,* for every man has become an enemy to every other and men live without other security, that what their own strength, and their own invention shall furnish them withal. In such condition, there is no place for Industry; because the fruit thereof is uncertain, and consequently no Culture of the Earth; no Navigation, nor use of the commodities that may be imported by Sea; no commodious Building; no Instruments of moving, and removing such things as require much force; no Knowledge of the face of the Earth; no account of Time; no Arts; no Letters; no Society; and which is worst of all, continuall feare, and danger of violent death; And the life of man, solitary, poore, nasty, brutish, and short.[2]

This is Hobbes's famous, or infamous, war of all against all.

TO PREVENT THE WORST FROM HAPPENING

Many, myself included, believe that Hobbes overstated his case. But there is a powerful element of truth in his depiction of the state of nature. Without civic peace—a basic framework of settled law and simple, everyday order—human life descends to its most primitive level. By primitive I mean rudimentary, the bare minimum—we struggle just to stay alive. The face of such worlds is known to us. We saw it in Somalia under the warlords. We saw it under the Taliban in Afghanistan, where horrible disorder prevailed in the name of order. When government becomes destructive of the most basic end for which it is instituted, *tranquillitas ordinis,* it abandons its minimal raison d'être and can no longer be said to be legitimate. This assumption is essential to political theory. All political theories begin with a notion of how to establish and sustain order among human beings. Some go beyond this minimal requirement to ask how human beings can work to attain justice, or serve the common good, or preserve and protect political liberty. But none of these other ends can be served without basic order. George Weigel defines *tranquillitas ordinis* as "the peace of public order in dynamic political community," insisting that there is nothing static about "the concept of *tranquillitas ordinis* as it evolved after Augustine."[3]

The primary reason for the state's existence is to create those minimal conditions that prevent the worst from happening—meaning, the worst that human beings can do to one another. How do we prevent people from devouring one another like fishes, as Augustine put it? This task is in the first instance one of interdiction: preempting horrible things before they occur. Not all misfortune, catastrophe, or crime can be prevented. What Augustine calls "carking anxieties" are part of the human condition. But we can try to eliminate as many of the conditions that give rise to catastrophe as possible. We can refuse to tolerate violent crime and arbitrary, chaotic disorder. It is horrific to stand in the ruins of a once flourishing city or a section of a city and to know that a government could not prevent what happened there—or was, even worse, the agent of destruction. Imagine such horror as a daily occurrence. If this were our circumstance, we would rightly seek the restoration of basic, minimally decent civic peace and order. And we would rightly ask: Could none of this have been prevented? Is the government somehow responsible for the chaos and destruction? If our answer to the former question is yes, we are likely to call for a new government.

It is difficult for us to imagine anarchy and dread unless we have been victims of random violence of some kind. Otherwise, it is easy for us to lose a sense of urgency. But government cannot and must not lose that sense of urgency. Any government that fails to do what is within its rightful power and purview in these matters is guilty of dereliction of duty. Order is "the condition for the possibility of virtue in public life," Augustine believed, and "such a peace was not to be deprecated: It allowed fallen human beings to 'live and work together and attain the objects that are necessary for their earthly existence.'"[4]

This does *not* mean that our absolute, unquestioned obedience to duly constituted authority is required. Given the temptations attendant upon the exercise of power, authority may overstep its rightful bounds, itself become lawless, and thereby lose its legitimacy.

Augustine appreciated that power is a basic reality of political life. How is power used? To what end? Augustine knew that questions concerning the ethics of power and its use or abuse are most exigent when it comes time to debate war and peace. Augustine launched a great tradition of reasoning on the ethics of the use of force called the *just war tradition*.

It is this tradition that provides a conceptual framework for interpreting and analyzing America's war against terrorism.

MAKING A CASE
FOR THE JUST USE OF FORCE

It is unsurprising that the events of September 11 inspired Americans, from President Bush to the average man and woman on the street, to speak of justice as a way to characterize our response to the intentional slaughter of almost three thousand innocent men, women, and children. When citizens evoke justice, they tap into the complex Western tradition called "just war." The origins of this tradition are usually traced from St. Augustine's fourth-century masterwork, *The City of God*. In that massive text, Augustine grapples with how best to think about force and coercion in light of the fact that the Christian Savior was heralded as the Prince of Peace by angels proclaiming "peace on earth and goodwill" to all peoples. Jesus resisted taking up arms in his own behalf or asking others to do so. How, then, can a Christian take up arms? That is the question that animated the just war tradition, which had several aims: to articulate occasions for the legitimate resort to force; to ensure that war derives from the use of right authority by those responsible for public order; to limit the means to be deployed even in a just cause; and to hold warfare, one outgrowth of political rule, up to ethical scrutiny.

Consider the terms: *justice* and *war*. The presupposition of just war thinking is that war can sometimes be an instrument of justice; that, indeed, war can help to put right a massive injustice or restore a right order where there is a disorder, including those disorders that sometimes call themselves "peace." This latter concern was part of St. Augustine's brilliant deconstruction of the official rhetoric of the Roman Empire. The Romans, Augustine argues, created a desert and called it peace. "Peace and war had a contest in cruelty, and peace won the prize," he notes, lacing his commentary with characteristically heavy irony. So peace should not be universally lauded even as war is universally condemned. Each must be evaluated critically. Many horrors and injustices can traffic under the cover of "peace." Indeed, there are worse things than war. The twentieth century showed us many of those worse things, including gulags and genocides. The world would have been much better off if the violence of particular regimes had been confronted on the battlefield earlier; fewer lives would have been lost over the long run.

Many Christians claim for early Christianity a uniform peace tradition and peace politics. They insist that for its first three centuries Christianity was pacifist and then fell away from a tradition of nonviolence, its only authentic tradition. They believe that the teachings of Jesus rule out any use of force, even force deployed at the behest and under the limits of legitimate authority and ethical restraint. But this characterization of early Christianity does not bear up under close scrutiny. For one thing, the strongest pacifist arguments in the early church are associated with theologians who fell outside the Christian mainstream, such as Origen and Tertullian. More powerful and more mainstream to the Christian tradition are the arguments of St. Augustine, St. Ambrose, and, later, St. Thomas Aquinas, all associated with the just war tradition.[5] These latter regarded their arguments as a consistent evolution from early Christian teaching, not a deviation from it. They knew that in a fallen world, filled with imperfect human beings, we cannot achieve perfection in earthly dominion, in religious life, or in anything else, and that—even more important—we all have a responsibility to and for one another to serve and to love our neighbors. If our neighbor is being slaughtered, do we stand by and do nothing?

Martial metaphors abounded in the early Church. One could be a nonviolent soldier who suffered violence bravely for Christ rather than assault others: These Christians were the *milites Christi*. And indeed, being a soldier for Christ, with all the explicit imagery of stalwart fortitude, fit with the lore of the early Church. Sacralizing suicide, or homicide, or other evils would certainly be inconsistent with Christian doctrine, but soldiering is another matter.

Christian involvement with force goes beyond metaphor, however. When Jesus made the distinction between serving God and serving Caesar, Christians were obliged to take the measure of earthly rule and dominion rather than condemn it or its necessities outright. The most famous—and to Christian pacifists nigh-infamous—passage in this regard is in St. Paul's Letter to the Romans, in which he calls upon believers to obey the governing authorities: "Let every person be subject to the governing authorities. For there is no authority except from God, and those that exist have been instituted by God" (Romans 13:l).[6]

Most important for our purposes, St. Paul claims that earthly dominion has been established to serve God and to benefit all human beings. It is the *rightful authority* of earthly kings and kingdoms to punish wrongdoers. Matters of temporal justice must not be left to self-help. The prospect of leaving questions of righting injustice and imposing penalties in the hands of each and every person conjures up a nightmare of private warfare, vengeance, and vendettas. And that is precisely what the historic record displays in abundance when no entity has been assigned the legitimate use of force to forestall the chaos of private warfare. Because the Church is to serve all, and because Christians believe evil is real, both justice and charity may compel us to serve our neighbor and the common good by using force to stop wrongdoing and to punish wrongdoers.

Of course, earthly rule can become a great disorder. In such a dire circumstance, the Christian may choose to suffer the evil of others, for protecting one's own life is not the highest value. But those in positions of authority and those who can help to spare others from suffering have an obligation to do so. Earthly peace, as imperfect as it is, is better than the nightmare of Thomas Hobbes's war of all against all. The early Christian community drew the line of obedience to the state at emperor worship, for "Thou shalt have no other gods before me." Because they refused to pay homage to the emperor, many early Christians were martyred. But in these first generations of Christian life after the crucifixion of Jesus, there is little evidence that the faithful were enjoined from serving in either the Roman army or police forces.

Augustine also tells us that Christians, if called upon, should take up the worldly political vocation of judge. This is a tragic vocation, since a judge can rarely be absolutely certain about the guilt or innocence of defendants. Truth is often hidden, or the full truth is. Inevitably, a judge winds up punishing some who are innocent and releasing some who are guilty. But Christians, if called, are obliged to do this work.

The dilemmas of judging speak to the nature of earthly rule more generally. It rarely admits of absolutes, and there are usually no bright lines separating alternatives. Carl von Clausewitz, the great German theorist of war, spoke famously of "the fog of war." Augustine would find that phrase apt as a characterization of governing overall. Responsible public authorities are always compelled to act in a kind of fog. As with waging war, the most certain thing about governing is its uncertainty. It is the armchair critics commenting from the sidelines who think the choices are absolutely clear. To be sure, a cause may be clear—opposing the indiscriminate horrors of terrorism, for example—but the means used to promote it may not admit of the same crystalline clarity. The just, or justified, war tradition recognizes this difference by giving us an account of comparative, not absolute, justice.

Although the just war tradition originated in early Christian history and was refined over the centuries by Christian theologians, it would become secularized, though not stripped of ethical content, when it was absorbed into the thinking of international law and many of its ethical restraints were encoded in both the Geneva and Hague Conventions.[7] By the beginning of the twenty-first century, the just war tradition had become part of the way in which much of the world spoke of war and peace questions, especially such matters as noncombatant immunity, proportionality, and the treatment of prisoners. International law states that intentional attacks on noncombatants violate not only recognized rules of warfare but universal humanitarian standards.

HOW TO DECIDE WHETHER A WAR IS JUST

What occasions or events justify the use of violence? Augustine begins by specifying what is not permitted: Wars of aggression and aggrandizement are unacceptable because they violate not only the civic peace but the framework of justice. Once again we see that, in deciding whether a war is just, we must get the critical distinctions right, beginning with a distinction between peace and justice. Some versions of "peace" violate norms of justice and do so egregiously. For the sake of keeping the peace, statesmen often acquiesce in terrible injustices.

Peace is a good, and so is justice, but neither is an absolute good. Neither automatically trumps the other, save for those pacifists who claim that "violence is never the solution," "fighting never settled anything," and "violence only begets more violence." Does it? Not always, not necessarily. One can point to one historical example after another of force being deployed in the name of justice and leading to not only a less violent world but a more just one.

Consider the force used to combat Japanese militarism in World War II. Defeating Japan in the war, occupying Japan in its aftermath and imposing a constitutional order did not incite further Japanese aggression of the sort witnessed in its full horror in what came to be known as "the rape of Manchuria." What emerged instead was a democratic Japan. Are there living Japanese who believe it is time to return to a violent world of militarist dominance or the world of violent self-help associated with the samurai tradition? When the great Japanese writer Yukio Mishima called for a mass uprising and restoration of the old militarism in 1970, only a couple of pathetic disciples responded. Mishima's bizarre fantasy of the return of a more violent world was regarded by the Japanese as daft and nigh-unintelligible.

All violence, including the rule-governed violence of warfare, is tragic. But even more tragic is permitting gross injustices and massive crimes to go unpunished. Just war stipulates that the goods of settled social life cannot be achieved in the face of pervasive and unrelenting violence. The horror of today's so-called failed states is testament to that basic requirement of the "tranquillity of order." In Somalia, as warlords have jostled for power for more than a decade, people have been abused cynically and routinely. Anyone at anytime may be a target. The tragedy of American involvement in Somalia is not that U.S. soldiers were sent there, but that the American commitment was not sufficient to restore minimal civic peace and to permit the Somalian people to begin to rebuild their shattered social framework. Can anyone doubt that a sufficient use of force to stop predators from killing and starving people outright would have been the more just course in Somalia and, in the long run, the one most conducive to civic peace?[8]

Organized force, fighting under rules of engagement in order to minimize civilian casualties, can help to create the safe surround that permits civic peace—*tranquillitas ordinis*—to flourish. Force used as an instrument of justice is not random, uncontrolled violence. It is not violence as an instrument of terror for terror's sake. It is not private violence. It is the use of force at the behest of *right authority*.

Some American films have done a better job of grappling with the question of force than many contemporary analysts and commentators.

One of the greatest, *The Man Who Shot Liberty Valence,* directed by the incomparable John Ford, offers up a reflection on violence in the service of politics and settled law in the absence of viable right authority. Liberty Valence is a vicious outlaw who preys on innocents, high and low. Everyone is terrified of him, including the local "right authority," the sheriff in the small town of Shinbone. Lawyer Ransom Stoddard (played by James Stewart) journeys west, but before arriving in town to set up a law office Stoddard is introduced to lawless Shinbone when his stagecoach is robbed by Valence and his gang. Stoddard is beaten to within an inch of his life.

Enter John Wayne as the tragic character, Tom Doniphon. The only way to deal with Valence, says Doniphon, is to run him out of the territory or disarm him, Doniphon tells the resistant Stoddard. Disarming Valence means killing him, for he will never disarm voluntarily and Shinbone's sheriff (played by Andy Devine) is too terrified to arrest him. Right authority has abandoned its post when confronted with untrammeled viciousness.

Doniphon's argument might be called an ethic of controlled violence. Law exists. Who will enforce it? The film tells us that settled law and its routine enforcement are possible only when random violence and the fear it instills have been pushed back. Doniphon proves to be right, although at the cost of personal tragedy to himself. *The Man Who Shot Liberty Valence* is a parable on the use of force at the service of civic peace in the fog of an undeclared war in which the forces of violence are pitted against all those who want to settle, raise their families, and educate their children. The film does not glorify the antiviolent use of force but shows it instead to be a tragic necessity.

Parables like *The Man Who Shot Liberty Valence* illustrate the just war tradition's nuanced recognition that justice and force are not mutually incompatible. Although Augustine never wrote a systematic treatise on war, he put into play the characteristic form of moral reasoning that enters into the just war tradition. This way of thinking carves out a stance that is neither pacifist nor what is usually called "realist" or *realpolitik.*

Absolute pacifists hold that the use of force is never justifiable under any circumstances. This form of pacifism is associated with the practices of early Christians who tied their pacifism to certain ascetical norms and withdrawal from the world. Leaders charged with right authority within organized political bodies cannot withdraw from the world, of course, and thus are never pacifists. Anyone who accepts political leadership understands that he or she may be compelled to sanction the resort to force in certain circumstances. The just war tradition limits those circumstances in part because it shares with pacifism a strong presumption against violence and force, all other things being equal.[9] The just war tradition does not discourage acts of forgiveness and reconciliation in political life but does recognize their limits in a world of conflicting human wills, one in which the ruthless would prevail if they faced neither restraint nor the prospect of punishment.

The other alternative to the just war tradition, *realpolitik,* is a tradition even older than Christianity. *Realpolitik* severs politics from ethics. There is no room in *realpolitik* for traditional ethical concerns about how and when to resort to force; for Machiavelli, the sixteenth-century Florentine diplomat and theorist after whom this way of thinking is named, this tradition of ethical restraint was synonymous with Christianity. By contrast, Machiavelli claimed that nothing should constrain the prince, the ruler of a principality, who can deploy even brutal techniques (some of which Machiavelli vividly describes) in order to seize and keep the reins of power. Justice is not the main concern for *realpolitikers.* Power is.

The just war thinker cannot accept the *realpolitikers'* "anything goes" approach to political violence.[10] In a landmark study that helped to revive the just war tradition in contemporary debate, Michael Walzer argues: "Our arguments and judgements shape what I want to call *the moral reality of war*—that is, all those experiences of which moral language is descriptive or within which it is necessarily employed."[11]

To sum up, at least provisionally: For pacifists, the reigning word is *peace*. For realists, the reigning word is *power*. For just war thinkers, the reigning word is *justice*. Peace may sometimes be served by the just use of force, even as power is most certainly involved. (Power is also involved in peace politics in ways that many pacifists ignore.)

If we try to avoid the complexity of what is at issue when we debate the use of force, simplistic solutions are likely to win the day, whether of a pacifist or militarist bent. The just war tradition requires that the philosopher, the moralist, the politician, and the ordinary citizen consider a number of complex criteria when thinking about war. These criteria shape a continuous scrutiny of war that judges whether the resort to force is justified, and whether, once force is resorted to, its use has been kept within necessary limits. Although never regarding war as desirable, or as any kind of social "good," the just war tradition acknowledges that it may be better than the alternative.

FORCE AS THE SERVANT OF JUSTICE

How is justice served by the use of force? For Augustine, a resort to force may be an obligation of loving one's neighbor, a central feature of Christian ethics. An offense that triggers a forceful response may be suffered by a third party. Suppose one country has certain knowledge that genocide will commence on a particular date and time against a group of people in another country. The group to be slaughtered has no means to defend itself. Within the just war tradition, the first country may be justified in coming to the aid of the targeted group and using force to interdict and punish their would-be attackers.

For Augustine, using force under such circumstances protects the innocent from certain harm. The historic just war tradition grappled with Augustine's statement that war may be resorted to in order to preserve or to achieve peace—and not just any peace, but a just peace that leaves the world better off than it was prior to the resort to force.[12] For early Christians like Augustine, killing to defend oneself alone was not enjoined: It is better to suffer harm than to inflict it. But the obligation of charity obliges one to move in another direction: To save the lives of others, it may be necessary to imperil and even take the lives of their tormenters. The latter response is the appropriate way, suggests the just war tradition, to meet the challenge of systematic violence. As the theologian Joseph E. Capizzi writes: "According to Augustine, nonviolence is required at the individual level and just-war is mandated at the societal level."[13]

In addition to preventing harm to the innocent, what are the other criteria that morally justify an armed response, the so-called *jus ad bellum?* First, a war must be openly declared or otherwise authorized by a legitimate authority, so as to forestall random, private, and unlimited violence. Second, a war must be a response to a specific instance of unjust aggression perpetrated against one's own people or an innocent third party, or fought for a just cause. Third, a war must begin with the right intentions. Fourth, a war must be a last resort after other possibilities for redress and defense of the values at stake have been explored. Another *ad bellum* criterion usually noted is the prudential one: Do not enter a conflict without reflecting on whether the cause has a reasonable chance of success. One should not resort to violence lightly or experimentally.

The just war tradition has been called upon repeatedly in criticisms of holy wars, crusades, and wars of imperial aggrandizement. Just war thinking could not be put to that use if it were just another way we have of talking about a crusade. But some critics have failed to see the deep and critical distinction between just war thinking—derived as it is from a religious tradition—and any other religiously based call to arms. Consider the vast gulf that separates just war restraint from Osama bin Laden's call for an unlimited attack by all Muslims everywhere against all infidels everywhere. This is the mentality of holy war, which aspires to limitlessness: One can never kill enough infidels. For holy warriors or crusaders, the occasion for war is the simple intention to spread their gospel, whether political or religious, through violence, whenever or wherever possible, against the infidels. For just warriors, both aims and means are limited, even if one has been grievously harmed.

4   IS THE WAR AGAINST
      TERRORISM JUST?

HOW WELL DOES THE post–September 11 war effort fare when assessed according to the just war framework?

The resort to force—or *jus ad bellum*—stipulates certain criteria for evaluation, as outlined in chapter 3. Let's begin with the triggering event. Surely there can be little doubt in anyone's mind that the attacks of September 11 constituted an act of aggression aimed specifically at killing civilians.[1] Indeed, when a wound as grievous as that of September 11 has been inflicted on a body politic, it would be the height of irresponsibility and a dereliction of duty for public officials to fail to respond. A political ethic is an ethic of responsibility. The just war tradition is a way to exercise that responsibility with justice in mind. Such an act of terrorism aims to disrupt fundamental civic peace and tranquillity. Good is forced into hiding as we retreat behind closed doors. Preventing further harm and restoring the preconditions for civic tranquillity is a justifiable *casus belli*.

But the argument need not end there. One could go on to make the case that love of our neighbor—in this case, the Afghan people—is implicated as well. Or, less theologically, one could speak of equal regard for others based on human dignity and our common humanity. In

Afghanistan under the Taliban, one of every four children died before the age of five; life expectancy was about forty-three years; only 12 percent of the population had access to safe drinking water; and barely 30 percent of the men and only 15 percent of the women could read or write. To be sure, the Taliban took over a country already weakened by war. But rather than restoring services and helping to rebuild the social framework, they devastated it further, becoming violent depredators of their own people. The five years of Taliban rule produced nearly one million refugees, and an estimated six million Afghans, fully one-quarter of the population, were unable to find sufficient food to eat.[2]

"In each of the last few years," writes *New York Times* columnist Nicholas D. Kristof, ". . . 225,000 children died in Afghanistan before the age of 5, along with 15,000 women who died during pregnancy or childbirth. There was no way to save those lives under the Taliban; indeed, international organizations were retreating from Afghanistan even before 9/11 because of the arrests of Christian aid workers." Since the fall of the Taliban, he continues, "aid is pouring in and lives are being saved on an enormous scale. UNICEF, for example, has vaccinated 734,000 children against measles over the last two months, in a country where virtually no one had been vaccinated against disease in the previous 10 years. Because measles often led to death in Afghanistan, the vaccination campaign will save at least 35,000 children's lives each year."[3] Kristof also calculated that 115,000 fewer children under the age of five will die in Afghanistan each year, and that there will be 9,600 fewer maternal deaths. Kristof's point is that military intervention that stops violence saves more civilian lives than are harmed or lost in the conflict itself. Vital human goods, such as healthy children and mothers, cannot be achieved without a minimal level of civic peace.

American forces operating in Afghanistan not only recognize this precondition but are authorized to act on it: As soon as an area is free from pervasive and random violence, troops working as civil affairs teams are paired with local officials. Their task is to reconstruct schools, rebuild hospitals, repair roads, and restore water systems. An article in the *New York Times* describes the reopening of a school that had been closed and gutted by the Taliban. An American civil affairs team paid local workers to ready the school for classes of four thousand girls, grades first through twelfth.[4] I am not arguing that enabling Afghan girls to return to school is a sufficient reason in and of itself to deploy force. But it is clear that the restoration of a fundamental human right to education is a direct outgrowth of the U.S. response to the attacks of September 11. As a result, Afghanistan will be a more just place than if no military action had been taken.

Examining the evidence, we can see that the U.S. military response in Afghanistan clearly meets the just cause criterion of being a war fought with the right intention—to punish wrongdoers and to prevent them from murdering civilians in the future. The right authority criterion was met when both houses of the U.S. Congress authorized statutes and appropriated monies for the war effort. To this we can add the right authority enshrined in Article 51 of the United Nations Charter on self-defense. The Bush administration honored the charter's requirements by giving advance notice to the UN Security Council of its intention to used armed force to punish aggression—for the first time in anyone's living memory, as this notification requirement had become a dead letter. The Security Council, for its part, acknowledged the threat posed by Al Qaeda to the international community.

What of the criterion of last resort? Properly understood, last resort is a resort to armed force taken after deliberation rather than as an immediate reaction. The criterion of last resort does *not* compel a government to try everything else in actual fact but rather to explore other options before concluding that none seems appropriate or viable in light of the nature of the threat. What *is* one to do with the likes of bin Laden and Al Qaeda? They present no accountable, organized entity to engage—no sovereign state. They are not parties to any structure of diplomacy and thus cannot be negotiated with; in any event, because what they seek is our destruction, there is nothing to negotiate about. As Michael Quinlan, a British commentator, writes:

> As we saw amid the wreck of Yugoslavia, to place military action at the very end of the line may mean invoking it only when matters have reached a desperate pass, and when its scale (with the inevitable damage) is larger than its robust use earlier might have entailed. The passage of time is moreover not neutral—if Saddam Hussein had been given longer in Kuwait, or Milosevic in Kosovo, while their mouthpieces filibustered, the delay would have furthered their malign aims.[5]

What about the prospect of success? This prudential consideration is always tricky, and in this instance I cannot pronounce with any degree of certainty that this criterion is met. Afghanistan has been successfully liberated, even though enormous difficulties lie ahead, including the continuing jostling between rival ethnic and tribal groups and the tension, as a result of military errors, between local authorities, the Afghan government, and American and coalition forces. It is important for the time being that the United States remain engaged there, as the Afghan government is urging us, so that Afghanistan does not fall back into the dismal company of failed states.

Interdicting terrorism of global reach is a tough war aim indeed, even though, and undeniably, the entire world—especially the Muslim world—will be better off if the effort is successful. It is faithful Muslims, more than any other group, who are threatened and tormented when radical Islamists and their terrorist arm hold sway.

THE LIMITS SET BY JUST WAR

Although it would be unusual for a just war to be fought in an unjustifiable manner, the tradition addresses that unhappy possibility. Unjust means may be employed even in a just wars. Take one example. There is widespread agreement—not unanimity—among just war thinkers that America's use of atomic bombs in the Pacific theater in the waning days of World War II did not pass muster under the so-called *in bello* criteria that are central to the just war tradition. How so? Because such weaponry by definition violated the most fundamental of all *in bello* requirements: noncombatant immunity. There is less agreement on whether Allied saturation bombing of German cities during World War II must be similarly criticized, if not condemned outright. Michael Walzer argues that the nature of the Nazi threat was such that this acknowledged violation of limitations on means is acceptable. I am critical of the bombing campaign.[6]

The important point for my purposes here is not to explicate the precise nature of this or any other disagreement between thinkers who otherwise agree on so much, but to note that such disagreements speak to the ethical and political debates opened up by just war thinking that are as certainly foreclosed by the arguments of pacifism as well as by those of *realpolitik*. Pacifists condemn any resort to force outright, whether administered by a musket or a nuclear bomb, so debating justifications for a resort to force is moot. Hard-core *realpolitikers* sever ethical considerations from strategic ones, thus also shutting down debate.

Within the just war tradition, by contrast, nuances are not only possible but necessary. For example: The rhetoric of justification in debating just war versus holy war helps to lay out the boundaries of these two options tellingly. In some versions of just war thinking, refraining from slandering one's enemy is part and parcel of respecting human dignity. Minimally, the very heart of the matter lies in doing all one can to discriminate between a broad category of persons—if one's foe is a variant on a religion—and those whose version of the religion has led them into remorseless enmity against another religion or an entire people. Thus, in his speech to the nation on September 20, 2001, President George W. Bush made it clear that the war against terrorism was *not* a total war, not a holy war, not an attack on a religion.

"I want to speak tonight directly to Muslims throughout the world," the president stated.

> We respect your faith. It's practiced freely by many millions of Americans, and by millions more in countries that America counts as friends. Its teachings are good and peaceful, and those who commit evil in the name of Allah blaspheme the name of Islam. The terrorists are traitors to their own faith, trying, in effect, to hijack Islam itself. The enemy of America is not our many Muslim friends; it is not our many Arab friends. Our enemy is a radical network of terrorists, and every government that supports them.[7]

Contrast this to the words of Osama bin Laden, who condemns all Americans and targets all Americans and infidels wherever they may be found as legitimate candidates for death, including children. To this one must add the *routine,* not exceptional, characterization of Jews by radical Islamism not only as infidels but as "monkeys and pigs." From official Baghdad television comes a report that America can save itself only if it ceases to be a "toy in the hands of criminal world Zionism and its accursed, freak entity, which has usurped the land of Palestine and the land of the Arabs." The Iraqi spokesman goes on to characterize America's "new terrorist plans against the world" as "[serving] Zionist-Jewish greed for unlawful funds and innocent blood."[8]

Egypt's leading newspaper, the *Al-Ahram Weekly*, which is "vetted and approved by the Egyptian government," also reported that: "A compilation of the 'investigative' work of four reporters on Jewish control of the world states that Jews have become the political decision-makers and control the media in most capitals of the world (Washington, Paris, London, Berlin, Athens, Ankara) and says that the main apparatus for the Jews to control the world is the international Jewish lobby which works for Israel."[9] All-out slaughter of one's opponents is made easier if one dehumanizes them, as happens when Jews are simultaneously depicted as subhuman (monkeys and pigs) and superhuman (they run everything and engineered the September 11 attacks themselves because they are diabolically, almost inhumanly, clever).

In an interview with Sheik Muhammad Gemeaha, who was the representative in the United States "of the prominent Cairo center of Islamic learning, al-Azhar University, but also imam of the Islamic Cultural Center of New York," the sheik stated that "'only the Jews' were capable of destroying the World Trade Center and added that 'if it became known to the American people, they would have done to the Jews what Hitler did.'"[10] Such rhetoric, which invites indiscriminate slaughter of all Jews, all Americans, all infidels, is routine, not exceptional, among radical Islamists. By contrast, President Bush and other responsible American officials embodying right authority have singled out for censure only terrorists acting in the name of a radical ideology that also targets moderate Muslims for threat, assault, and death. These same officials praise faithful Muslims and honor their religion as one of the great world faiths. It is tendentious and wildly distorting to equate this approach of distinction with one that issues vicious blanket condemnations of all Americans, all infidels, all Jews, and all Muslims who are unfaithful in the eyes of bin Laden and other radicals.

I was a principal author and signatory of the statement "What We're Fighting For," in which sixty academics and intellectuals evoked the just war tradition explicitly and called for friendship between Americans and "our brothers and sisters in Muslim societies." Modeling our rhetoric after Abraham Lincoln's great Second Inaugural, we made the "forthright" statement: "We are not enemies, but friends. We must not be enemies. We have so much in common. There is so much that we must do together. Your human dignity, no less than ours—is what we believe we're fighting for. We know that, for some of you, mistrust of us is high, and we know that we Americans are partly responsible for that mistrust. But we must not be enemies." Our attempt to evoke commonalities and open a dialogue flowed directly from the statement's reliance on the just war tradition as the conceptual framework for explaining not only why we fight but how we fight. We must never lose the language of justice, for it reminds us of what is at stake and of the importance of keeping justice itself alive in how we fight.

JUST AND UNJUST MEANS

The two key *in bello* requirements are *proportionality* and *discrimination*. Proportionality refers to the need to use the level of force commensurate with the nature of the threat. If a nation faces a threat from a small, renegade band carrying out indiscriminate assassinations, it does not call in a tactical nuclear strike; rather, it puts a mobile unit in the field to track down this band and stop them. Discrimination refers to the need to differentiate between combatants and noncombatants. Noncombatants historically have been women, children, the aged and infirm, all unarmed persons going about their daily lives, and prisoners of war who have been disarmed by definition.

Knowingly and intentionally placing noncombatants in jeopardy and putting in place strategies that bring the greatest suffering and harm to noncombatants rather than to combatants is unacceptable on just war grounds.[11] According to just war thinking, it is better to risk the lives of one's own combatants than those of enemy noncombatants. In the case of U.S. military strikes in Afghanistan, of course, the noncombatants were not foes because they too had been victims of Al Qaeda and the Taliban. Even as U.S. forces attempted to strike only legitimate war targets, however, the campaign in Afghanistan renewed an old debate about what constitutes a legitimate war target.

Legitimate war targets may vary from conflict to conflict depending on what is deemed essential to the war effort of one's opponents. It is always suspect to destroy the infrastructure of civilian life. People should not be deprived of drinking water, for example. In the early formulations of the principle of proportionality, it was stipulated that wells from which persons and animals drink are never to be poisoned.

Although civilian casualties should be avoided if at all possible, they occur in every war. Inevitably, civilians fall in harm's way because a shell or bomb goes astray and misses its primary target or because war fighters are given faulty intelligence about where combatants are hidden, whether intentionally or unintentionally. The question of "collateral damage" should never be taken lightly. That the United States takes this matter very seriously indeed was noted in chapter 1. Every incident in which civilian lives are lost is investigated and invokes a reevaluation of tactics in an attempt to prevent such incidents in the future. The First Geneva Protocol of 1977, additional to the Geneva Conventions of August 12, 1949, relating to the Protection of Victims of International Armed Conflicts, codified basic just war norms on civilian and nonmilitary targeting, building these into the interstices of international norms on warmaking.

The demands of proportionality and discrimination are strenuous and cannot be alternately satisfied or ignored, depending on whether they serve one's war aims. The norms require that a war-fighting country ask itself critical questions about each criterion. The United States knows that it must try to answer these questions about its war on terrorism, even with all the difficulties attendant upon separating combatants from noncombatants when fighting a shadowy entity that is not a state actor and has neither de jure nor de facto accountability to any wider international community.

During and after a conflict, those animated by the just war tradition assess the conduct of a war-fighting nation by how its warriors conducted themselves. Did they rape and pillage? Were they operating under careful rules of engagement? Did they make every attempt to limit civilian casualties, knowing that, in time of war, civilians are invariably going to fall in harm's way? It is unworthy of the solemn nature of these questions to respond cynically or naively.

Since the Vietnam War and the restructuring of the U.S. military, those who train U.S. soldiers have taken pains to underscore the codes of ethics that derive from the just war tradition. No institution in America pays more attention to ethical restraint on the use of force than does the U.S. military. Thus, we do not threaten to kill and target explicitly three thousand civilians because that number of our own civilians were intentionally slaughtered. The soldier, by contrast to the terrorist, searches out and punishes those responsible for planning, aiding and abetting, and perpetrating the attacks, the act of aggression that served as the trigger for going to war. Preventing future attacks is a critical motivation. Just punishment, which observes restraints, is different from revenge, which knows no limits.

Have *in bello* criteria been met in the U.S. war on terrorism? On the rule of discrimination, it is clear that every effort is being made to separate combatants from noncombatants, and that targeting civilians has been ruled out as an explicit war-fighting strategy. As the author and war historian Caleb Carr puts it: "Warfare against civilians must never get answered in kind. For as failed a tactic as such warfare has been, reprisals similarly directed at civilians have been even more so—particularly when they have exceeded the original assault in scope. . . . Terror must never be answered with terror; but war can *only* be answered with war, and it is incumbent on us to devise a style of war more imaginative, more decisive, and yet more humane than anything terrorists can contrive."[12] What the terrorists are planning, if they can acquire effective biological, chemical, and nuclear weapons, are attacks on civilians. What we are planning is to interdict their plans: to stop them without resorting to their methods.

The improved accuracy of the U.S. air war, conducted with weaponry that is more precise and does less damage to the surround than was possible only a few years ago, serves the ends of discrimination. A senior navy officer, quoted by the *New York Times,* observed that: "With precision-guided weapons, you don't have to use as many bombs to achieve the desired effects, and using fewer weapons reduces the risk of collateral damage."[13] It is difficult to assess civilian casualties in a war theater, particularly in the patchwork that is Afghanistan, where different areas are under at least partial control of contesting tribal leaders (some of whom may have called in U.S. strikes against the Taliban when they were in fact trying to kill their own ethnic or tribal rivals, and this on more than one occasion). But attempts to come up with an accurate estimate of civilian deaths in Afghanistan have been made by human rights groups, the U.S.

military, and the *Los Angeles Times*. As of July 3, 2002, the consensus was that Afghan civilian casualties numbered between 1,000 and 2,000.[14] The *Los Angeles Times* reviewed more than 2,000 news stories covering 194 incidents. Their count was between 1,067 and 1,201. Relief officials of the Afghan government gave the same figures.

The *Los Angeles Times* concluded that the numbers suggest a very low casualty rate compared with earlier Afghan conflicts. In the early battles between competing Afghan warlords, an estimated 50,000 civilians were killed, according to the International Committee of the Red Cross. Soviet air raids in March 1979 killed 20,000 civilians in a few days in the western city of Herat—just a fraction of the estimated 670,000 civilians who died during the ten-year Soviet occupation. In the current conflict, Afghans themselves report that the big problem is not the accuracy of U.S. weaponry but flawed intelligence.

For example, before it fell, the Taliban put out false information about U.S. warplanes hitting a hospital in central Kabul. "Lies—all lies," said Ghulam Hussain, an emergency room nurse who said he was on duty that night. "Not a single person in this hospital was hurt. No rockets, no bombs, no missiles. Not even a window was broken."[15] The president of the Afghan Red Crescent (the Islamic equivalent of the Red Cross), a foe of the Taliban, is quoted as saying: "The Taliban propaganda created a huge distortion in the outside world, especially early in the war. . . . Civilians were killed, of course, but not nearly as many as the Taliban said, or in the way they said. . . . The Americans were careful and their bombs were very accurate. They checked to see for sure that they were targeting Taliban or al-Qaida bases or convoys. The people who died—it was accidental, not deliberate."[16]

To signal the serious nature of mistaken bombings in which civilians are harmed, Deputy Defense Secretary Paul D. Wolfowitz visited Afghanistan in July 2002 to explore recent incidents and to insist that these incidents be fully investigated.[17] The *New York Times* reported the results of an investigation in which on-site reviews were conducted of eleven locations where airstrikes had killed an estimated four hundred civilians. These reviews "suggest that American commanders have sometimes relied on mistaken information from local Afghans." Another factor was an understandable preference to use airstrikes with precision, high-tech weaponry rather than to put more soldiers in harm's way. American military commanders reiterated that "they take pains to ensure that civilians are spared, often verifying their targets with several sources of information. In many of the cases . . . they insist that they struck valid military targets."[18] The investigation concluded that too many men in the field had been given cell phones to call in intelligence; not all of them shared the interest of the coalition fighting terrorism in trying to uproot the last of the Al Qaeda–Taliban nexus.

The *New York Times* report also suggested that there might be a pattern in the U.S. military of overreliance on air power. During the Kosovo war, I criticized the Clinton administration for its stated zero-casualty policy. In that conflict, we aimed to sacrifice Serbian civilians rather than risk the life of a single American soldier. Such a policy is not acceptable on just war grounds. To his credit, President Bush warned from the beginning that American lives would be at risk and some would be lost. That commitment must always be carried through on the battlefield in order to protect civilians as thoroughly as possible in a theater of modern war.

The United States must do everything it can to minimize civilian deaths—and it is doing so. The United States must express remorse for every civilian death in a way that is not simply rote—and it is doing so. The United States must investigate every incident in which civilians are killed—and it is doing so. The United States must make some sort of recompense for unintended civilian casualties, and it may be making plans to do so—an unusual, even unheard of, act in wartime.

Finally, what about proportionality? Proportionality is a daunting challenge in the fight against terrorism. As the British analyst Clifford Longley writes: "Proportionality is a central concept of conventional just war theory. Under the principle of double effect, for instance, it may be justified to shell or bomb an enemy position even though there may be civilian casualties as a result. But shooting off rounds of ammunition that unintentionally kill civilians would not be justified simply to demonstrate . . . that the gunners are keen and up to scratch."[19] Terrorism aims to kill as many civilians as possible. Terrorists do not assess casualties against traditional war aims: The war aim *is* the death of civilians and the terrorizing of living civilians. How do we develop a proportional response to a disproportionate intended threat?

We begin by being clear about what we cannot do. We cannot use biochemical, biological, or counter-population nuclear weapons against civilians just because our enemies are setting about doing it. We cannot knowingly target any number of civilians because our opponents are doing it. We can attempt to interdict, disarm, and demolish training camps, weapons stashes, and active combatants, and we can deploy the weapons appropriate to that purpose.

It is fair to say that in Afghanistan the U.S. military is doing its best to respond proportionately. If it were not, the infrastructure of civilian life in that country would have been devastated completely, and it is not. Instead, schools are opening, women are returning to work, movie theaters are filled to capacity, and people can once again listen to music and dance at weddings. This observation is not intended to minimize the suffering and grief that has occurred in too many places, some of it the result of American mistakes in the war effort. But the restoration of a basic structure of civilian rule and a functioning state is a great benefit. We must stay engaged to this peaceful end.

•   •   •

The just war tradition of moral argument affords criteria for determining whether a resort to force is justified. Just war thinking provides guidance as to how a war should be fought and offers a framework of deliberation, evaluation, criticism, and moral challenge. Particularly useful is the tough-minded moral and political realism of just war thinking—not a Machiavellian "anything goes" realism, but an Augustinian realism that resists sentimentalism and insists on ethical restraint. Estrangement, conflict, and tragedy are constant features of the human condition, and just war thinking laced with Augustinian realism offers no assurances that we can ever make the world entirely safe. Augustinianism is skeptical about the exercise of power even as it recognizes the inescapability of power. Augustinian realists are not crusaders, but they do insist that we are called upon to act in a mode of realistic hope with a hardheaded recognition of the limits to action. You do not yourself have to be an Augustinian to recognize the abiding truths and strengths of this position.

Why, and how, have so many in our intellectual and religious life abandoned any such tradition or framework? That question will occupy us in the next four chapters.

5   THE ACADEMY
       RESPONDS TO TERROR

SOMEWHERE ALONG THE LINE, the idea took hold that, to be an intellectual, you have to be *against* it, whatever *it* is. The intellectual is a negator. Affirmation is not in his or her vocabulary. It was not always so. Throughout the World War II era, when the stakes were high, American intellectuals signed on for the war effort. Our foreign policy enjoyed bipartisan support: As everyone fought fascism, liberal, conservative, moderate, even radical intellectuals and academics found common ground without fearing that they would be accused of betraying a lofty stance of dissent. Unfortunately, signing on to fight Stalinism would have been a different thing. Many on the left were reluctant to face the truth about the Soviet Union: The body count numbering in the millions was even higher than the Nazis had managed. Sadly, left-wing denial has resurfaced in the wake of 9/11, as we shall see.

During the Cold War era, the bipartisan consensus held, but pre–World War II divisions come to the fore again. The hard left broke into sectarian factions. The anti-anti-Communists, aided and abetted by the hyperbole of professional anti-Communists, displayed a naivete about anything that paraded under the name "socialism" and continued to insist that the Soviet Union was no threat. The anti-anti-Communists were primarily opposed by anti-Communists (both Republicans and Democrats) and anti-anti-Communists (some Democrats, but primarily people of the far left). These divisions illustrated the lack of agreement after the war as to what to unite against, given the strange lapse of political conscience concerning the Soviet Union, with its millions killed and its gulags. (Albert Camus is the most famous honorable exception.) The massive trove of archival materials made available with the collapse of the Soviet Union proves—as if more proof were required—that, indeed, the Communist regime had posed the aggressive threat the reasonable anti-Communists always claimed. But anti-anti-Communists are loathe to acknowledge this, even today.

A BRIEF HISTORY OF POSTWAR DISCONTENTS

The Vietnam War era opened up a fissure that transfixes us yet and freezes our thinking. At that time the old Cold War consensus broke up and former allies split bitterly. The radical young saved their most vehement ire for those they called "the establishment," which was liberal. The United States entered an era of political vituperation and paranoia. The assault against the liberal "establishment" is an important part of the backdrop to the simmering discontents of the intellectual class in America today. It also helps to account for the time warp in which so much antiwar protest seems stuck, whether during the 1991 Persian Gulf War or the current war against terrorism. All the antiwar rhetoric of the Vietnam War era has been dusted off and sent marching yet again, often in a manner that displays a disconnect between the slogans and chants and current realities.

For those of us who entered young adulthood in the 1960s, to be an intellectual was to be in opposition. To be an academic was to be on the left, minimally a liberal. It was unfashionable to suggest that, although the Vietnam War was unjust and needed to be brought to a halt as quickly as possible, communism posed a real threat. Yet the historic record was clear: In the process of destroying freedom, Communist regimes slaughtered millions of their own people. Although that was an empirical reality, many denied it. Facts themselves came in for a beating, partly because the country had been lied to on so many occasions that the cynical view arose that no one ever tells the truth in public life, and partly because this period saw the beginning of a rush into the arms of subjectivism. From the subjectivist perspective, how I *feel* about something triumphs over serious thinking; this worldview prevailed in too many circles, the academy by no means exempted.

To the consternation of many, one key architect of the collapse of the old Cold War world and the Soviet Empire—which, to the people living under it, had indeed been an evil empire—was a conservative American president, Ronald Reagan. But the true voice of moral protest against what Albert Camus called "the socialism of the gallows" was that of an unarmed prophet and impassioned defender of human rights, Pope John Paul II. Holding two doctorates in theology, John Paul II had read the works of Marx and Engels and could counter the defenders of "really existing socialism" on their own grounds. Yet Pope John Paul II was ignored in intellectual circles, and Ronald Reagan was treated with contempt. Indeed, I recall very well colleagues telling me that Reagan's election would mean nuclear war. Dire predictions of this sort proliferated. People murmured darkly of moving to Canada or somewhere else where movie stars do not get elected president. I had not voted for Reagan, but this sort of thing struck me as preposterous and self-important. It still does.

What actually happened, of course, was a nuclear détente and standdown as Reagan and his Soviet counterpart, Mikhail Gorbachev, developed an extraordinary working relationship. Things were not moving the way left-wing ideology had dictated. This outcome should have prompted a bit of rethinking for scholars and intellectuals, not necessarily as a volte-face, but as a critical recognition of altered circumstances and the mounting evidence putting pressure on their categories and conclusions. But that rarely happened. One wag's somewhat bitter depiction of the dominant intellectual class as "the herd of independent minds" struck me as all too apt all too often.

Over time such automatic oppositionism seems to harden into identity. That is the only way I can make sense of the vituperation that so often accompanies attacks from those who consider themselves radicals, as well as other dominant voices both inside and outside the academy, against those with whom they disagree. The people who were hotly dismissive when Western observers articulated and condemned what was taking place behind the Iron Curtain, calling these assessments just so much CIA propaganda, now dismiss or diminish (or their successors do) attempts to take the measure of the threat that terrorism poses to America and Americans—and indeed, to peoples everywhere who fall under indictment by Islamist fundamentalists, including moderate, reformist, and civic Muslims. Many intellectuals seem to believe that those of their number who support their country's effort are betraying their calling. The late Christopher Lasch dubbed this sort of automatic negativism "pseudo-radicalism."[1] It fails to make critical distinctions and fails to take the measure of what is at stake *now*, not a quarter of a century ago.

The fact that the vast majority of one's country men and women disagree with the view that America brought the attacks on herself, and say so, is called "stifling" dissent, we are told, as if the only true measure of dissent is whether the majority of one's country men and women agree with what one is saying.[2] If a majority agrees with oppositionists, dissent is alive; if a majority does not agree with them, dissent is being stifled. The unstated purpose in such proclamations of quashed dissent is to discredit the policymakers under attack and to silence serious opponents by linking them to dissent stifling. If they succeed in such efforts, these intellectuals declare that dissent is alive and well; if not, it must be that dissent has been silenced.

The repeated post–9/11 insistence that no space exists within American society today to make contrarian arguments is risible. One hears and reads such arguments all the time. Less frequently heard, in fact, is intellectual *assent* to something the government is doing or that America is undertaking from outspoken academics and intellectuals—as a number of us have learned over the years.

"WHAT WE'RE FIGHTING FOR": AMERICAN INTELLECTUALS DEFEND THE WAR AGAINST TERRORISM

As discussed in chapter 4, I was part of a group of sixty academics and intellectuals who, on February 12, 2001, issued a statement, "What We're Fighting For: A Letter from America," that outlined what we believe is at stake in the war against terrorism. We were concerned about the fate of five fundamental truths that, we insisted, "pertain to all people without distinction": that all human beings are born free and equal in dignity and rights; that the basic subject of society is the human person, and the legitimate role of government is to protect and help to foster the conditions for human flourishing; that human beings naturally desire to seek the truth about life's purposes and ultimate ends; that freedom of conscience and religious freedom are inviolable rights of the human person; and that killing in the name of God is contrary to faith in God and the greatest betrayal of the universality of religious faith. We stated that we were fighting to defend ourselves and to defend these principles.[3]

We associated these five principles with "American values" because America is premised on some version of these truths—not that America alone is the bearer of them. We insisted on freedom of religion. We lamented our society's shortcomings and frequent failures to live up to its highest ideals. We defended the resort to war on just war terms and reaffirmed without reservation just war restraints on how the war was to be pursued. Finally, we called for brotherhood and sisterhood with Muslims, urging that what unites us is greater than what divides us. Finally, we pledged ourselves to stay on guard against jingoism and extremism in our own efforts.

We hoped that the statement would do two things. First, we wanted to demonstrate to our counterparts in other countries that American intellectuals and academics are not uniformly in the opposition where the war effort is concerned. We sought to begin a dialogue with intellectuals in other countries who are ambivalent about or disagree with the American effort. Second, we hoped to offer a conceptual framework within which to assess critically America's efforts.

The statement was almost completely ignored by the media in America. Those who did comment domestically rose up and, as this particular company tends to do, vocally denounced the statement as a pro-war celebration.

Because this all-too-predictable response of a cohort of American academics and intellectuals to "What We're Fighting For" illustrates the weak arguments and severe rhetoric that spring up like a mushroom overnight, it is worth reviewing their rejoinders in some detail, as well as items from academic journals, the news media, and the popular press.

The reactions I criticize share four characteristics. One or more of these features is *always* present in ideological attacks that refuse to come to grips with current realities: they distort or ignore facts; they deploy tired categories that give one a sense, as Václav Havel put it, of returning to the tired categories of a previous era; they assert a false clarity that makes things much simpler than they really are and that ignore the "fog of war" and politics by deploying inflammatory rhetoric and deeply flawed historic analogies; and they attack American motivations, aims, and, not infrequently, Americans themselves as dupes of these motivations and aims. The remainder of this chapter will consider the first two characteristics of ideological attacks on America's war on terrorism, and I discuss the other two in chapter 6.

IGNORING OR DISTORTING THE FACTS

It is difficult to make a case that facts are being distorted if one's opponent believes there is no such thing. I have already noted the commonplace distortion of the number of civilian casualties, both in the 1991 Persian Gulf War with Iraq and in Afghanistan. Those who provide inflated casualty figures do so casually and matter-of-factly but cite no hard evidence from credible sources. In "Letter from United States Citizens to Friends in Europe," a rejoinder to "What We're Fighting For" and presented as an attempt to set the record straight, the third paragraph begins with an example of the fact-shunning hyperbole I have in mind. The statement claims that the "material destruction envisaged" by the U.S. military in the war effort in Afghanistan is "immeasurable." The human damage is also tagged "immeasurable," to which is added "the moral desperation and hatred that are certain to be felt by *millions of people who can only watch helplessly as their world is devastated*" by the United States.[4]

Are the authors of this statement aware of the ongoing assessments made by the U.S. military itself, as well as by international observers and analysts attempting to get as accurate a reading as possible of the material damage in Afghanistan? How do they square their dire picture of "millions" of Afghanis growing in hatred toward the United States with the witnessed scenes of celebrating in the streets of Kabul, dancing at weddings, women going to school and teaching, moviegoers crowding into theaters, and small shops and enterprises springing up? Of course, we must note the tragic effects of military errors or miscalculations in order to take stock honestly. But what is remarkable up to this point—and I write in the summer of 2002—is the fact that so little anti-Americanism has developed in Afghanistan despite the inevitable losses from bombing mistakes.[5]

Perhaps those who suffered under the Taliban have a clearer sense of what is at stake than do those who claim to be on their side but ignore the Afghanis' own reactions. The Afghan government has repeatedly and insistently argued that Afghanistan needs America to remain engaged in their country for a long time to come in order to stabilize and rebuild the devastation wrought, not by American military action, but by the actions of the Taliban and the years of war against the Soviets. The citizens of Afghanistan appreciate what is at stake in the attempt to create an infrastructure of law to succeed the brutal lawlessness that was Taliban rule. Should we tolerate a regime that routinely shot women in the back of the head for alleged adultery, that slit throats before spectators, that toppled walls on homosexuals?[6] If not, what sort of effort would the critics mount to disrupt Al Qaeda training camps and the Taliban's active support of these camps? This we are never told. Instead, America's critics lump America and her allies together with the Taliban and Al Qaeda victimizers of the Afghan people as guilty of brutality.

If what the United States is doing in Afghanistan has been so uniformly awful, why do Afghanis continue to seek our presence in their country? The likeliest response to this question is what Marxist and pseudo-Marxist ideology call "false consciousness." To put it simply: The Afghani government and people do not know what they are talking about. Their consciousness has gone bad, and they cannot appreciate their own best interests. To call such arguments condescending is to understate, but people still make them. Thus, all the Afghanis in exile who are returning to their country in huge numbers to help rebuild now that the Taliban is removed from power and Al Qaeda is on the run; all the women and girls who are back at work and in school; these and more who credit the United States with making these changes possible—all are being duped.

WAS THERE A MAD RUSH TO WAR?

America's response to the attacks of September 11 has been characterized as a "mad rush to war," and there has been much flutter about Bush the reckless cowboy. What are the criteria for a "mad rush" by contrast to deliberate movement? "Mad rush" suggests that, on September 12, America wildly began striking back. But that is not what happened. There was no rush to war. The Bush administration did immediately start thinking in terms of war, but this should come as no surprise. By all known standards of international law and under the terms of the United Nations Charter, the attacks of September 11 were acts of war. The United States, as a sovereign state, has a fundamental right to defend herself.

In 1625, Hugo Grotius, a Dutch jurist, wrote *Rights of War and Peace,* widely acknowledged as the beginning of what is now called "international law." Grotius took it as stipulated that states "have first and foremost the right to defend themselves. And, tangentially, just as a society of human beings has the right to punish a member who has committed a crime against another, so a nation or a group of nations have the right to punish a state or ruler that has injured another unjustly."[7] The claim that the United States is behaving like a trigger-happy cowboy flies in the face of the facts and does not comport with settled standards of international law and centuries of practice. Remarkably, the condemnatory "Letter from the United States" document confounds matters by claiming on behalf of "humanity as a whole" a "right to defend its own survival against the 'self defense' of an unchecked superpower." All "victims of U.S. military power" are enjoined to act in "solidarity" against the United States, including outraged American citizens. Because Osama bin Laden and others like him count as victims in this scenario, the implication is that only those with a grievance against America, real or imagined, are fighting the good fight for "whatever universal values we claim to cherish." This muddled document does not articulate these universal values. So we are left to ponder *how* such values are to be protected and defended save to somehow *stop* everything the United States is doing. Then our "victims"—like bin Laden and the Taliban—can presumably carry on unchecked.

There are, by contrast, many reasonable ways to debate the matter, including the argument that the United States, on prudential grounds, should not have committed itself to armed conflict. But to make a false claim about what happened is not a legitimate point of departure for debate. The argument of those who do not get the basic time line right, or who cannot account for facts verifiable by widely available evidence, is going to collapse under the weight of its initial distortions. Almost invariably, distortions of the facts of a situation—of what is actually happening or has happened—go hand in hand with inflammatory rhetoric. The great twentieth-century political theorist Hannah Arendt famously claimed in her masterwork, *The Origins of Totalitarianism,* that the first victim of totalitarian ideology is the truth. Totalitarianism obliterates the basic distinction between truth and falsehood; indeed, Arendt insisted, the ideal candidate for totalitarian rule is someone for whom truth and falsehood no longer exist as distinct categories.[8] Arendt argued that politics depends on getting the facts right. She noted that the French Prime Minister Georges Clemenceau, in discussing the origins of World War I, acknowledged that disputes about who, or what, led to the calamity would be long debated. "But I know one thing for certain," he insisted. "They will not say Belgium invaded Germany."[9]

The number of unintentional civilian casualties matters, but the number of intentional civilian casualties matters as well. This is a point Michael Walzer makes in his hard-hitting essay "Can There Be a Decent Left?"

> A few left academics have tried to figure out how many civilians actually died in Afghanistan, aiming at as high a figure as possible, on the assumption, apparently, that if the number is greater than the number of people killed in the attacks on the Twin Towers, the war is unjust. . . . But the claim that the numbers matter in just this way—that the 3,120th death determines the injustice of the war—is wrong. It denies one of the most basic and best understood moral distinctions: between premeditated murder and unintended killing. And the denial isn't accidental, as if the people making it just forgot about, or didn't know about, the everyday moral world. The denial is willful: unintended killing by Americans in Afghanistan counts as murder.[10]

Such denials and distortions are the stock-in-trade of polemics that play fast and loose with the evidence. As I have argued, scholarly integrity is not served when a commentator skips over the facts before going on to interpret a situation in a way that makes his or her "side" look good. Instead, any sound evaluation flows from as full a factual account as one can make of critical events. Interpretation is intrinsically tried to a description of the situation. To see how this works in the breach, let's consider one "truism" that is not "true" at all.

DID AMERICA CREATE OSAMA BIN LADEN?

We have heard repeatedly since 9/11 that Osama bin Laden and the Afghan Arabs who formed the core of Al Qaeda are creatures of the United States. (Many have responded that if this charge were true, our responsibility would be doubled, not negated.) Peter L. Bergen, one of the leading experts on bin Laden and his organization and someone who knows the Afghan situation intimately, writes: "Various books and multiple news reports have charged that the CIA armed and trained the Afghan Arabs and even bin Laden himself as part of its operation to support the Afghan rebels fighting the Soviets in the 1980s. They argue, therefore, that the United States is culpable in the jihads and terrorism those militants subsequently spread around the world. As we shall see, those charges are overblown and are not supported by the evidence."[11]

Frequently heard in academic debates and discussions is the claim that the CIA helped bin Laden build his first terrorist training camp.[12] As Bergen writes: "This defies common sense. American officials did not venture into Afghanistan during the war against the Soviets for fear of handing the communists a propaganda victory if they were captured." In fact, the CIA "had very limited dealings" with the Afghans, let alone the Afghan Arabs, Bergen writes, "and for good reason. . . . The CIA did not need the Afghan Arabs, and the Afghan Arabs did not need the CIA. So the notion that the Agency funded and trained the Afghan Arabs is, at best, misleading."[13]

Some of those who claim American culpability for the creation of Islamist terrorism make an allegation of historic vintage, namely, that the beginning of Western offenses is located in the medieval Crusades, which they pronounce to be a "root cause" of September 11. I have no interest in defending the Crusades. I oppose any triumphalist undertaking, and the Crusades were a kind of holy war, hence unacceptable. But it is a real stretch to go all the way back to the eleventh century to start building a bill of particulars against the West, as if Western perfidy popped out of nowhere in the high Middle Ages and has continued unabated ever since. As the historic evidence shows, the Crusades were a complex series of events that began as a direct response to four centuries of conquest and attack by an energetic and expansionist Islam. Christians had been routed and expelled from Palestine, Syria, and

Egypt. By the eighth century, Christian North Africa, the home of St. Augustine, was gone. You would never know about this prehistory of the Crusades, however, if you read and listened to contemporary reports. Some critiques of the West "reach back a millennium into Christian crusades into Arab homelands," notes the *New York Times*, without adding that these were Arab homelands because the indigenous Christian population had been attacked, defeated, and displaced.[14]

Considering that Islamic warriors nearly advanced into the heart of what became Western Europe at the Battle of Poitiers in what is now the south of France in 732 A.D., it is unsurprising that the crusaders saw the reconquest of Jerusalem as an act of restoration rather than an imperial adventure. If there are grievances left over from the crusading era, the aggrieved would include all parties. Few seem to appreciate that Christendom was *not* the dominant power in the Middle Ages: Islam was. Western efforts to seize what they had once controlled and regain the lands inhabited by the earliest Christians—indeed, the lands in which the Christian religion began—were often bloody. Nobody played by Marquis of Queensbury rules in that day and age. (What is fascinating is that, in light of the general brutality of the era, protesting voices did emerge in the West in the writings of churchmen who opposed the Crusades on just war grounds.) Nevertheless, any simplistic condemnation of the Crusades, whether as Western imperialistic adventuring or as noble religious endeavor, fails the test of complexity.

What is fascinating is that simplistic denunciations of the Crusades have become "the fact of the matter" to some commentators, who roundly denounce anyone who offers an equally simplistic defense. Imagine the reaction if Western intellectuals and political leaders justified for even a second a Western attack on the Muslim world as an appropriate response to leftover grievances from the Islamic conquests that lasted for centuries and then picked up again from the fourteenth through the seventeenth century. (Turkish forces advanced as far as the gates of Vienna in 1683.) A Western religious leader, politician, or polemicist who pointed to Islam's attacks on Western Europe, whether in the eighth century or the seventeenth, as a continuing grievance would be dismissed from the company of serious interlocutors very quickly. We would find such a charge preposterous, inflammatory, and unacceptable. Why, then, should a historic narrative based on an ideologically charged, partial reading of the historic record as a narrative of remorseless Christian aggression be taken seriously? Surely it makes good sense to oppose such exculpatory strategies from any direction.

WORN-OUT CATEGORIES AND FALSE ANALOGIES

Signs of what Václav Havel calls "evasive language" are everywhere in evidence in response to American efforts to combat terrorism and punish those responsible for September 11. To Havel, the ideological thinking that lies at the heart of evasive language ignores concrete truths and realities in favor of abstract claims. Politics as a sphere of dialectical maneuvers that always seem to underwrite one's prefabricated claims and conclusions trumps politics as a sphere of concrete responsibility.[15] Havel argues that ideologues think that the world conforms to a simple linear scale, with "progressive" at one end of a continuum and "reactionary" at the other. So America is criticized as a society that must be taken to task on principle because it is "bourgeois," or "capitalist," or "imperialist," or "racist," or "patriarchal"—hence, not "progressive" by definition. These categories substitute for analysis.

When Hannah Arendt was asked whether she was a liberal or a conservative, she criticized the question. No real illumination ever comes out of "thinking" in ideological categories, she noted, for that does not constitute thinking at all. Categorical rigidities inhibit thought rather than promote reflection; Michael Walzer has been led to call the (academic) leftist critique of U.S. foreign policy, with its blanket condemnations, "stupid, overwrought, grossly inaccurate."[16]

Such critics argue, for example, that the attacks of September 11 are "blowback": a reaction we brought on ourselves by being engaged with the world.[17] Characteristic of these arguments is a paper by the Princeton theologian Mark Taylor, who depicts the "organized terror experienced by ever larger numbers of world communities today as a result of U.S.-led, sponsored or supported activities in its so-called 'war on terrorism.'" We are not told what these "ever larger numbers" are, nor which communities Taylor has in mind; neither does he provide details of the "organized terror" they allegedly experience at our hands. The charge alone will do. If one asks for concrete specifics, the response is silence. The historian Louis Menand explains the dilemma with the concept of blowback:

> Blowback, as the term is used in the literature on September 11th, is intended to carry moral weight: if you insist on tramping through other people's flower gardens, you can't complain when you get stung is the general idea. But this is true, without moral implication, of any sufficiently complex undertaking. It's like saying, If you keep building huge passenger ships, sooner or later one of them is going to hit an iceberg. . . . The destruction of the World Trade Center—an almost inconceivably long-odds operation itself—was at the extreme of the imaginable consequences of supporting an Afghan resistance movement in 1979. On some level it's just a consequence of participating in global affairs at all. This is why the notion . . . that September 11th was a "wake-up call" is empty. Wake up to what? The fact that the United States is involved in the affairs of other nations? *If that is a problem, we are left with only two alternatives: isolationism or conquest. Anything in between is bound to produce results that Americans do not like but could not have foreseen.* (emphasis mine)[18]

Apparently convinced that America has opted for conquest, Taylor accuses the United States of being the number-one exporter of terror worldwide. He offers the "evidence" of "the large number of civilians in Afghanistan, whose deaths now exceed in number those lost at the New York World Trade Center," thereby eliding the central distinction between the intentional murder of civilians and the unintended deaths that happen in any war. The legally authorized response to the September 11 attacks— when the United Nations Security Council for the first time in its history declared that the attacks constituted an assault on all members of the UN—strikes Taylor as "imperial retaliatory terrorism." The World Trade Center was attacked, he alleges, not because that was the way to kill the largest number of civilians as well as assault an international symbol and center of economic life (nationals from eighty-six countries died in the attacks), but solely because it is a "symbol of today's financial wealth and trade."[19]

In a deeply flawed analogy that, sadly, ties a prophet of peace to an advocate of indiscriminate slaughter of civilian populations, Taylor claims that Jesus, like Osama bin Laden, attacked the "'World Trade Center' of

Jerusalem" in his day, though without violence.[20] This grotesque analogy not only associates Jesus with the September 11 attackers, it assimilates our destroyed World Trade Center towers, the epicenter of "financial wealth," to Jerusalem, the so-called World Trade Center in Jesus' day. Jerusalem was the capital of Jewish Palestine. The association of Jerusalem with "financial wealth" is troubling given the foundational anti-Semitism of the September 11 attackers, who claimed that Jews control world finance. It is astonishing that Taylor assimilates two "financial centers" as appropriate targets for attack, the one explicitly Jewish, the other rhetorically proclaimed as such by the terrorists. Whatever the specific grievances of the contemporary Muslim world, it is distorted at best to collapse the wrath of Jesus against those who would defame a holy temple by using it for activities that were not sacral with the violent murder of almost three thousand innocent human beings.

Michael Walzer believes that the left is haunted by leftover ideology from the Marxist theory of imperialism and "the third worldist doctrines of the 1960s and 1970s," and that this helps to account for claims as wild as those I have just examined. One consequence is "the inability of leftists to recognize or acknowledge the power of religion in the modern world. Whenever writers on the left say that the 'root cause' of terror is global inequality or human poverty, the assertion is in fact a denial that religious motives really count."[21]

This is an important insight. Walzer suggests that there is a "suppressed discourse," but it is not, as usually claimed, the voices of academic dissent, for that discourse is flourishing. What we hear far too little of is serious reflection on religion. Religion is epiphenomenal to Marxists and its various offshoots. It is "false consciousness" par excellence. Osama bin Laden's talk of infidels and the will of Allah is thus just a quaint rhetorical turn; the "real" reasons for his murderous rampages must lie elsewhere. As a result of the suppression of any view of religion more thoughtful than this one, we remain unable to appreciate what is going on in the war on terrorism and what is really at stake.

6   TAKING TERRORISTS
        AT THEIR WORD

THE YALE HISTORIAN Donald Kagan is right: It is time to take Osama bin Laden and others at their word. They are not "reluctant to reveal their motives." "In countless statements," Kagan notes,

> he and other terrorists have made it clear that the U.S. is "the great Satan," the enemy of all they hold dear. And what these terrorists hold dear includes the establishment of an extreme and reactionary Muslim fundamentalism in all currently Muslim lands, at least—which is a considerable portion of the globe. Such a regime would impose a totalitarian theocracy that would subjugate the mass of people, especially women. . . . No change of American policy, no retreat from the world, no repentance for past deeds or increase of national modesty can change these things. Only the destruction of America and its way of life will do, and Osama bin Laden makes no bones about this.[1]

In a videotaped statement after the attacks on New York and Washington, Osama bin Laden claimed that God Almighty himself had struck America through the terrorists. John Paul II responded that it was grotesque and wholly unacceptable to drag God into this kind of thing and to claim that God's will led to the intentional slaughter of civilians. But such responses will not deter bin Laden, who proclaimed that God had blessed a group of "vanguard Muslims" who successfully carried out the attacks. The end is clear, he thundered: to destroy America.

What does one do when confronted with such rhetoric? A common tactic is to pretend to have not heard it and to turn bin Laden's words into a political platform that comports with one's own prejudices: Israel must get out of the occupied territories entirely; the United States must withdraw from the world; and so on. Perhaps becoming an isolationist America that has wholly abandoned Israel would buy us a little time, if we take bin Laden seriously. But, we are told in so many words, his religious messages are window dressing and the heart of the matter lies elsewhere, in leftover colonial ire or antiglobalist chagrin.

In an essay in Egypt's *Al-Ahram Weekly,* the celebrated American academic Edward Said does precisely this, beginning with the claim that Arabs and Muslims in the United States now face "targeted hostility." He speaks of "many reported instances of discriminatory behavior against Arabs," who draw "unwelcome attention" if they speak Arabic. He claims that Arabs are "usually made to stand aside for special attention during airport security checks."[2] (I fly at least twice a week, usually more often, and I have never seen this happen; indeed, the directives sent down by the secretary of Transportation prohibiting ethnic and racial profiling make it less likely that persons of Arab descent will be singled out. This is *not* to say it never happens, but it is *not* official policy.) Remarkably, however, views of mainstream Islam became more favorable in the wake of September 11, thanks in important part to President Bush's visit to a mosque, his words of reconciliation to Muslims, and his generous characterizations of authentic Islam, which he consistently contrasts to radical Islamicism.[3]

Said reports being "stunned when a European friend asked me what I thought of a declaration by 60 American intellectuals that was published in all the major French, German, Italian and other continental papers but which did not appear in the U.S. at all." He implies that there was some sort of underhanded attempt in the United States to downplay our statement "What We're Fighting For" for domestic consumption (which he condemns), but the truth of the matter is that the U.S.

press just didn't care—after all, the signatories were *affirming* an effort rather than condemning it, and that, apparently, was not newsworthy.[4]

Said scores the signatories for refusing to note the "hundreds of thousands killed . . . by Israel with U.S. support, or the hundreds of thousands killed by U.S.-maintained sanctions against the innocent civilian population of Iraq."[5] Where is the evidence for these figures? Let it be said that I do not know how many have died over the years at the hands of Israel, but hundreds of thousands is a preposterous claim. One would also have to discriminate between combatant and noncombatant deaths, a distinction that Said appears to disdain. (At least it plays no role in his argument.) No doubt estimates on those killed at the hands of the Israelis are available from respected historians and human rights groups. There is no doubt that too many Palestinian civilians have suffered and died in the ongoing travail. Too many Israelis have suffered and died as well. There is misery enough to go around.

Concerning Iraq, we do have figures. Civilian casualties in the Persian Gulf War—and these are Iraq's own figures—are 3,200 killed and 6,000 wounded. Lawrence Freedman, a British professor of war studies at King's College, explains part of the discrepancy between the figures often cited and the actual figures:

> Critics of the U.S. often cite a ludicrous figure of 200,000 Iraqis dead. It originates in the comment of a U.S. general puzzled at the discrepancy between the number of Iraqis taken prisoner and those who were assumed to be in position waiting for coalition forces. . . . Moreover, one reason why George Bush senior stopped the ground war when he did was because of reports that U.S. aircraft were engaged in a turkey shoot of a retreating Iraqi convoy. . . . In fact, most of the Iraqis had fled as soon as the shooting began.[6]

Said also speaks of the alleged "hundreds of thousands" killed as a direct result of the "U.S.-maintained" embargo as if United Nations authorization had nothing to do with it. Freedman takes on such claims, including the oft-cited figure of 500,000 Iraqi children dead because of "inadequate nutrition and medical treatment." The sanctions do not work this way. They were adapted by the UN to "allow unlimited funds for food and medicine." Rather than using available monies for food and medicine for his people, Saddam Hussein has used the resources to "strengthen the state apparatus." Thus, to suggest that "Iraqi suffering is caused by the U.S., while neglecting to mention the direct responsibility of Saddam, is a gross distortion."[7] If hundreds of thousands of Iraqi children have died—and the figure, most credible analysts agree, is wildly inflated—their deaths are the direct responsibility of Saddam. In Said's world, the West, especially the United States, has always blocked the legitimate aspirations of Arab peoples, despite many examples of U.S. support for Arab countries; for example, President Eisenhower in 1956 required that Israel return territories seized from Egypt during the Suez Crisis.

Finally, for Edward Said, the authors of "What We're Fighting For" are culpable because they "align themselves so flagrantly with . . . power"; our position "augurs a new and degraded era in the production of intellectual discourse." He warns about a return to the bad old days when intellectuals during the Cold War worked for the CIA and were "militantly unreflective and uncritical."[8] This "shameful episode" now is being repeated, he cries. What is remarkable in this commentary is the undefended view that intellectuals must always be oppositionists—unless, presumably, they are for the causes that Said supports. Not only are intellectuals who support the war effort collaborationists, but they use their "bullying way" in order "to cow foreign readers into submission"—a statement that shows very little confidence in, or respect for, foreign readers. Once again we see that within the framework of American intellectual life at present the dissenters are likely to be those who defend U.S. foreign policy, at least in part. As one tenured professor of modern Middle East politics put it to Franklin Foer, a reporter from *The New Republic:* "You don't get tenure by praising American policy."[9]

FALSE CLARITY DERIVED
FROM FLAWED ANALOGIES

Let's turn now to the third characteristic of ideological attacks: a false clarity derived from flawed analogies. Consider one frequently voiced analogy. We are told that the federal government's initial detention of some 1,200 men of Middle Eastern descent in the wake of September 11 (with many more questioned and released) was as indiscriminate and brutal as the notorious Palmer Raids. In the early 1920s, anarchists had been carrying out violent attacks in American cities. Attorney General A. Mitchell Palmer's reaction (a suicide bomber had blown himself up outside Palmer's home, so it got personal) is regarded by historians as a grievous overreaction to these events and to the peril supposedly represented by anyone accused of being a "Red."

The "Red Scare" extended to groups that had legitimate grievances and were active in trying to right some wrongs. The writer Clancy Sigal claims that "between 4,000 and 10,000 people were secretly efficiently rounded up." Whether these figures are accurate, I do not know, but the 6,000-person gap between the lowest and highest estimates suggests considerable malleability. Whether the high or low estimate is most accurate, it is true that tremendous injustices were supported and sustained at the highest levels of government. Those rounded up during the Palmer Raids, Sigal continues, "like today's detainees, . . . were often held without bail, habeas corpus rights or access to lawyers."[10] Is this an accurate depiction of the present? Is the current situation analogous to the Palmer Raids? Is our Bill of Rights dangerously imperiled?[11]

To be sure, it is *always* in order to worry about threats to civil liberties in a time of war and crisis. But it is not responsible political argument to claim that a current situation is "just like" some previous and widely acknowledged horrible situation unless it actually is. The Palmer Raids are an example of bigotry officially sustained, supported, and encouraged by the U.S. government from the top down. The behavior of the president, the head of the FBI, the attorney general, and all responsible officials in the wake of September 11, by contrast, was to insist that *no vigilante action against Arab Americans and Muslims was acceptable.* Period. Rather than encouraging such action, these officials specifically condemned it. The president stated that "no one should be singled out for unfair treatment or unkind words because of their ethnic background or religious faith." How is this response "like" the Palmer Raids?

A zealous young J. Edgar Hoover was A. Mitchell Palmer's enforcer. Current FBI Director Robert Mueller, by contrast, "authorized hate-crime investigations into 40 attacks against Arab-American citizens and institutions. . . . Indeed, not one prominent member of either party has stoked anti-Arab or anti-Muslim racism."[12] The "face of terror" is "not the true face of Islam," the president has said again and again. I can see no similarity here to the brutal attacks against immigrants and "Reds" initiated by A. Mitchell Palmer, nor to the internment of 120,000 persons of Japanese descent in World War II (about half of whom were American citizens).

What, then, of the 9/11 detainees? The Patriot Act of 2001 authorizes the attorney general of the United States, as part of the Justice Department's response to terrorism, to detain *unlawful aliens* for the purpose of determining whether they pose a threat to the United States. Notes the *New York Times:* "The roundup that followed the attacks, conducted with wartime urgency and uncommon secrecy, led to the detention of more than 1,200 people suspected of violating immigration laws, being material witnesses to terrorism or fighting for the enemy. . . . Most of the detainees have since been released or deported, with fewer than 200 still being held."[13] The complicated issue involved is whether the constitutional guarantees of procedural and substantive due process have been violated and what guarantees pertain, if any, to noncitizen illegal aliens. The Supreme Court has ruled that aliens, even those present illegally, do have procedural protections under the Fourth and Fifth Amendments. At the same time, Congress has considerable latitude regarding the substantive issues of immigration policy—and the detainee situation does fall under the jurisdiction of the Immigration and Naturalization Service (INS). Case law suggests that a person who poses a threat to the community can be held civilly, provided that the affected persons constitute a narrow class who are particularly dangerous to the community.

In *Zadvydas v. Davis,* decided in 2001, Justice Stephen Breyer, writing for the majority, held that holding aliens for an indefinite period violates substantive due process. But civil confinement might well apply—and this for unlimited detention—to a small segment of particularly dangerous persons, such as suspected terrorists. The upshot is that the detention does not violate per se the due process rights of detainees. The real question is: How long can they be detained? What constitutes a reasonable length of time? In the case of an emergency, additional detention is provided for under an amended regulation that became effective September 17, 2001.[14]

The Patriot Act requires a review of the cases of aliens held as suspected terrorists every six months. This requirement is scarcely the stuff out of which police states are made. The Palmer Raids and the World War II detentions of entire families of Japanese and Japanese Americans bear no similarity to the carefully targeted and delimited detentions, with built-in safeguards, of today. To reiterate: It is not only appropriate but necessary for vigilant citizens and watchdog civil liberties groups to raise questions about these matters. There is real danger, however, in hyperbolic accusations that the government has run amok. When the hysteria charged to the government is instead to be found in words of accusation that are demonstrably false, our confidence in responsible criticism and careful examination of what is happening to civil liberties may be undermined.

Alarmist accusations based on flawed analogies do not—as their defenders sometimes claim—"open up" debate. Instead, they have the opposite effect. These accusations push subtlety into the shadows and lead persons who may have qualms about the government's actions to defend the government against outlandish charges. Whether charges of government abuse come from the left, the right, or the middle, it is vital to politics that concrete and accurate evidence lie at the heart of any argument. At present, the overheated distortions emanate primarily from the far left. Michael Walzer describes these efforts as a search for "the moral purism of blaming America first," rather than assessing with the seriousness it deserves what can be laid at the doorstep of America, or of a particular administration, and what cannot.[15]

ATTACKING AMERICAN MOTIVES AND ACTIONS

In a game called "gotcha," the rules are pretty simple. One makes blanket charges about the motives and actions of others, acting as if these charges flow from widely acknowledged truths. If one says something long enough, and if it pops up on the Internet and is repeated frequently enough, it comes to have the status of a given. Examples abound. We have been told that the president of the United States is a dictator who unilaterally and summarily went to war even though it upset some in the

European Union and war was not legally declared. The facts: The determination on the part of the United States to respond (under Article 51 of the UN Charter and under the standards and stipulations of international law) to the attacks of September 11 was conveyed to the secretary-general of the United Nations, to the Security Council, and to our allies. The war was authorized by Public Law 107–40 (S.J. Res. 23) on September 18, 2001, through a joint resolution of Congress: "To authorize the use of United States Armed Forces against those responsible for the recent attacks launched against the United States." The president, the act stated, "has authority under the Constitution to take action to deter and prevent acts of international terrorism against the United States."

Section 2 of the authorization broadens the authority given to the president to those who harbor terrorists and terrorist organizations, including nations, and gives him authority to prevent "any future acts of international terrorism against the United States by such nations, organizations, or persons."[16]

There may be good grounds to debate the wisdom of particular provisions of the Patriot Act, but the claim that the president is acting unconstitutionally because there was no official declaration of war is preposterous. There was such an authorization. Because there was no sovereign state to declare war against, the authorization had to be nuanced in order to deal with the particular situation confronting us.

As well, we have been told repeatedly that the proposed use of military tribunals to try accused terrorists is an unheard-of act of presidential usurpation. But such tribunals have been used previously in our history, particularly during the Civil War, which witnessed their greatest expansion. Both *USA Today* and the *New York Times* claimed that the specter of military tribunals constitutes an abandonment of American principles (the former newspaper) and that President Bush was throwing out the constitutional rulebook (the latter). False once again—and an easy call to make with but a cursory glance at our history. Whether such tribunals are wise or not is debatable, but the claim that they are unknown to American history and therefore prima facie illicit is false.

There is enormous reluctance in intellectual circles to credit the U.S. government or the Congress as a whole with responding appropriately in any particular way to September 11, under the presumption that their motives are venal. Looking back at President Franklin D. Roosevelt's presidential order establishing a military tribunal to charge eight German agents who landed secretly on the U.S. coast during World War II, one can debate whether this was a wise move on Roosevelt's part, or whether the men in question received due process. But we would be appalled by any suspicion about Roosevelt's motives or any suggestion that he was promoting narrow party interest rather than the common good of the country, as he understood that exigency, during a time of terrible crisis. In President Bush's case, all U.S. citizens are excluded from the jurisdiction of any tribunal.[17] Safeguards of the sort that did not pertain in the Roosevelt tribunal have been set to try to ensure that war prisoners receive fair trials.[18] Again, such tribunals may or may not be a good idea, but they do not constitute a radically innovative act of presidential usurpation.

A second case in point: A group of clergy who went to court claiming that military detainees were being held unconstitutionally lost that case. A U.S. district court held that prior cases that gave the military power "to exercise jurisdiction over . . . enemy belligerents, prisoners of war or others charged with violating the laws of war" were controlling.[19] Here too there is much to debate, and debate it we should. Reasonable discussion goes forward—in essays by Ronald Dworkin and Ruth Wedgwood, for example—but the staccato drumbeat persists that U.S. motives are reducible to imperial ambition, or a lust for vengeance or hatred of that vague all-purpose entity, the "Other"—all in the interest of extending the sway of an international bully.[20] Repeatedly the worst possible gloss is put on American motivations and the best on the motivations of those who attacked us. Terrorists are given the benefit of the doubt. After the obligatory caveat that it is not a good thing to fly hijacked commercial aircraft into skyscraper office buildings, we are told to consider the provocations. These range from "the fascism of U.S. foreign policy over the past many decades," in the words of a Rutgers professor cited by Andrew Sullivan, to the historian Mary Beard's declaration that, "however tactfully you dress it up, the United States had it coming."[21]

People who routinely insist on the illegitimacy of blaming victims now do it. No one deserved what happened to them on September 11, neither the immediate victims and their families nor the country itself. Cannot a powerful country bleed? Are not its citizens as mortal as those anywhere? Simple human recognition along these lines does not deter the literary theorist Frederic Jameson from seeing in these horrific events "a textbook example of dialectical reversal." Rather, what we are being treated to in such comments is a textbook example of what Hannah Arendt called the handy magic of "the dialectic," which puts "to sleep our common sense, which is nothing else but our mental organ for perceiving, understanding, and dealing with reality and factuality."[22]

Those who do not argue outright that the United States is the author of its own destruction often profess mystification at the motives of the attackers, despite the fact that the attackers have told us repeatedly what their motives are. *The Nation* editorialized, "Why the attacks took place is still unclear."[23] Suddenly the far left is perplexed as well as isolationist: If we had not poked our nose in where it did not belong, maybe people would leave us alone. However, either we really do not know what drove the attackers—which requires that we ignore their words and those of Osama bin Laden—or we really *do* know what motivated the attackers—which also requires that we ignore their words and those of Osama bin Laden. Why? Because we cannot take the religious language seriously. Donald Kagan cites an example of the latter when he recalls the words of a fellow Yale professor who opined that the "underlying causes" of the 9/11 attacks were "the desperate, angry, and bereaved" circumstances of the lives of "these suicide pilots," who were responding to "offensive cultural messages" spread by the United States.[24]

There is considerable hubris on display in such assertions of certainty about what drives terrorists, when doing so requires ignoring the terrorists' own words. This scenario usually plays out like this: First, one professes ignorance of the real motives, although one can do so only if one ignores the words of the attackers, who have scarcely been secretive. Or second, one ignores the real motives because one knows better than the attackers themselves what their motives were. "What is striking about such statements is their arrogance," writes Kagan. "They suggest that the enlightened commentator can penetrate the souls of the attackers and know their deepest motives. . . . A far better guide might be the actual statements of the perpetrators."[25] Kagan is not alone in this observation. Tony Judt writes that Osama bin Laden's stated motives are "to push the 'infidel' out of the Arabian peninsula, to punish the 'Crusaders and the Jews,' and to wreak revenge on Americans for their domination of Islamic space." Judt cannot help noticing, however, that bin Laden "is not a spokesman for the downtrodden, much less those who seek just solutions to real dilemmas—he is cuttingly dismissive of the UN: 'Muslims should not appeal to these atheist, temporal regimes.'"[26]

Not surprisingly, Salman Rushdie, the Muslim writer against whom a fatwa ordering his death was issued in 1989, makes the trenchant observation that the

> savaging of America by sections of the left . . . has been among the most unpleasant consequences of the terrorists' attacks on the United States. "The problem with Americans is . . . "—"What America needs to understand. . . . " There has been a lot of sanctimonious moral relativism around lately, usually prefaced by such phrases as these. A country which has just suffered the most devastating terrorist attack in history, a country in a state of deep mourning and horrible grief, is being told, heartlessly, that it is to blame for its own citizens' deaths.[27]

The *New York Times* columnist Thomas Friedman expresses amazement

> at the ease with which some people abroad and at campus teach-ins now tell us what motivated the terrorists. . . . Their deed was their note: we want to destroy America, starting with its military and financial centers. Which part of that sentence don't people understand? Have you ever seen Osama bin Laden say, "I just want to see a smaller Israel in its pre-1967 borders," or "I have no problem with America, it just needs to have a lower cultural and military profile in the Muslim world?" These terrorists aren't out for a new kind of coexistence with us. They are out for our non-existence. None of this seems to have seeped into the "Yes, but . . ." crowd.[28]

Even the courage and grief of those Americans who came to the rescue of the victims and their lost comrades, or of those at home who lost wives, children, or friends, has been treated with what perhaps was supposed to be knowing sophistication but wound up simply being cruel and tasteless commentary. To some, a horror with enormous geopolitical consequences seemed to have been little more than a story line for a new series—"Grief and the City" perhaps. For instance, only five short weeks had passed since the attacks when the *New York Times* featured two articles, "Heavy Lifting Required: The Return of Manly Men" and "Not to Worry: Real Men Can Cry." In mocking tones, the former article told us: "The operative word is men. Brawny, heroic, manly men." Susan Faludi, a feminist author, opines that we want "to feel Daddy is going to take care of us." The feminist Robin Morgan locates the "roots of terrorism" in the "breeding of masculine aggression," so the terrorists are examples of the dark side.[29] "Not to Worry: Real Men Can Cry" features a photo of a man, eyes closed, wiping a tear off his cheek, and the snide caption: "Wiping a post-terror tear." The article begins: "Real men cry. They cry before the camera, and they do so unapologetically." Since September 11 we have been inundated with images of weeping men, we are told. But fortunately, they could still be manly because they didn't seem to be losing control.[30] The cheapening of sorrow is not limited to the tabloids, and this from a newspaper that published the extraordinary vignettes on the victims of 9/11.

•   •   •

The weak arguments and overheated rhetoric that I have criticized in the last chapter and this one are united by cynicism and a blame-the-victim mentality. Framing the whole is a refusal to grapple with the fog of war and politics. St. Augustine defined politics as the attempt to reconcile conflicting human wills. It is a dauntingly complex task, made ever more so in the arena of international politics, constituted as it is by distance, estrangement, common misunderstanding, irreconcilable goals—and this on the good days. The difficulty of fighting a war and protecting our freedoms is not confronted in the commentary I have criticized. It is easier by far to condemn the government and to launch broadsides than to grapple with the dilemmas involved.

Secretary of Defense Donald Rumsfeld, in one of his press briefings, summarized one of these dilemmas succinctly:

The problem we've got is the one you're seeing manifested in the press [and] to a certain extent in our society. That is the tension between treating something as a law enforcement problem and treating it as an intelligence-gathering problem, and that is not an easy thing to deal with for a country that has historically [not had] a domestic intelligence-gathering entity. Most countries do. Anything that comes up in the United States tends to be looked at as a law enforcement matter. . . . Your interest is what in the world do you do to find out what that person [a person arrested for an infraction who may have knowledge of an impeding terrorist attack] knows so that you can prevent an attack with thousands more Americans being killed, and that is a mind-set that does not even exist domestically in our country. It doesn't exist in the population, it does not exist in the press, it does not exist in how our government is organized and arranged. . . . Therefore, the question is, How do you deal with that? *It is not an easy question for us, and we've got a lot of good, fine people who are worrying that through and wondering what that all means in our society* (emphasis mine).[31]

Not an easy problem at all. It is easier by far to occupy a stance of lofty condemnation than to try to puzzle it through. Justice Robert Jackson, in the case *Terminiello v. Chicago* in 1949, stated that "the Bill of Rights is not a suicide pact." We are not obliged, in other words, to hand avowed enemies the weapons with which to destroy us. But we need to exercise meticulous care so as not to overstate what poses a mortal threat. Those who struggle with such matters are not above criticism. In a democracy, we should never treat our public officials with inappropriate reverence, although people who commit themselves to the pressures of public life deserve our respect. Unlike those who specialize in the verbal equivalent of a hit-and-run accident, politicians cannot evade responsibility for their words and deeds. They cannot talk blithely about "blowback" and "dialectical reversals" and "imperial retaliatory terrorism" when a country and its people face possible biological, chemical, and nuclear attack—not to mention explosions and suicide assaults.

"The complete indifference to the real dilemmas of foreign policy produces an indiscriminate critique," writes Lawrence Freedman. He scores the litany of attacks on American foreign policy as "tendentious" and "selective in the use of evidence." They evince "scant regard for international context" by giving no weight to "Iraq's invasion of Kuwait and its pursuit of weapons of mass destruction," and they fail to note that "on many critical issues . . . the U.S. has worked *with* rather than against Muslim states." Such indiscriminate critiques ignore "the fact that even if Iraqi sanctions were lifted and the Palestine issue solved, al Qaida would not be appeased."[32]

Have religious scholars and officials done any better in responding to September 11? The record is mixed, and it is to this that we turn next, perhaps with the question on our lips: Where have you gone, Reinhold Niebuhr?

7

WHERE IS THE LEGACY OF NIEBUHR AND TILLICH?

H. RICHARD NIEBUHR, brother of the more famous Reinhold Niebuhr, wrote what is widely regarded as a modern theological classic, *Christ and Culture*. In it, he tackles the complex relationship between religious belief and worldly matters, an "enduring problem" for Christians precisely because Jesus articulated a distinction between what is God's and what is Caesar's. For some Christian thinkers, the "injunctions of the Sermon on the Mount concerning anger and resistance to evil, oaths and marriage, anxiety and property, are found incompatible with the duties of life in society," writes Niebuhr.[1]

In many ways, Jesus preached an ethic for the end time. He praised those who never married or had children. He was stringent in his teachings on divorce, forbidding it rather than accepting the regulation of divorce in traditional Jewish law. He recommended following the example of the birds and the lilies, who "toil not, neither do they spin." Human beings, whatever their glory, cannot array themselves with the beauty of simple creatures and plants, he told his followers. Jesus urged his disciples to rely on grace and, in anticipation of the end time, directed them away from temporal pursuits.

Given this message, it is unsurprising that Christians have struggled for centuries with how they are to live in the here and now. Christ's ethic seems unattainable in principle, save by the few saints among us, and even they are not without sin, as all believers know. To these complexities one must add the argument of many contemporary critics that an ethic derived from Christianity is sectarian or exclusive. They do not believe that Christians should engage the public world as Christians at all. The Christian teacher of ethics is likely to respond that the claims of a gospel-derived ethic speak to universal human dilemmas and universal human capacities and therefore offer insight that all may draw upon, believer and unbeliever alike.

Misunderstandings of Christian teachings are rife. Christianity is not an exalted or mystical form of utilitarianism. Jesus preached no doctrine of universal benevolence. He showed anger and issued condemnations. These dimensions of Christ's life and words tend to be overlooked nowadays as Christians concentrate on God's love rather than God's justice. That love is sometimes reduced to a diffuse benignity that is then enjoined on believers. This kind of faith descends into sentimentalism fast. But how do believers translate the message of the Christian Savior into an ethic of worldly engagement if an ethic of universal niceness misses the point? Because Christianity is far and away the dominant faith of Americans, these are exigent matters of concern to *all* citizens, believer or no. For a minority of believers, worldly engagement already marks a capitulation. But the vast majority of Christians, both now and in the past, have sorted things out in more nuanced and complicated ways.

CHRISTIANITY IN RELATION TO CULTURE

H. Richard Niebuhr delineates five "Christs," by which he means five characteristic models of how Christians have engaged the world: the Christ against culture; the Christ of culture; the Christ above culture; Christ and culture in paradox; and Christ as transformer of culture. Believers have occupied each of these positions historically, sometimes more than one at a time. An example would be the great Thomas Aquinas, who was faithful as a monk to his vows "against" the culture—poverty, celibacy, and obedience—even as he belonged to a church that had "achieved or accepted full social responsibility for all great institutions" and that had "become the guardian of culture, the fosterer of learning, the judge of nations, the protector of the family, the governor of social religion." For Aquinas, Christianity is, among other things, a structure of practical wisdom "planted among the streets and marketplaces, the houses, palaces, and universities that represent human culture."[2]

This kind of believer neither despises the world nor retreats from it. Rather, this believer engages the world, sustains it, and seeks to transform it—all at the same time. Ordinary vocations are the responsibility of believers. They should not shirk their vocations, including political vocations like soldiering or judging. Such vocations are necessary to sustain a common life. This Christian believer undertakes the tasks of vocation as an act of service and performs them in humility and with a strong commitment to their often tragic, sometimes joyful nature. Tension, even paradox, emerges in situations when "what is required of man in his service of others is the use of instruments of wrath for the sake of protecting them against the wrathful."[3] This point is made most vividly by Luther, with his insistence that there is a "time of the sword," but it has been widely, if not universally, shared in the historic Church. For Christians living in historic time and before the end of time, the pervasiveness of conflict must be faced. One may aspire to perfection, but living perfectly is not possible. To believe one is without sin is to commit the sin of pride and to become ever more boastful in the conviction that a human being can sustain a perfectionist ethic. For St. Augustine, for Martin Luther, and for the anti-Nazi martyr Dietrich Bonhoeffer, the harsh demands of necessity as well as the command of love require that one may have to commit oneself to the use of force under certain limited conditions, and with certain intentions.

There are dangers in taking up worldly vocations: Those who commit themselves to the care of cultural institutions must remain fully aware of just how fragile these institutions are. For instance, imagine that for one entire generation no child was educated. Consider how much of civil society would collapse. The danger in responding to this and other realizations is that the believer may become too reconciled to the world, lose critical distance, and efface the "Christ and Caesar" distinction that the believer *must* maintain.

For believers, the created order is fundamentally good: God saw it and said it was good. This order includes human beings. But our wills can be directed wrongly. What are we to do with those whose wills direct them to claim that every man, woman, and child in a particular group or nation is an infidel and they must be wiped out and destroyed? Do we permit such wickedness to happen? Or do we attempt to interdict such violence, even if this requires the use of violence to stop evil before it unleashes unlimited violence to meet its ends? Up until the last fifty years or so, most Christians, with the exception of the radical peace churches, would have answered: As an act of neighbor love and of service, we may at times be obliged to commit ourselves to active intervention in order to prevent evil from having its day, even as we give evil its due.[4]

There has never been a single Christian answer to the dilemmas of culture, however, including the resort to force. All responses are carried out in the twilight that falls over human deeds in history. All are concerned with relative value. Nothing has absolute value save God.[5] One way or another, Christians, together with other citizens, face moments when they are asked: Where do we stand? Refusing to answer is itself an answer. But the duty of conscience and of witness demands more from us. Two great twentieth-century theologians, Reinhold Niebuhr and Paul Tillich, can help us understand these demands.

TILLICH AGAINST NAZISM

Human wretchedness is a given for St. Augustine. Our wretchedness consists, in part, in being forced to confront certain necessities in which our judgment is unavoidable, even as ignorance is similarly unavoidable.[6] Our knowledge will never be perfect. There is a fog of politics as there is a fog of war. We act knowing that action can never dispel the fog. But action may forestall the worst. And it is only when the worst is interdicted that certain human goods—those associated with everyday civic peace—can be manifest.

For Paul Tillich, a German émigré to America, Christians are obliged to confront and take the measure of evil. As we confront evil in our own era—the terrorism whose perpetrators are described by the political analyst and commentator Michael Ignatieff, writing in the *New York Times Magazine,* as "apocalyptic nihilists"—it is worth taking a look at how Paul Tillich and Reinhold Niebuhr confronted political evil in their own era, World War II.[7]

Both Tillich and Niebuhr possessed the capacity to peer into the heart of darkness and to name it correctly. They did not equivocate, exculpate, or "understand" to the point of losing their own dignity as human subjects. Evil, they saw, is that which diminishes. It takes away from the good, including the goodness of created being, and aims to destroy it. Neither Tillich nor Niebuhr had any difficulty in making this judgment, nor did Dietrich Bonhoeffer, who called National Socialism demonic.

Tillich delivered 112 addresses in German for broadcast into occupied Europe from March 1942 through May 1944. These powerful political sermons were broadcast into Germany by the U.S. Office of War Information. The radio programs, interestingly enough, were "forbidden to use falsehood"; they were not to be crude propaganda. Tillich's aim was to draw Germans away from loyalty to the Third Reich and to bring German Christians into a hard reckoning with what their country was doing. Tillich cried that Germans had to stand against the terror, and in particular they needed to confront "the Jewish question," which, he insisted, was fundamental.[8]

How did Tillich help Germans understand they were facing a demonic order? For one thing, a demonic order surrounds a people with "symbols of death," and these dominate in rhetoric, slogans, and iconography. (Here one is reminded of Osama bin Laden's claim that he will prevail because Islamist young people are in love with death and seek it, whereas the soft Americans love life too much.) Tillich knew that a Christian is called to love life even as he or she is prepared to face death, perhaps by looking evil in the eye and attempting to stay its hand. This love of life he contrasted to the mind-set of "German youth," who were trained from childhood, writes Tillich, to "seek the meaning of life in death."[9]

The drive toward death on the part of German youth was horrifically on display in the final battle for Berlin. Few know about the hideous sacrifice of young people on the altar of death constructed by National Socialism. In the final months of the war, starving, bewildered Hitler Youth were drafted into a children's militia organized by Hitler and his cadre of faithful SS. It was in effect a suicide mission, a way to offer up the young as a final tribute to the Nazi cult of death. Five thousand children between the ages of eight and seventeen, male and female, perished in suicidal sabotage attempts and last-ditch stands in the last spasm of the agony of Berlin. Only five hundred survived. What was most astonishing to observers was the determination of these children to "do their duty until they were literally ready to drop. They had been fed on legends of heroism for as long as they could remember. For them the call to 'ultimate sacrifice' was no empty phrase."[10]

A willingness to sacrifice children is one sign of a culture of death. One is reminded not only of the drive toward death lauded by bin Laden and extolled by Islamist radicals everywhere, but specifically of how thousands of Iranian children were thrown into the horror of the eight-year war between Iran and Iraq from 1980 to 1988. These children were decimated: sent out as human minesweepers, they were either killed outright or left limbless and scarred. Yet families spoke of the honor of being parents of such martyrs.

Contrast this hideous will to sacrifice children with the ethic of training adult soldiers to fight in a manner that preserves as many lives as possible, both of their own number and of noncombatants. This ethic obliges soldiers to take prisoners when enemy combatants surrender and prevents them from just laying down a line of fire when they feel like it. This ethic informs an army that clears a minefield by sending in special teams, trained for the job, rather than flooding it with innocents and watching as they are blown to pieces.

In the context of the bloodletting of World War II, Paul Tillich took his German listeners to task. In a radio broadcast of April 20, 1942, he told them that they had been seduced by the notion of "internal freedom" associated with the great German philosophers Kant, Fichte, and Hegel. An obsession with internal freedom leads to an "upbringing for bondage, . . . for the negation of that which is human in the person," even as a tyrannical government violates and oversteps its legitimate mandate. When individuals believe that, by remaining free "inside" they can somehow hope simply to ride out the horrific events unfolding around them, a sense of fairness and decency is destroyed and people lose their dignity. All Germans acting in this way, he maintained, would become either slaves or tyrants.[11]

There are times when human dignity must be defended, Tillich told his listeners, and that can only be done by honoring the dignity and rights of all. In his broadcast of August 28, 1942, Tillich called his German friends to political responsibility. Why was it that Germany seemed to lack a "politically responsible intellect," he asked, one that could resist criminals and political pathology? Tillich argued that those who are incapable of standing up against criminal violence are politically immature and irresponsible. They live in a dream world in which they imagine that in the inwardness of their own hearts they remain pure.

In helping his listeners discern how to fight the foe of political terror, Tillich was clear that terror must be fought, but without hatred. Prevailing over evil is not the same as giving oneself over to evil. What Tillich called a will of retribution, repaying evil for evil, is to be avoided. But there is another will, that of justice. Those combating evil with a will to justice wish only to stop it, not to commit evil in turn. This is the more difficult course, Tillich insisted, but it is the only one compatible with Christian understanding.[12]

There is a nonretributive power that flows from justice. It works to clear the space for justice to operate in situations where justice has languished. The idolatry of power destroys justice, in the name of vengeance. For his broadcast delivered near the time of "the fourth war Christmas," Tillich was impassioned about the crimes of National Socialism, which he saw as crimes against all that is fragile and profound in humanity. Of course it is true, he conceded, that "there has never been a time when love alone ruled; that is impossible in this world. There has always been violence and injustice and falsehood." But those who advocate hatred and ridicule love are compelled, he observed, to "persecute the child in the manger."[13]

What of the necessities of war itself? Tillich resolutely maintained that the German people had brought destruction down on themselves through their capitulation to Hitler. The majority might not have been actively involved. But Germans had permitted their country to be a host for the proliferation of Nazi hatred and the destruction of innocent persons, within and without. No, cried Tillich, when the German army took over a city, then abandoned it by laying it to ruin. Tillich spelled out the difference between such atrocities and true military necessities:

It is a military necessity to bombard and to reduce places to rubble in which the enemy is entrenched. It is a military necessity to destroy factories, bridges, and depots on a forced retreat. But it is not a military necessity to make a wasteland out of a country, to drive the inhabitants before you, or to leave them for death. It is not a necessity to wipe out the enemy nation. . . . It is not a military necessity to massacre millions of women and children and old people, directly or indirectly![14]

Tillich offered the powerful example of a theologian confronting the social and political reality of his time. It does little good to speak simplistically of turning the other cheek so as to remonstrate against Tillich and show that he defected from a purist nonviolent position. Tillich himself was both clear and subtle. In his writings directed at the horrors of National Socialism, he is clear that he is not speaking of how Christians should respond to slights, insults, or cruelties committed against their own person. Rather, he addresses the question of the obligations of whole nations and peoples and makes us think about what the world would look like if those who know no limits in their frenzy to destroy indiscriminately were given free rein.

Tillich's great wartime contribution was to remind all of his radio listeners that it is not Christian to permit the cruel destruction of the civic peace that occurs when violence is not confronted. Looking the other way is irresponsibility cloaked in Christian terms.[15] It is no surprise that the great majority of Christian ethicists and theologians who support the war against terror do so with a proviso to forestall the emergence and ratification of hatred or vengeance. "A just response . . ." is the way most of these documents begin. This is language that would have been endorsed by Reinhold Niebuhr, to whom we now turn.

NIEBUHR AGAINST UTOPIANISM

How does one discern the signs of the times and respond appropriately? This question preoccupied Reinhold Niebuhr, who died in 1971 and was the greatest public theologian of his time. Niebuhr argues that: "To discern the signs of the times means to interpret historical events and values. The interpretation of history includes all judgments we make of the purpose of our own actions and those of others; it includes the assessment of the virtue of our own and other interests, both individual and collective; and, finally, it includes our interpretation of the meaning of history itself."[16] Discernment is never easy. Our conclusions may not be pleasant. The tasks called for in light of our understanding may be troubling or tragic, but we cannot shrink from them. We must also be honest about our own interests and avoid promoting narrow interests under cover of a common good.

Writing shortly after the world had only just passed through the horror that was World War II, Niebuhr chided those who had shrunk from doing what was necessary to combat Nazi tyranny, especially those who made the claim that in the process of fighting fascism, "we would all become fascists."[17] This did not happen. Liberties were "fairly well preserved" even during a prolonged, total war (with some notable exceptions, like the internment of Japanese and Japanese Americans). We are always well advised to fly the flags of warning about descending into terror as we fight terror, or authoritarianism as we fight authoritarianism. But these perils do not negate the need to respond; rather, they make self-examination even more necessary.

The peace of God, writes Niebuhr, "cannot be equated with the peace of detachment." There is a role for forgiveness in human affairs, but forgiveness does not allow us to avoid facing the facts and confronting a disharmonious world. Forgiveness is possible "only to those who have some recognition of common guilt," for all have fallen short.[18] Those struggling against brutality cannot forget their own sins as they engage in that struggle. The world of political action is one that may give rise to moral regret as we confront what political theorists call the problem of "dirty hands," for we cannot remain pure in a difficult and often dangerous world. Christian realists, as they are often called, appreciate that "political units—cities, provinces, and nations— . . . gather up all people within a given geographical area, and so must create a workable community from those who have not come together sharing a set of beliefs or commitments."[19] Politics is the way these plural, diverse groups of people order a life together.

The theologian Robin Lovin reminds us that the starting point for Christian realists (and for the just war tradition, as I construe it) is Augustinian and hence quite different from Aristotelianism, which held that politics somehow fulfills and completes our nature (or at least the nature of the more completely rational free male). The primary and most compelling reason Christians enter politics, by contrast, is to restrain evil.[20] If the restraint of evil remains their exclusive concern, however, they may become complacent toward systematic inequities, so long as violence is kept at a minimum. By the same token, a politics of the common good, which always sounds good, may prompt its adherents to evade doing what is necessary to curb violence, domestic and international; they may indulge in naive advocacy and refuse to engage with the least pleasant realities of a world in conflict. "Justice" and "nonviolence" too easily become mantras divorced from the realities of a world descending into a vortex of horrible threats and even more terrible realities.

By contrast, those who, like Niebuhr, link the restraint of evil to a politics of justice and the common good gain a rich and complex perspective. Above all, Niebuhr insists, Christians dare not lose the language of justice. No doubt he would have cautioned us against calling September 11 a tragedy: If it is a tragedy, we can simply succor the wounded and grief-stricken and avoid dealing with the knowledge that planned terror remains a clear and present danger. Usually when a true tragedy occurs—a flood roars through a canyon, for instance, and kills vacationers—there is no one to punish. When acts of terror destroy lives, however, there are specific persons we do, rightly, punish. It is this task of punishment, essential to any workable vision of political justice, that many contemporary Christians shun.[21] Perhaps because our culture, steeped in a therapeutic ethos, is tuned in to syndromes but resistant to sin, we prefer not to conjure with humanly willed horror.

Tied to this recognition is another: We have particular moral responsibilities to those nearest and dearest to us—parents to children, friends to other friends, but also citizens to fellow citizens. Vague talk about our responsibility for the entire human race is meaningless.[22] Unless we tie our responsibility to concrete tasks, we are simply issuing greeting card nostrums. To call myself a "citizen of the world," as Hannah Arendt rightly insisted, is to strip citizenship of concrete meaning and to flee the world of political actuality for a world of vague goodwill. Those who take on the vocation of concrete political responsibility have a special obligation to their fellow citizens. Their obligations are not exclusive to their own citizenry, but they are far more meaningful and demanding than any thinned-out obligations to those who are not citizens. One dimension of a Niebuhrian ethic is to insist that, when Christianity is interpreted as an ethos of universal benevolence, it loses the concrete neighbor love we should always connect with it.

Niebuhr's larger contribution to the ongoing debate about Christ and culture and what is demanded from believers lies in his hardheaded insistence that Christianity is not solely a religion of love. Because the God of mercy is also a God of judgment, justice and love go together. Chiding what he calls "Christian moralism," Niebuhr reminds us that justice "requires discriminate judgments between conflicting claims." By contrast to simplistic moralism, a "profounder Christian faith must encourage men to create systems of justice" in a realm that presents "tragic choices, which are seldom envisaged in a type of idealism in which all choices are regarded as simple."[23]

Unfortunately, what presents itself as true Christian idealism, the idea that "pure moral suasion could solve every social problem," may be a form of self-delusion. This kind of idealism ignores the fall and the inheritance of sin and embraces an overly optimistic view of human nature and possibility. Niebuhr continues: "Whether the task of reconciliation is conceived in terms of pure moral suasion or whether it recognizes the inevitabilities of conflict in society and only seeks to avoid violence in such conflicts, it is interesting that the consequence of such conceptions is to create moral idealists who imagine that they are changing the world by their moral ideals." Or, one might add, by their condemnations. But either stance evades "responsibility for maintaining a relative justice in an evil world," a stance that Niebuhr insists is central to biblical understanding.[24]

Whether Niebuhr was calling for repeal of the Neutrality Act of 1939 as an immoral law promoting isolationism, urging Christians into the fight against Nazism, or opposing the war in Vietnam, he held that the world must be engaged. Sentimentality in the name of Christianity must be avoided and idolatry of the state—any state—eschewed. Christians must understand that their own freedom is entangled with political realities and possibilities. It follows that Christians as citizens have "an important stake in politics" and in all the institutions that are the warp and woof of a democratic society.[25] Niebuhr was especially scathing in his criticism of those who advocate a withdrawal from what he called "world responsibility"—people who keep their own hands clean by refusing to confront the inevitable moral ambiguities of politics.

Most pertinent to the contemporary war against terrorism are Niebuhr's World War II–era writings. In a potent essay, "Love Your Enemies," Niebuhr argued with a "certain rather hysterical" strain of Christian idealism that believed that, since Christians are enjoined to love all men, and "it is impossible to love an enemy, you must have no enemy." Is this really so? he queried. He challenged those who were then "touring the country with the message that all people who are participating in the war will become so corrupted by hatred that they will be incapable of contributing to a decent peace." Niebuhr called, in cutting tones, on "the handful of nonparticipants to hold themselves in readiness to build a new world after the rest of us have ruined it."[26]

A summary of Niebuhr's response to this idealistic message—here one is reminded of Camus's see-no-evil "humanists"—is reducible to one word: balderdash. Of course, war and conflict tempt some to hatred, but "this hatred is not nearly as universal as our idealists assume. And it is least general among those who are engaged in the actual horrors of belligerency." Niebuhr points to a commonly accepted fact of war-fighting: combatants themselves usually do not hate. Bloodthirstiness is more often found on the sidelines. Niebuhr also mulls over the poverty of the idealists' deployment of terms like "love." Christian agape, the love of the Kingdom of God, is more than a "refined form of sympathy, for it does not depend upon the likes and dislikes that men may have for each other."[27] We may struggle against a determined foe intent on our harm and destruction without hating that foe.

Yet criticism of, and contempt for, the military comes readily to the lips of many religious people, perhaps because they put the worst possible interpretation on those who have determined that a resort to force is justified. Niebuhr insists, however, that such contempt flows from a sentimentalized Christianity whose adherents have reduced the complexities of the Christian message to slogans that exalt alleged victims, encourage condemnation of responsible authorities, and traffic in attention-getting breast-beating. Sometimes what looks like self-effacement is really a form of self-promotion.

On December 18, 1940, pondering America's entry into World War II, Niebuhr published an essay, "To Prevent the Triumph of an Intolerable

Tyranny," in the journal *Christian Century*.[28] America was not, as some alleged, plunging recklessly into conflict, Niebuhr argues. To the contrary, "contemporary history refutes the idea that nations are drawn into war too precipitately. It proves, on the contrary, that it is the general inclination, of democratic nations at least, to hesitate so long before taking this fateful plunge that the dictator nations gain a fateful advantage over them by having the opportunity of overwhelming them singly, instead of being forced to meet their common resistance." (Niebuhr was referring to appeasement of the German National Socialists, who, by the time the essay was written, had already overrun Poland and Czechoslovakia.) It is naive to assume that "all war could be avoided if only you could persuade nations not to cross each other's borders." Those who counseled neutrality for America in 1940 so as to avoid entering the conflict, Niebuhr claims, exhibited the fruit of a "moral confusion that issues from moral perfectionism, whenever moral perfectionism seeks to construct political systems." The result is that evil flourishes, as in Germany, "its fury . . . fed by a pagan religion of tribal self-glorification; . . . it intends to root out the Christian religion; . . . it defies all the universal standards of justice," and it threatens the Jewish people "with annihilation."

How can one not respond to such attacks? To condemn America's alleged rush to war, to make that the focus of critique rather than the statements and aims of those on the attack, is a rhetoric of perfectionism of the sort that informs much of liberal Protestantism in America. This brand of Protestantism, Niebuhr stated rather bitingly during World War II, is "wrong not only about this war and the contemporary international situation. It is wrong about the whole nature of historical reality." Sadly, he concludes, much pacifism in America (he calls it "perfectionist pacifism") springs from this same well of historic utopianism rather than from solid scriptural resources. Liberal pacifism, for Niebuhr, is a position that relies far more on a general faith in human perfectibility and a teleology of historic progress than it does on the teachings of Jesus of Nazareth. It is, in other words, an ideological, not a gospel, stance.[29] Are Christians not obliged to respond, even at the risk of dirtying their hands?

With the powerful voices and witness of Tillich and Niebuhr in mind, let's turn to the remarks of various voices from the pulpit since September 11. It is not an entirely happy picture.

8

THE PULPIT
RESPONDS TO TERROR

ONE MIGHT THINK THAT terror of the sort on display September 11 comes close to the horrors depicted by Niebuhr and that the debate about the use of force would be on how best to respond with restraint rather than on whether to respond at all. But the language in which Niebuhr spoke in his early writings signified his frustration at the political innocence or irresponsibility of many believers. In taking the measure of current responses that are surprisingly unwilling to come to grips with political realities, I am not claiming that I have anything like a social scientific sample at hand. Rather, in reading sermons posted on Internet sites, going over contemporary journals, both print and online, perusing op-ed pages, I have been struck by the widely repeated approaches and broad patterns emanating from our pulpits and from statements put out by church bodies or groups. My assumption is not that the Niebuhr-Tillich tradition has been altogether abandoned, but rather, that a position best described as "pseudo-" or "crypto-" pacifism now dominates, certainly from our mainline pulpits.[1]

My own experience attending church on September 16, the first Sunday after September 11, was rather depressing. All of us were in a state of shock. We were looking for words of forthright encounter with what had happened and for guidance. But instead, we were told that "it has been a terrible week. But that is no reason to lose your personal dreams! We need to hold on to our own dreams." Thousands dead in lower Manhattan and at the Pentagon, and this was the best the minister could muster? The disconnect between the words of the sermon and the reality of Ground Zero was stunning. It was as if the Christian tradition had no way to take the measure of the horror and to reflect on possible responses to it. Dream on, we were told. We were not reminded that God's gift of forgiveness and mercy is available to those who, in acting against evil, themselves incur guilt. We were not warned that this guilt could invite despair and lead to inaction in the hope of escaping the tragedies of politics and power, that we could fall into what Niebuhr called self-deception. We were not told that there was no way out of the dilemmas posed, nor reassured that there was, instead, a way *in* if we kept alive theological discernments, concepts, and recognitions in all their complexity.

The Christian religion in America has not escaped our cultural tendency to conflate the personal and the political. In what some call "the American religion," we assume that our inner barometer is the measure of all things. Add to this the thinning out of a vocabulary of discernment and comparative justice, and the result is saddening. This conflation of the personal and the political is evident in many of the reactions from persons in our religious communities to the attack on America. To be sure, many powerful words were uttered from the pulpit, and moving essays were written by theologians and ethicists, but overall, our religious leaders seemed to have lost touch with the tradition articulated so brilliantly by Tillich and Niebuhr.

There are four characteristics of the weak arguments and strong rhetoric I discern emanating from the communities of the religious: a radical oversimplification of the issues involved in the attacks of September 11 and in the U.S. response; a tendency to traffic in utopianism and sentimentality concerning politics; easy criticism, if not condemnation, of America and her leaders; and the loss or distortion of central theological categories.

An example that exhibits all four tendencies and stands as paradigmatic for the genre was offered by the Reverend John Dear, S.J., in his "Open Letter to George W. Bush" of February 8, 2002. Not content to warn against what he takes to be an ill-advised move to counter terror with force, Father Dear does what many student protesters in the 1960s frequently did: He calls upon political leaders to do the impossible in response to the September 11 "wake-up call." By making a set of utopian and non-negotiable demands that no responsible official could possibly meet, Father Dear confirms his view of their essential immorality and venality. (I recall one student protest in which the demands upon the chancellor of the university were to do the following: [1] create an Afro-American studies program; [2] create a separate dormitory for African-American students; and [3] end racism and imperialism everywhere. The irony of the chancellor's dry response that he would get to work on demands number 1 and 2 but that number 3 might take a little longer was lost on many of the protesters, if memory serves.)

Consider Father Dear's shopping list of non-negotiable demands on the president of the United States:

> I am writing to you to ask you to stop immediately the bombing of Afghanistan, to stop your preparations for other wars, to cut the Pentagon's budget drastically, not increase it; to lift the sanctions on Iraq, end military aid to Israel, stop U.S. support of the occupation of the Palestinians, lift the entire third world debt, dismantle every one of our nuclear weapons and weapons of mass destruction, abandon your Star Wars Missile Shield plans, join the World Court and international law, and close our own terrorist training camps, beginning with Fort Bennings's "School of the Americas."[2]

Contrast this bizarre list to the strategy enshrined by such geniuses of nonviolent direct action as Mahatma Gandhi, who insisted that, in principle, any demand made of a responsible official must be one that he can carry out. How could a president of the United States lift the entire Third World debt, for example? Father Dear invokes the principles of Gandhi when he speaks of "loving, non-violent resistance to U.S. war-making," but the statement bursts with contempt for the United States and its leaders. Moreover, Dear's shopping list of demands shows that he is not serious, and his theology leaves a great deal to be desired as well. He tells us that Jesus "commanded us not to bomb our enemies, but to love our enemies." What Father Dear is obliged to do is to offer us his understanding of what the injunction to love one's enemies means. Does it mean we should refuse to protect the innocent against harm? Does it mean we should forsake any concern with justice?

Hurling charges and setting up impossible demands flies in the face of one of the great strengths of the Catholic tradition, with its commitment to the concept of a common good and its centuries-old effort to grapple with the question of force and its possible legitimate use, a tradition one might reasonably assume Dear would take seriously. This struggle takes place largely, if not exclusively, within the framework of the just war tradition, which resists oversimplifying the issues involved. But there has been a falling away from the just war tradition in much Catholic thinking on war and peace over the past twenty-five years.

Consider, for example, the "Pax Christi USA Statement on the Devastation of September 11," a statement addressed to Americans and American officials by the Catholic peace organization. The statement beings by noting the "horrific loss of life" and then goes on to argue that Christians must be disciples of nonviolence. The principles of nonviolence require not only that they refuse to go to war but that they refuse to "demonize and dehumanize any ethnic group as 'enemy.'"[3] But who is demonizing and dehumanizing whom? No American public official on the national front has demonized Muslims. All political leaders from both parties have warned against any such tendency. The demonizing has come from the other side. The demand for restraint is enjoined on one side only—this nation and its leaders. The strong rhetoric deteriorates further when the authors of this statement assume that the "despicable act" of September 11 should not be followed by "a despicable act of violence *in kind.*" We are not told what would constitute such an "in kind" act. Presumably, it would have to be the intentional slaughter of three thousand civilians. That has not been done. We recognize soon enough that the authors of this statement use "despicable" to cover *any* resort to force. By refusing to distinguish between combatants and noncombatants, they weaken their argument altogether.

Such erosion of distinctions is characteristic of this and many similar statements emanating from our churches. Think of how we would react if someone argued that a motorist who unintentionally killed a pedestrian—not from any recklessness on her part but as a result of other circumstances—and a motorist who *knowingly* ran over a pedestrian should be treated identically where the law is concerned. This would violate a basic principle of justice. Scripture has a lot to say about justice. Christian teaching down the centuries discusses punishment carried out without hatred of wrongdoers and visions of peace, earthly and heavenly. Too often nowadays church men and women ignore the call to reflect theologically. Instead, they assert the political commitments they made in a prior era and have not rethought since in many cases. Then they cast about for religious justification of a prior political stance. From this posture, they castigate a response to the intentional slaughter of civilians with the use of force that does its utmost to avoid civilian casualties as "reckless retribution."[4]

Consider in this vein a sermon delivered by the Reverend Canon John L. Peterson, Secretary General of the Anglican Communion, on December 16, 2001. He cites the warning from an Anglican bishop in Nigeria that "'If the United States bombs Afghanistan, the front line will not only be Kabul, but Kano and Kaduna as well.' What was meant by this warning is that there was no way this 'new crusade' would not be interpreted by the Muslims living in northern Nigeria as yet another crusade, another show of force by the most powerful nation in the world. A new colonialism."[5] What are the theological categories in this argument? So far as I can tell, there are none, for the argument seems to rely on expediency alone—that and the easy criticism once again of America and her leaders.

The Reverend Canon Peterson's sermon is marked by radical oversimplification as well. Where does the locution in quotes—"new crusade"—come from? Who has put that label on the war against terrorism? I noted that the president let slip the word *crusade* (in the moral sense) in an impromptu press conference soon after the attacks. But he excised the word from his vocabulary thereafter and *explicitly* enjoined the American people to avoid a "crusading" mentality. Let's be clear about the situation in Nigeria. Does the Reverend Canon Peterson mean to suggest that the war in Afghanistan will inflame a previously becalmed community? I have good friends, a Nigerian professional couple, who returned to Nigeria with considerable trepidation after ten years in the United States. They fear the violence flowing from the north of Nigeria that has been spearheaded by Islamist radicals, especially the brutal treatment of women. No action or inaction from the United States or any other country is needed to set off the already inflamed zealots in Nigeria.

What of the casually tossed-in phrase "a new colonialism"? How is the war against terrorism colonialism? Are Americans going to move in everywhere to occupy and colonize the territory of other nations? The Reverend Canon Peterson and the many who share his views should tell us in what this new colonialism consists, so that we can evaluate their use of such language. Not only do they rarely offer any such explanation, but they claim that the words emanating from the United States after September 11 were words of "retaliation and revenge" only. The Reverend Canon Peterson owes us a few examples. Who spoke such language? The man in the street? Yes, some did—but remarkably few. American public officials? No, very few did.

Most interesting in this statement and many others like it is the apparent lack of interest in offering up a critique of the war effort based on theological criteria. One would think this is a minimal expectation for statements emanating from church men and women. One would be wrong. Many terms are thrown around that have emotional impact but little factual or theological basis. All the buttons of Western Christian guilt are pressed. Our contemporary tendency toward self-loathing—part of a destructive dynamic that Nietzsche limned rather brilliantly as *ressentiment*—is put on display. The upshot is not strength to face what is before us, but emotionality that winds up reveling in Western guilt rather than confronting honestly Western responsibility.

Consider the words of Dr. Tony Compolo, an evangelical minister best known as one of former President Bill Clinton's spiritual advisers during the Monica Lewinsky affair. One month after the attacks he explored with students the events then unfolding. He harkened back to the Crusades. "We don't know much about the Crusades, but there isn't a Muslim in the world that doesn't know about the Crusades. Where, in the name of Jesus, we slaughtered how many hundreds and thousands of innocent people, a lot of them women and children."[6] This allusion taps the vein of Christian guilt, but does it enhance historic acumen or offer students concrete understanding of the complex events we call "the Crusades"? Certainly not, for Compolo's words lack historic depth and particularity. He provides no context and makes no mention of the prior wars of Islamic conquest that had expelled Christians from lands they had long inhabited.

Nothing, of course, excuses indiscriminate slaughter. But Dr. Compolo deploys the Crusades in a mood of self-flagellation while speaking to young American students who cannot in any way be held accountable for what a group of European horsed warriors did in the eleventh and twelfth centuries. "The Crusades" now functions as a loaded term that conjures up guilt in the absence of concrete responsibility. It becomes a form of what Dietrich Bonhoeffer called "cheap grace"—or "cheap guilt" in this case. We can feel good about feeling bad. How on earth does this serve young people in the early years of the twenty-first century facing a world of dangers in which determined people are embarked on a course to kill as many Americans as possible? How can they sort out America's role in the world and American responsibility, whether current or historic?

Is "rage" against the West justified because of events that go back more than a thousand years? Reverse the situation. Would Compolo find it acceptable were Western Christians to nurse a grudge dating from the twelfth century? ("There isn't a Christian in the world that doesn't know about the [fill in the blank].") In *that* circumstance, he would come down hard against the Christian grudge-holders: What about forgiveness? he would say. What about getting past a horrible event and not nurturing anger and rage, with all their corrosive effects, over the centuries? In the powerful argument of the theologian David S. Yeager, this double standard—setting up a different set of exculpations and expectations for Christians and Muslims—is insulting to Muslims:

> To suppose that Islamic faith, or Arab culture, or poverty and the experience of oppression somehow lead young men directly, of themselves, to be capable of flying an airliner full of passengers into a building crowded with unsuspecting civilians, is deeply denigrating to Muslims, to Arabs, and to the poor and oppressed. It requires us to suppose that Muslims, or Arabs, or the poor lie almost beyond the borders of a shared humanity, that however much we pity and excuse them, we cannot rely on them, simply *because* they are Muslims, Arabs, or oppressed, to behave in humanly and morally intelligible ways. I would suggest that this is a dangerous line of thought, however humanely motivated it may initially be.[7]

Indeed, the very notion that "poverty breeds terrorism" is false, although this claim is a theme that runs like a red thread through post–September 11 sermons.[8] As everyone knows by now, the hijackers of September 11 were not poor. Paul Marshall, Roberta Green, and Lela Gilbert, in *Islam at the Crossroads,* write:

> The terrorist organizations that attacked the United States are not composed of uneducated people who grew up in poverty and know nothing of the world. . . . Most poor people do not fight, and have never fought as terrorists. The people from the poorest countries in the world, such as Haiti or Mozambique, are not attacking the United States or anyone else. The terrorists themselves are usually wealthy and privileged. . . . The stress on poverty as a cause of Islamic terrorism is misguided or, at the least, very exaggerated.[9]

Alan B. Krueger, a professor of economics at Princeton, and Jitka Maleckova, a professor of Middle Eastern studies at Charles University in Prague, have explored in depth the relationship, if any, between economic deprivation and terrorism. They conclude that a "careful review of the evidence provides little reason for optimism that a reduction in poverty or an increase in educational attainment would, by themselves, meaningfully reduce international terrorism." The issue is important, they aver, because drawing a false causal connection between poverty and terrorism is potentially quite dangerous. We may be led to do nothing about terrorism, and we may also lose interest in providing support for developing nations should the terrorism threat wane. By "falsely connecting terrorism to poverty," policymakers, analysts, and commentators only "deflect attention from the real roots of terrorism," which are political, ideological, and religious.[10]

The strength of Krueger and Maleckova's study is that it relies on an examination of the best available empirical evidence rather than on hunches or truisms that turn out not to be so true. As they discovered, cohorts of terrorists, compared with the relevant population, have relatively high education levels. Despite the availability of evidence that undermines any direct causal connection between impoverished circumstances and terrorist activity, this drumbeat goes on without surcease. The effect is similar to the collapse of moral agency noted by Stephen Carter in his indictment of those who excuse crimes committed by African Americans because of their history of oppression. Those making this claim wind up construing those of another race or religion as less than full moral agents, as people who do not make choices but whose lives are determined. This judgment diminishes the dignity of those human beings who live in desperate circumstances but do not rob and kill and assault their fellow human beings. In fact, drawing a connection between poverty and terrorism is a very odd thing for Christians to be doing given the fact that Christianity is premised on human free will.

Of course, there are extenuating circumstances that may play a role in both crimes and terrorist acts. But conceding that possibility is *not* the same thing as positing an exculpatory condition that demotes a whole category of persons to something less than the status of responsible agents.

There are many more examples along these lines. When Konrad Raiser, the general secretary of the World Council of Churches, condemned the war on terrorism, he insisted that it has been presented as a defense of freedom, but instead, it is claiming "untold numbers of new victims." Recall here my earlier analysis of overstated statistics. The number of civilian casualties is not "untold." Many agencies and groups, as well as the U.S. military, are continually trying to get an accurate count. General Secretary Raiser also proclaimed that a "demonic character . . . captivates even the mind and soul of the victims" in light of the U.S. "will to dominate and to exercise power over instead of with others."[11] Once again, and tellingly, a religious leader analyzes cataclysmic events without any fundamental indebtedness to the theological categories of his faith, save to assert that the American victims of terror have exhibited a "demonic character" in their response. What is billed as a "religious" voice makes just another partisan attack.

Consider, in this light, a statement issued by the U.S. Episcopal bishops on September 26, 2001, calling for the United States to "wage reconciliation." The bishops do not tell us with whom and precisely how this reconciliation should be waged, considering that the terrorists are not responsible political leaders with a legitimate mandate and they have not issued a set of negotiable political demands. Concerns with justice where the United States is concerned are conspicuous by their absence. Moreover, the bishops make the causal argument that it is "crushing poverty" that "causes the death of 6,000 children in a single morning"—a claim that is false, as I have already noted.[12] We are back in a moral universe in which Muslims cannot be expected to respond in any way other than violence to social inequities, real or perceived. The assumption of the Episcopal bishops is that citizens of the Muslim world will, of course, blame the conditions of their lives on the West rather than indict the authoritarian regimes under which the overwhelming majority of the world's Muslims live.

STRONG ARGUMENTS
AND RESPONSIBLE RHETORIC

Some religious voices have had strong responses that try to understand what happened on September 11—how best to name it—and what our reaction should be, by deploying fundamental theological and ethical concepts. They have done so in the belief that theological responses need not be narrowly sectarian, hence available in principle only to the company of believers, but rather, that all citizens can take up such arguments with benefit, whether they agree with them or not. Catholicism has an advantage in this regard because of its centuries-old tradition of pressing moral argument in and through the language of natural law, the common good, and, more recently, the dignity of the human person and human rights associated with the papacy of Pope John Paul II.

John Paul II's response to September 11 was admirable. It is important to note that he has offered a higher valuation of authentic Christian pacifism than any previous pontiff, in part because such pacifism lifts up the "incomparable worth of the human person." But he insists that there *is* such a thing as a just war, under quite specific, carefully delimited circumstances. The pontiff always reminds the faithful that the God of Abraham, the God of Isaac, and the God of Jacob are closely linked, and that the Christian Savior arose out of the Jewish community. God is a god of justice. God does not leave crimes unpunished, even as God holds forth the possibility of mercy and grace. "Vengeance is mine," says the Lord. But justice is the job of human beings as part of their earthly vocation.

In the encyclical *Evangelium Vitae,* which contrasts cultures of life and cultures of death, Pope John Paul II notes that there are

> situations in which the values proposed by God's law seem to involve a
> genuine paradox. This happens for example in the case of legitimate

defense, in which the right to protect one's own life and the duty not to harm someone else's life are difficult to reconcile in practice. Certainly, the intrinsic value of life and the duty to love oneself no less than others are the basis of a true right to self-defense. The demanding commitment to love your neighbor presupposes love of oneself as the basis of comparison. . . . Consequently, no one can renounce the right to self-defense out of lack of love for life or for self. . . . Legitimate defense can be not only a right but a grave duty for someone responsible for another's life, the common good of the family or of the State.[13]

The pope's peace message for New Year's Day 2002 again insists that there exists a right of self-defense against terrorism. The pope writes: "When terrorist organizations use their own followers as weapons to be launched against defenseless and unsuspecting people, they show clearly the death wish that feeds them. Terrorism springs from hatred, and it generates isolation, mistrust and closure. . . . Terrorism is built on contempt for human life. For this reason, not only does it commit intolerable crimes, but because it resorts to terror as a political and military means it is itself a true crime against humanity."[14] Unlike those who insist that poverty and injustice *cause* terrorism, John Paul II credits those tempted by terrorism with the capacity to repudiate this option. He acknowledges the millions who suffer injustice but do *not* capitulate to indiscriminate hatred.

Most reprehensible, the pope reminds us, is the terrorist who claims to be killing in God's name. Such a person is in the grip of a "fanatic fundamentalism which springs from the conviction that one's own vision of the truth must be forced upon everyone else." This fundamentalism is, in fact, "radically opposed to belief in God. Terrorism exploits not just people, it exploits God: it ends by making him an idol to be used for one's own purposes."[15]

Nor should those fighting terrorism turn their belief in God into an ideological weapon. It is one thing to ask God for wisdom and guidance and to acknowledge that God judges the nations. It is another to say that we alone fight with God on our side. Other Catholic responses might be noted in which theological categories, or terms with a long tradition within Christian theology (like hope), are deployed as central to understanding and interpreting the present moment. The United States Conference of Catholic Bishops urged that when military action is necessary, it alone is not sufficient; that military force must be directed only against perpetrators and combatants; and that a constructive engagement with the Muslim world is necessary. Vengeance must be eschewed, the Catholic bishops said, and deliberate hatred repudiated utterly, even in—or especially in—the fighting of a war. "National leaders bear a heavy moral obligation to see that the full range of nonviolent means is employed," the bishops write. "We acknowledge, however, the right and duty of a nation and the international community to use military force if necessary to defend the common good by protecting the innocent against mass terrorism. *Because of its terrible consequences, military force, even when justified and carefully executed, must always be undertaken with a sense of deep regret.*" (emphasis mine)[16]

Finally, the Reverend Billy Graham, dean of American evangelism, reminded us of the fog of history's unfolding in his remarks at the service in the National Cathedral for the National Day of Prayer and Remembrance on September 14, 2001. Reverend Graham insisted that he did not know the answer to why God allows tragedy, and that there is a mystery at the heart of this question. September 11 did teach some lessons, however—lessons about "the mystery of iniquity and evil, but, secondly, it's a lesson about our need for each other," and in this need lies hope. This may be the only true Christian message to have come out of the horror of that day—a message of hope and human solidarity.[17]

SHOULD NON-CHRISTIANS
EXPECT SOMETHING FROM CHRISTIANS?

In a statement made at the Dominican Monastery of Latour-Maubourg in 1948, Albert Camus, an unbeliever, insisted that the "Christian has many obligations" and that the world "today needs Christians who remain Christians." Camus professed that he did not share the Christian hope. But he did share "the same revulsion from evil." Christians must speak out "loud and clear," he admonished, and they "should voice their condemnation in such a way that never a doubt, never the slightest doubt, could rise in the heart of the simplest man. That they should get away from abstraction and confront the blood-stained face history has taken on today."[18] Camus's ire was roused by what he took to be the muted voices of many Christians in condemning Nazi horrors. If Christians do not guard against reducing the human person to a mere instrument of blind historic forces, he asked, who will?

For Camus, Christians should link arms with others in articulating and embracing a philosophy of limits that affirms rather than breaks human solidarity. This logic of the rebel, by contrast to that of the violent revolutionary, repudiates all philosophies and ideologies that stoke unlimited violence and countenance such, whether radical Marxism or various fundamentalisms. Down that path lies nihilism. By contrast, rebellion "cannot exist without a strange form of love. . . . Rebellion proves in this way that it is the very movement of life and that it cannot be denied without renouncing life. . . . Revolution without honor, . . . in preferring an abstract concept of man to a man of flesh and blood, denies existence as many times as is necessary, puts resentment in place of love."[19] In the voice of terrorism and the radical Islamist advocacy of hatred and destruction, we see the face of nihilism, hear the voice of resentment, and are confronted by the celebration of death.

A week or so after the attack of September 11, with the anthrax threat looming, one of my daughters and I found ourselves discussing the need for a plan should there be a biological or chemical attack. Who would pick up her children, my grandchildren? Should we buy gas masks? How does one discuss this with two five-year-olds and a seven-year-old? Already the children were drawing pictures of planes flying into buildings and asking whether more buildings would be knocked down and more airplanes hijacked. What happens if Grandma's plane is hijacked? they pondered.

Of course, we must all die one day. But the Christian gospel calls people to life, to have it more abundantly. There are times when that call to life requires action against those claimed by death. How best to do that? Unless Christians grapple with this reality, they ignore the heart of the message that they purport to embrace.

THE PROBLEM
WITH PEACE

THE HISTORY OF HUMANKIND is littered with the ruins generated by wars of conquest. Such wars, and the subsequent enslavement and exploitation of those conquered, were the way of the ancient world. But even these sorts of wars become more complicated the longer one looks at them. St. Augustine pointed out that everyone who goes to war wants peace. War seems to be a means to that end. Peace is construed as the elimination of all those who pose an immediate or hypothetical threat. It follows that not only war but contrasting visions of peace must be examined critically. All too often people cry, "Peace, peace," when there is no peace, or when the call for peace is dubious or destructive in its means and its proclaimed end. For that reason alone, peace needs to be examined. Let's begin by looking at different visions of peace.

CONTRASTING VISIONS OF PEACE

The conqueror, the just warrior, and the pacifist are all inspired by a vision of peace, but each construes peace differently. For the conqueror, justice is beside the point. For the just war advocate, the demands of justice may require that peace be suspended temporarily in order to prevent or to rectify a grievous harm. For the pacifist, peace is the highest good and if injustice prevails, it must be contested with nonviolent weapons.

Let's begin with the conquest mentality. Tacitus's sober words describing Rome's destruction of its enemy Carthage—"Where they make a desert, they call it peace"—are a solemn reminder that the quest for peace can bring ruin too. This kind of peace seeks a world in which adversarial politics as we know it—Augustine's conflicting human wills—has disappeared. Interested only in total domination, the conqueror can never rest. There is always opposition somewhere that must be quashed. This is a utopian vision of peace, although it is often not construed as such.

There are other utopian visions of peace. There is the biblically inspired vision in which the lion lies down with the lamb and the lamb does *not* have to be replaced frequently. Harmony reigns. Everyone "gets along." Liberal humanists in the seventeenth and eighteenth centuries grafted their own concerns onto this biblical template. Rather than speaking of sin or evil as that which destroys peace and promotes injustice, this "liberal conscience," as the historian Michael Howard calls it, talked of war as an atavism that arises from misunderstandings.[1] They placed a premium on defeating superstition, promoting rationalism, and communication, and thereby bringing peace along as a side benefit—especially as nations became mutually dependent through trade. The aim was to overcome what the social theorist Joseph Schumpeter called "bloody primitivism."[2]

Just before the unleashing of the Great War, there were some 425 peace organizations throughout the world. Numerous peace treaties had been signed, and many peace congresses had been held. The liberal humanist conscience envisaged a world in which each state submits gracefully to vague entities that the "world" or "humanity" have somehow endowed with the legitimate power to bring an end to any and all disputes that threaten to erupt into open conflict. In some utopian visions, the peoples of the world will one day speak a single language, everything will be shared equally, and all armies will disappear—and so, eventually, will states. In other visions, there is a veritable carnival of diversity. Multiple cultures flourish unhindered. Many languages are spoken. Here too vague international or universal entities keep the peace, and all peoples everywhere bow to their ministrations because of a belief that all outcomes are fair.

Notice that in such utopias, as in the utopia of the conqueror, politics disappears. The conflict and reconciliation of human wills that is politics no longer mars the beatific landscape. One way or another, the "eschatological moment" of the Kingdom of God at the end of time is brought down to earth, secularized, placed within time, and embraced as a realizable goal—despite the fact that over the long course of humankind's bloody history nothing remotely approximating this vision has ever been attained.

Other images of peace are far less grand. The baseline aspiration of peace is the absence of open warfare. This hoped-for absence of conflict is made possible once other ways of settling disputes have been instituted and acquired sufficient legitimacy in the eyes of persons and states. According to this vision, states will one day be obliged to submit willingly to arduous processes of negotiation in which settlements are imposed by impartial third parties. Or institutions will be created to provide attractive incentives for states to handle their disputes peacefully— and equally potent disincentives to avoid warfare. Another minimalist vision is that associated with balance-of-power advocates and *realpolitik*. This vision takes as a given that states invariably defend their interests and promote their own well-being. In the process of doing so, they secure allies and incur foes. *If* the configuration of forces on both sides is roughly equal, "peace" may well ensue, because the costs of going to war are too high and a favorable outcome is by no means guaranteed.

Another cluster of visions of peace goes beyond the severe strictures of *realpolitik* minimalism but avoids rationalist or sentimentalist utopias. These pictures of a peaceful future tease out what advocates take to be the capacious possibilities of liberal internationalism. Peace is an international system in which multiple entities engage one another, sometimes cooperating, sometimes contesting. The most important players (politically speaking) are states. But there are also hundreds of institutions and associations—NGOs (nongovernmental organizations)—in the arena pressing their demands and intervening in the affairs of states. Most often these interventions are called humanitarian. Some certainly deserve the appellation. Other interventions are more directly political, although they operate under the slogan of protecting human rights, an activity often presented as being above politics. Amnesty International is a good example. Such groups believe they are helping to create the preconditions for "lasting peace" with justice.

The peace through NGOs approach, however, fails to answer one vexing question: To whom, or before whom, are NGOs accountable? States must justify their legitimacy before their own people and in the eyes of the international community. But what about entities that are not authorized in this way? Most observers would agree that these entities cannot continue to receive support from states unless their mission is clearly humanitarian. At the same time, however, many such groups press for a world beyond what they view as the hopelessly flawed world of states and sovereignty.

Complicating the picture even more are the international organizations whose members are individual states in concert, beginning with the United Nations and its endless list of acronym offshoots (UNICEF, UNESCO, and so on). Powerful entities like the World Bank and the International Monetary Fund also play an enormous role in today's international affairs. Various tribunals and juridical entities usually associated with The Hague fit this category as well. Many peace advocates place their hopes in the growing power (or at least they hope the power of such institutions is growing) of trans-state entities that can put states, or particular persons acting in the name of states, in their place, up to and including imprisonment for violating human rights. A significant cohort of multilateralists here and abroad hold up the European Union as a model toward which all states and peoples should be moving.

OMITTING RELIGION FROM THE VISION

Note that these visions do not include the great world religions. This omission can be accounted for by the continued power of the so-called secularization hypothesis, articulated by the great German sociologist Max Weber, among others, and adopted as a paradigm by Western social science. This hypothesis promises a world denuded of religion. The argument holds that as humankind modernizes, it disentangles itself from religion. So powerful has this theory been that it remains difficult for many who write about international affairs and political life to take religion seriously to this day. If religion enters the picture at all, it is as what social scientists call a "dependent variable." As such, religion cannot be the real reason for the behavior of groups of peoples. The real reason lies elsewhere, according to the secularization hypothesis, and religion is a cover-up, mere window dressing covering the real interests involved. We have seen this sort of thinking in analyses that ignore Osama bin Laden's words and recast his fatwas in the language of political interests that comport with the presuppositions of the secularization argument.

Anyone with a Marxist cast of mind does this consistently. Within Marxism, religion is a form of "false consciousness" that traps people, making it impossible for them to see their real class interests. There is also the view that people who take their religious beliefs too seriously present a clear and present danger. The Inquisition is trotted out as if it were a real possibility in twenty-first-century Europe or anywhere else in the West. The wars of religion are referenced as lurking just beneath the surface if religious "fanatics" are not appeased or their influence is not stymied. Whether as "false consciousness" or inflamed extremism, religion is cast as a negative force.

What does this prejudice do to our understanding of international affairs? For one thing, we often overlook the role that religious bodies and groups play in positive and transformative ways. Martin Luther King was no generic social reformer but an African-American Baptist minister; Pope John Paul II's pastoral identity deeply informs his extraordinary diplomatic missions. A range of developments, from civil rights struggles in the United States to Solidarity in Poland and the end of the Soviet Empire, are incomprehensible if religion is left out of the picture.

Throughout Western Christianity there have been prophets set afire by visions of more just and peaceful worlds. To the utopians among them, a world of perfect peace can be brought about in the here and now and the Kingdom of God made manifest on this earth. Many adherents of this vision have behaved nobly in a variety of situations. But this and other pacifist visions also invite people to retreat into moral purism and isolationism. The vast majority of Christians reserve a vision of perfect peace for the end of history. Here and now, nations and human wills are in conflict with one another. One is obliged to keep alive on this earth a rich vision of peace that places justice and injustice front and center without assuming perfection is possible.

For most Christians, justice is a complex term consisting of several parts. There is retributive justice, which refers to restraining and punishing wrongdoers. There is distributive justice, which helps to bring about more equitable circumstances for citizens of a particular nation or nations in general. And there is what those involved in the Truth and Reconciliation Commissions in South Africa called restorative justice—a way to help a community deal with a cruel and unjust past so that it can both acknowledge the horror and move on to reconciliation and the constructive building of a future. It is important to note that murderers are still brought to justice under such a system of restorative justice, but there are several "just" options. One is a prison sentence, especially for offenders who remain recalcitrant. Another option is making restitution to the injured community.

As a way to honor the cause of both justice and mercy, political restorative justice is shaped significantly by Christianity. The goal is civic peace marked by justice. The value of this approach in dealing with not just one state's internal efforts to build a constitutional order but with relations between states is untested; political restorative justice seems likely, however, to fall prey to the classic dilemmas of international politics. The fog of politics grows thicker and less penetrable when states whose cultures are alien to each other try to interact. To be sure, there are many ways to promote understanding. But understanding cannot be premised on either blatant presuppositions of superiority or collective guilt and self-loathing. In the one case, one simply asserts the superiority of one's way of life and bids to extend it through force. In the second, one finds nothing worth defending.

The decent middle way is to ponder the ethics of how Western cultures can defend themselves against threats within and without. One step in this process is appreciating what we face in the fierce and dogmatic assertions of supremacy mounted in contemporary Islamist extremism. Let's begin with Islamic teaching on war and peace.

JUSTIFICATION OF WAR
AND WAR-FIGHTING IN ISLAM

The student of war and peace quickly discovers some interesting areas of overlap and difference in how the Christian and Islamic traditions reflect on force and its justification or condemnation. In January 1993, I participated in a conference, "The Ethics of War and Peace," held at the Notre Dame Center in Jerusalem. This was my first serious encounter with the similarities and differences between Islam and the Christian just war tradition. The distinguished Muslim scholars and experts on the Islamic ethics of war and peace gently chided those of us articulating the just war tradition when we moved too quickly to assimilate Islam and Christianity. Bassam Tibi, a professor of international relations who has written on Islam, war, and modernity, told us:

> [The] Western distinction between just and unjust wars linked to specific grounds for war is unknown in Islam. Any war against unbelievers, whatever its immediate ground, is morally justified. Only in this sense can one distinguish just and unjust wars in Islamic tradition. When Muslims wage war for the dissemination of Islam, it is a just war. . . . When non-Muslims attack Muslims, it is an unjust war. *The usual Western interpretation of jihad as a "just war" in the Western sense is, therefore, a misreading of this Islamic concept.* (emphasis mine)[3]

There are moral restraints in the conduct of war, but such restraints are more likely to appeal to a warrior's *honor* rather than to a soldier's sense of *justice*, a point that Michael Ignatieff makes in his book *The Warrior's Honor*. Ignatieff articulates the difficulties involved in teaching "the warrior's code of honor to men trained in Islamic jihad."[4] The intentional slaughter of civilians is a dishonorable thing to do, according to an honor code. But within Islamist fundamentalism, such slaughter can be a noble act. Traditionally, the Islamic goal of war against unbelievers, as Tibi notes, was to "force them to submit to Islam, not to destroy them," but this goal appears to have changed in modern fundamentalism.[5]

One fundamental feature of Islamic teaching is that an effort to extend the boundaries of the territory of Islam is a prima facie case of a just cause. In Tibi's words: "It is . . . in line with the Qur'anic revelation dividing the world into a peaceful part (the Islamic community) and a hostile part (unbelievers who are expected to convert to Islam, if not freely then through the instrument of war). In this sense, Muslims believe that expansion through war is not aggression but a fulfillment of the Qur'anic command to spread Islam as a way of peace."[6] The theologian and scholar of

Islam John Kelsay adds that the resort to force may require something additional, for example, in the case of "the refusal of a non-Islamic political entity to acknowledge the sovereignty of Islam through the rulers converting to Islam or through the payment of tribute."[7]

By contrast, Christian theology has never taken the primacy of territory or earthly sovereignty as a foundational claim or principle. St. Augustine in the fourth century was clear, as was Jesus of Nazareth before him, that belief cannot be coerced and spread by force of arms. When Christian believers and historians of Christianity look back on acts of forced conversion carried out by rulers acting in the name of Christianity, it is with a great sense of shame. Not only do such deeds have no justification, but there are ample grounds for condemning them.

The basic foundation of Islamic concepts of war and peace is a "worldview based on the distinction between the abode of Islam (dar al-Islam), the 'home of peace' (dar al-Salam) (Qur'an, Jon. 10:25), and the non-Muslim world, the 'house of war' (dar al-harb). . . . The establishment of the new Islamic polity at Medina and the spread of the new religion were accomplished by waging war. The sword became the symbolic image of Islam in the West."[8] The Sword of Islam was feared and even respected. The question to be put by contemporary analysts is this: What prophylaxis exists within Islam to curb or limit the waging of war in the name of spreading the house of Islam, given the historic legitimacy and reality of this approach?

There is no single, and no singularly clear, answer to this question. A version of this question must be put to any traditional way of thinking about war and peace, religious or secular, because any tradition could generate excess or deteriorate into violence. As I demonstrated in my discussion of the just war tradition, there are a variety of ways in which the excesses of Christian zeal throughout history have not met the standards of just war ethics. A limitless war to propagate the faith is *never* legitimate within the Christian just war tradition.

What about Islam? Scholars of Islam make it clear that Islamic views on war and peace vary depending on whether one is a Sunni or Shiite Muslim, for example, and on whether one is interpreting the Qur'an metaphorically or with a strict literalness. Although analogies between Christianity and Islam concerning the conduct of war are certainly made, scholars often dispute one another. Bassam Tibi claims that, by contrast to justifying occasions for war, when "it comes to the conduct of war, one finds only small differences between Islam and other monotheistic religions or the international laws of war. Islam recognizes moral constraints on military conduct, even in wars against non-Muslims."[9] John Kelsay argues that *jus in bello* considerations are prominent in the classical materials, but in more contemporary discussion, "one is struck by the scarcity of *jus in bello* materials."[10] Sunni and Shiite differences emerge here too. The Shiites historically "considered religion the only legitimate cause for war," and this to extend the sway of Islam.[11] Faith could be spread by the sword; indeed, in the West, the Sword of Islam symbolized the Islamic world and its aggressive expansion.

The Sword of Islam makes more sense if one keeps in mind that the Prophet Muhammad was a war leader and fighter. He was, as the great scholar of Islam Bernard Lewis puts it, "his own Constantine." By contrast, Jesus of Nazareth insisted that his Kingdom was not of this world, and he rejected earthly dominion. Muhammad founded a "religiously conceived polity . . . and his successors confronted the realities of the state and, before very long, of a vast and expanding empire. At no time did they create any institution corresponding to, or even remotely resembling, the church in Christendom."[12] There was no separate church to call the prince or the state to account. The state-church distinction makes no sense within classic Islam, because there is no church as such. It is worthwhile to quote Lewis at some length here:

> In Islam the struggle of good and evil very soon acquired political and even military dimensions. Muhammad, it will be recalled, was not only a prophet and a teacher, like the founders of other religions; he was also the head of a polity and of a community, a ruler and a soldier. Hence his struggle involved a state and its armed forces. If the fighters in the war for Islam, the holy war "in the path of God," are fighting for God, it follows that their opponents are fighting against God. And since God is in principle the sovereign, the supreme head of the Islamic state—and the Prophet and, after the Prophet, the caliphs are his viceregents—then God as sovereign commands the army. The army is God's army and the enemy is God's enemy. The duty of God's soldiers is to dispatch God's enemies as quickly as possible to the place where God will chastise them—that is to say, the afterlife.[13]

Within the Christian just war tradition, by contrast, all notions of moral absolutism smack of triumphalism and a crusading mentality of war without limits and must therefore be repudiated. The Islamic concept of jihad has quite a different interpretation within the faith. In discussing Ibn Rushd, a medieval Islamic writer, Sohail H. Hashmi, another distinguished scholar of Islam, traces the Islamic tradition's detailed discussions of jihad, which emerged, he writes, "in the context of offensive struggles aimed at expansion of Islamic hegemony, an expansion aimed ultimately at the universal propagation of Islam. . . . Because the ultimate end of jihad is the propagation of the Islamic faith, not material gain or territorial conquest, Ibn Rushd, like other medieval writers, implicitly, if not always explicitly, separates the grounds for jihad from the grounds for war."[14]

This is not good news for those in the West who are targets of jihad, as well as for adherents of humanistic, civic, or moderate Islam, who are under tremendous pressure within Muslim societies. Some live under the threat of death or imprisonment. As radical fundamentalism has risen, tolerance of multiple tendencies within Islam has fallen. This fact helps to account for the muted voices of condemnation and criticism from the Islamic community in the wake of September 11.

THE CRISIS WITHIN ISLAM

After September 11, bookstores were flooded with materials on Islam.[15] There was always a wealth of material on Islam in the years before 2002, but Westerners paid scant attention until the attacks on the World Trade Center and the Pentagon. One learns that no one really speaks for Islam. There are no strong centers of theological transmission or anything equivalent to the Catholic magisterium; there are no central, foundational texts, other than the Qur'an itself, that are accepted as such by all believers. The political scholar Richard W. Bulliet argues that this is one reason Islam is currently in crisis. The absence of clear lines of authority and legitimacy helps to make possible a fanatic like bin Laden, who, "despite his lack of a formal religious education or an authoritative religious position, [is able] to assume the role of spokesman for the

world's Muslims." Bulliet attributes the "strange silence" of Muslims
since September 11 to the fact that there is no "clear, decisive, and unequivocal religious authority able to declare that the killing of innocents
by terrorist attacks is contrary to Islam and to explain how Muslims can
stand firmly against terrorism without seeming to embrace the United
States and its policies."[16]

To be sure, there were a few Islamic scholars and ethicists who insisted
that Osama bin Laden and his minions "could be charged with violating
well-codified provisions of Islamic law concerning safe passage, or *aman*
in Arabic," in the words of Khaled Abou el Fadl, a distinguished professor of Islamic law at the University of California at Los Angeles. "When
the terrorists entered the United States on visas and when they got aboard
those airplanes," he argues, "they were asking for *aman,* and when they
turned around and did harm, they were committing treachery, which is
forbidden."[17] In an interview with National Public Radio, Abou el Fadl,
who has been threatened by Islamist extremists inside the United States,
described his own absorption in fundamentalism as a youth and the feelings of power that this orientation gave him. Confronted on one occasion
by the complexities of Islamic law and its multiple interpretations, he defected from radical Islam and the "power-hungry" people who flock to it.
His criticism of American Muslim leadership is sharp. The extremists, he
argues, are transforming Islam into a system of thought that is destructive
of civilization itself, and it is time to speak up loud and clear. Why didn't
Muslim leadership make a thunderous, unequivocal condemnation of the
attacks of September 11? Why did they not organize a massive march to
Ground Zero and issue a unified statement, signed by all Muslim organizations, rejecting the Taliban and bin Laden?

Such questions were posed in the wake of September 11 across the
U.S. political spectrum, by liberals, moderates, and conservatives alike.
The theologian Gilbert Meilaender, writing in the liberal journal *Christian Century,* stated that "we need to hear from Islamic leaders sincere
condemnation of the attacks. Not ambiguous comments designed to
ward off military reprisal, and not condemnations which—in the same
breath—condemn Israel. We cannot do this for them; they must do it
themselves."[18] Some Muslim student groups on American college campuses rose to the occasion, offering powerful condolences and prayers
and charging that the terrorists could not claim to represent Islam.[19]

Sadly, other Muslims mounted what amount to strategies of evasion to avoid dealing head-on with the question of whether the Islamic tradition includes justification for acts of mass murder in the name of jihad or justification for opposition to such acts. One frequently voiced comparison used to deflect this question is to the mass murder committed by Timothy McVeigh. McVeigh no more represented Christianity than they represented Islam, some Muslims told us. But this is one more of the strained and flawed analogies that have proliferated in the wake of September 11. Timothy McVeigh never claimed to be acting in behalf of Christianity. He never cited scriptural justification or divine sanction for what he did. His last testament was the poem "Invictus," the defiant screed of an agnostic ("I thank whatever gods may be/For my unconquerable soul"). By contrast, the September 11 terrorists claimed to act in behalf of Islam and in fulfillment of the justified necessities of a holy war against infidels. That is why Muslims must address the matter head-on.

Evasions like the McVeigh analogy inspired Charles Krauthammer, writing in the *Washington Post,* to score the silence of the imams who have not spoken out against the fanatics who have declared holy war against America. He asks readers to imagine that nineteen murderous Christian fundamentalists

> hijacked four airplanes over Saudi Arabia and, in the name of God, crashed them into the holy cities of Mecca and Medina, destroying the holy Kaaba and killing thousands of innocent Muslim pilgrims. Could anyone doubt that the entire Christian world—clergy and theologians, leaders and lay folks—would rise as one to denounce the act? . . . The pope himself would rend his garments at this blasphemous betrayal of Christ. . . . Where were the fatwas against Osama bin Laden?[20]

The political analyst Jack Tapper, writing for the online *Salon Magazine,* exposes what he takes to be the flawed leadership of Muslim groups on the Council on American-Islamic Relations (CAIR) and the American Muslim Council (AMC), "even as public officials, from President Bush on down, [were making] a public show of support for American Muslims, [and] as ugly acts of violence and intimidation were made against Muslims and Arab Americans."[21] What Tapper objects to is that these groups have refused to condemn specifically either Osama bin Laden or Islamist extremism. The criticisms are vague and generic. When interviewed, some of the Muslim clerics blamed the pro-Israel lobby for promoting negative views of them and of Islam.

I mention such criticisms because they express the general disappointment many people felt when the attacks were not emphatically and specifically condemned by Muslim leaders. There are other critics, within and outside Islam, who are even stronger in their assessments. Second to none in this regard is the writer Salman Rushdie. In editorials in the *New York Times* and elsewhere, Rushdie insists that the struggle really is about Islam and not just extremism. He points to the "worldwide Muslim demonstrations in support of Osama bin Laden and Al Qaeda" and notes:

> Why did those 10,000 men armed with swords and axes mass on the Pakistan-Afghanistan frontier, answering some mullah's call to jihad? . . . Why the routine anti-Semitism of the much-repeated Islamic slander that "the Jews" arranged the hits on the World Trade Center and the Pentagon. . . . Of course, this is "about Islam." The question is, what exactly does that mean? . . . For a vast number of "believing" Muslim men, "Islam" stands, in a jumbled, half-examined way, not only for the fear of God—the fear more than the love, one suspects—but also for a cluster of customs, opinions and prejudices that include their dietary practices; the sequestration or near-sequestration of "their" women; the sermons delivered by their mullahs of choice; a loathing of modern society, in general, riddled as it is with music, godlessness and sex; and a more particularized loathing (and fear) of the prospect that their own immediate surroundings could be taken over— "Westoxicated"—by the liberal Western-style way of life.[22]

Rushdie observes that it was already routine twenty years ago in the Muslim world "to blame all its troubles on the West and, in particular, the United States."[23] This tendency has, if anything, become even more pronounced. Bernard Lewis makes essentially the same point, noting that "it is usually easier and always more satisfying to blame others for one's misfortunes."[24] The demonized picture of the Jew illustrates most of the conspiracy theories mounted about the West, which frequently make the massive projection that the West is still determined to conduct a religious crusade against Islam. This adds up to a self-exculpatory strategy that refuses to take a hard look at troubles internal to the Muslim world, among them: appallingly low standards of education and literacy; the absence of political freedom, a human rights culture, and solid economic development; and the officially sanctioned second-place status of women. When we also consider the pressure on humanistic or moderate Islam by extremists, it seems more than fair for Muslim and non-Muslim scholars alike to speak of a crisis within Islam. Those who confront the crisis head-on insist that repressive fundamentalist regimes like the late and unlamented Taliban do not exhaust the possibilities of Islamic law, which has a rich and varied tradition.[25] It is that rich and varied tradition they hope to recover.

10   ENCOUNTERING ISLAMIST FUNDAMENTALISM

ISLAMIST FUNDAMENTALISM is a twentieth-century phenomenon. Its adherents purport to be the only authentic voice of Islam, despite the fact that Islam provides a "vast variety of responses" to ethical questions, "from the quietism of silent disapproval, advocated by some of the most revered and respected figures in the development of Muslim law, to government-directed coercion, supported by the threat of imprisonment or death and sustained by the reports of pious informers."[1]

Fundamentalist Islam threatens the sleep of the world wherever it is established.[2] The more virulent Islamism becomes, the more difficult life becomes for moderate Muslims. In many parts of the world, extremism appears to have won the day. Texts are drawn upon to support a harsh version of Islam, including texts proclaiming that infidels should be seized, besieged, ambushed, and destroyed. With the tolerant Islamic tradition on the wane, with virulent anti-Semitism, anti-Christianity, and anti-Western attitudes triumphant in so many places, it is unsurprising that commentators with perspectives as varied as those of Andrew Sullivan, Christopher Hitchens, and Salman Rushdie declare that the current struggle is, indeed, a religious one. How does one respond to Islamic fundamentalism, however, without descending into a religious war mentality? Writes Sullivan:

> This coming conflict is indeed as momentous and as grave as the last major conflicts, against Nazism and Communism, and it is not hyperbole to see it in these epic terms. What is at stake is yet another battle against a religion that is succumbing to the temptation Jesus refused in the desert—to rule by force. The difference is that this conflict is against a more formidable enemy than Nazism or Communism. The secular totalitarianisms of the 20th century were, in President Bush's memorable words, "discarded lies." They were fundamentalisms built on the very weak intellectual conceits of a master race and a Communist revolution. But Islamic fundamentalism is based on a glorious civilization and a great faith. It can harness and coopt and corrupt true and good believers if it has a propitious and toxic enough environment.[3]

Dealing with this challenge will be a task requiring great nuance. But the threat must be faced, because it is not going to go away of its own accord.

ISLAMIST FUNDAMENTALISM AND THE CHALLENGE TO MUSLIM LEADERSHIP

Two sorts of situations confront us. The first is the internal threat represented by centers that preach hatred and urge the destruction of infidel societies from within those societies themselves. The second is the takeover of Muslim countries by fundamentalists, as embodied most vividly in the Taliban regime in Afghanistan. The overriding issue in both cases is a literalist, frequently bloody-minded understanding of jihad and its justification. Rising attacks on Christian schools, churches, and hospitals in Pakistan; the bombing of several popular dance clubs and watering holes in Bali by Al Qaeda–backed indigenous extremists; the resurgence of grotesque anti-Semitic propaganda, including "blood libel" slanders and the forgery *The Protocols of the Elders of Zion*—all receive official or quasi-official sanction in many Islamic societies. The first step in determining what to do is to appreciate what is already being done and said by extremists. In established fundamentalist regimes governed by a severe version of Shari'a law, there is no distinction between a sin and a crime. Criminalized sins are dealt with harshly. Sayyed Nadeem Kazmi comments that "the Islamic world needs to rethink its strategy and offer a clear and workable framework for peace and stability in Afghanistan now that the Taliban have been relieved of their artificial stranglehold on power."[4]

There are strains of self-criticism in the wind, including the fact that Sheik Muhammad Hisham Kabbani, a prominent Sufi cleric living in America, just two short years ago issued a "chilling admonition to Americans to beware the Muslims in their midst," a warning that was widely regarded as overwrought. "Sheik Kabbani said that American Muslim groups were dominated by Sufi-hating Wahhabis, and that when he tried to distribute pamphlets at the annual conference of the Islamic Society of North America, organizers called the police."[5] For his troubles, Sheik Kabbani received FBI protection because of threats against his life.

Wahhabism specializes in anti-Americanism as a central feature of its extremist ideology, whether among its Saudi-funded epigones in the United States or in Saudi Arabia itself. The Saudis have only just begun to do the very thing that Wahhabism puts off limits: criticizing and questioning themselves. This tentative voice of self-critique is under enormous pressure. When Saudi religious scholars and academics issued a statement in response to "What We're Fighting For" and, in the mildest possible terms (dotted with the rather contemptuous suggestion that if the United States got out of the world outside its own borders, Muslims would no longer mind what it does), suggested there were possible grounds for dialogue between Muslims and the West, the reaction in Saudi Arabia, according to the *New York Times*, was immediate, negative, and severe.[6] Subsequently, the Saudi regime banned the distribution of *Al-Hayat,* the Arab-language newspaper of record, which had published in full our response to the letter from Saudi scholars. Apparently such an exchange is regarded as too dangerous by those in charge in Riyadh. They are unwilling to accord their intellectuals the preconditions for genuine debate, namely, an open and public forum.

For every voice calling publicly for tolerance or at least for dialogue, or condemning attacks on innocent civilians, there are other, often official, voices eschewing the possibility of dialogue altogether. Too many imams in Western Europe as well as in Muslim countries "preach murderous hatred of the United States," including the admonition that "Christians and Jews should have their throats slit," according to an article in the *New York Times*.[7] Sadly, wild conspiracy theories are also current in much discourse promulgated by extremists but picked up and apparently given wide currency in the Arab streets. One Saudi Arabian scholar who issued his own personal response to the statement "What We're Fighting For" backed up his anti-American and anti-Semitic posture by repeating some of the canards of the conspiracy theories disseminated from crackpot sources on the Internet: For instance, the CIA knowingly injected black babies with the HIV virus, and the AIDS and ebola viruses are "both products of American biological war laboratories." Although it is always difficult to pinpoint how ideological madness gets started, the slander that Jewish doctors, or the CIA, or both, knowingly began the AIDS epidemic among blacks already had wide currency a decade ago. One spokesman for the Black Muslim movement traveled the United States giving talks on college campuses proclaiming this "fact."

Such slanders, paraded as fact, make serious dialogue between radical Islam (and those who accept these canards) and others impossible. Furthermore, discourse between moderates and radicals within Muslim majority cultures also seems unlikely under such circumstances. The "still, small voice of reason" is difficult to hear above the din from the official press. For example, the leading Egyptian daily, *Al-Ahram Weekly,* reported that the United States deliberately filled humanitarian food drops with land mines in order to kill or maim as many Afghani children as possible.[8] This conspiracy theory penchant is also evident in the conviction that Israel engineered the World Trade Center attacks—a view current with young American Muslims, among others.[9] Those immersed in conspiracy theories are unmoved by empirical evidence or counterevidence, and they have a ready answer to every query or quandary. Because conspiracy theories proliferate on the Internet, such views gain a currency and pseudolegitimacy heretofore impossible. This too is part of the challenge we face.

In the meantime, and tragically, the problems faced by the Arab world are real and deep. The journalist Thomas Friedman describes a "brutally honest" report of the Arab Fund for Economic and Social Development that analyzed "the three main reasons the Arab world is falling off the globe. (The GDP of Spain is greater than that of all 22 Arab states combined.) In brief, [Arab underdevelopment is] due to a shortage of freedom to speak, innovate and affect political life, a shortage of women's rights and a shortage of quality education." A serious "freedom deficit undermines human development," says the report. Friedman cites one remarkable statistic that speaks volumes: "The whole Arab world translates about 300 books annually—one-fifth the number that Greece alone translates. . . . In spite of progress in school enrollment, 65 million Arab adults are still illiterate, almost two-thirds of them women."[10]

The West has a responsibility to partner with Arab societies to help them as they dig out of this deep hole. How best to do that without stoking resentment is no easy task. And although a strong positive correlation between undereducation, poverty, and terrorism is weak at best—according to serious scholarly studies—it is reasonable to expect that greater political stability and discernible improvement in the lives of the population in general would promote ordinary rather than extremist politics—or perhaps better said, anti-politics.

The task for the United States and the West in their dealings with Islamic, especially Arab, societies is twofold. The first and most immediate task is interdiction: Violence and terrorism must not be allowed to spread and to take more lives. We must accept the fact that terrorism aims to destroy, not to build. As St. Augustine argued about the nature of evil, destruction depletes and diminishes that which is good in society by destroying lives, human artifacts, and the delicate web of human sociality. We must do what we can to stop the spread of evil when we recognize it. This task entails making the necessary distinctions and deploying a proper economy of force. We must do minimal damage in order to forestall greater damage. Only when we stop the spread of evil can good flourish and manifest itself. We prevent harm so that good might flourish.

At the same time we must work to build an international culture in which people are secure in their homes and their cultures and in which human sociality is honored rather than quashed and stifled. Within Christianity, neighbor love is implicated in each instance: in the interdictive task of preventing harm not only to ourselves but to innocent third parties, and in the positive task of serving and assisting in an active way. Here it is worth noting that just war thinking is not only about war but about politics. Robust debate of political issues is possible only when arbitrary violence is curbed. In the aftermath of a conflict in which force has been deployed, politics is more likely to flourish if the temptations of religious triumphalism and nationalistic chauvinism have been avoided during the conflict.

At play throughout all such considerations is a central feature of Christian theology and ethics, namely, the importance of reflecting on what both individuals and collectives of individuals can or must do to redress evil. The theologian Joseph Capizzi argues that:

> According to Augustine, nonviolence is required at the individual level and just-war is mandated at the societal level. In other words, when a person is confronted by evil his duty is to turn the other cheek toward the evil (cf. Matt. 5:38). In these cases, Augustine did not counsel nonviolent resistance; he advised nonresistance. A state, on the other hand, has a moral obligation to defend itself against evil. The distinction between moral duties for individuals and states is classic in Christian theology, and was reaffirmed by Pope John Paul II in *Evangelium Vitae*.[11]

The Christian imperative, for both individuals and society, is to keep love of life and a commitment to human dignity in the forefront. In his New Year's Day message of 2002, Pope John Paul II argued that "peace born of justice and forgiveness" is assaulted by "international terrorism." Terrorism is fed by a "death wish," "springs from hatred, and . . . generates isolation, mistrust and closure. . . . Terrorism is built on contempt for human life. For this reason, not only does it commit intolerable crimes, but because it resorts to terror as a political and military means it is itself a true crime against humanity." From this indictment, John Paul moves to a general "right of self-defense against terrorism, a right which, as always, must be exercised with respect for moral and legal limits in the choice of ends and means." Forgiveness is vital, but what does it actually mean? the pontiff asks. Only when "an ethics and a culture of forgiveness prevail," he suggests, "can we hope for a 'politics' of forgiveness, expressed in society's attitudes and laws, so that through them justice takes on a more human character."[12]

The burden of power is not easily borne if we take justice seriously. We have to discern where self-defense begins and ends, where just punishment begins and ends, how to distinguish each of these from revenge and vengeance, how to build in limits against foes who practice and preach violence and killing without limits, and so on. Unfortunately, such distinctions seem lost not only on Islamist extremists but on many European intellectuals as well. Indeed, reading much of the material flowing from European capitals since September 11, 2001, we must confront the unpleasant reality that America is construed as a much bigger threat to human freedom and justice than anything that violent terrorists have done or plan to do. What is striking in these polemical, often caustic commentaries and poses of cultural superiority over the "American cowboy" is an inability, once again, to make the critical distinctions.

THE CORROSIVE EFFECT
OF MORAL EQUIVALENCE

It is worth discussing here Václav Havel's bemused observations on Western "peace people" during the Cold War and the nuclear stand-off between the United States and the Soviet Union. As I discussed in a previous chapter, these peace activists mistrusted Eastern European dissidents, whether they were in or out of jail at the time, because of their argument that there was a qualitative difference between the U.S. and Soviet systems and that the West, whatever the problems it faced, had political freedom and the possibility of protest. Havel found it amusing that dissidents like himself were paying a heavy price for seeking and defending the very freedoms that many Western activists either took for granted or seemed to reckon very cheaply.

Something similar seems to be going on in the wake of September 11. Confronted with an aggressive foe preaching hatred of any and all things Western, many have responded with a disturbing strain of Western self-loathing. How else to describe the lack of justifiable ire at demonstrations of hatred toward the West conducted within Western societies? In the section of London called "Londonistan," rallies supporting the Taliban and bin Laden sprang up after September 11; only a minority of the two million Muslims in the United Kingdom participated, but it is a significant minority. In France, Muslim thugs have fire-bombed synagogues and promulgated a wave of anti-Semitism of a sort not seen since the dark days of World War II.

An article in the *New York Times* on deepening anti-Semitism among Muslims notes that hateful images of Jews are embedded in Islamic popular culture. "The use of Nazi imagery, the newspaper caricatures of Jews with fangs and exaggerated hook noses, even the Arab textbooks with their descriptions of Jews as evil world conspirators—all of that, Arab leaders often insist, reflects a dislike for Israelis and Zionism but not for Jews and Judaism," notes the *Times*.[13] It is unsurprising, if shocking, that anti-Semitism is enjoying a resurgence. The French government acknowledged "a sharp increase in anti-Semitic incidents since September 2000, when fighting between Israelis and Palestinians intensified. One government report says acts of violence against Jews have increased from one in 1998 to nine in 1999 to 116 in 2000, the most recent figure available. Other anti-Semitic incidents, ranging from threats to arson, went from 74 in 1998 and 60 in 1999 to 603 in 2000."[14] The extremist anti-Western message in Arab school curricula, especially in Saudi Arabia, spills over into materials that circulate in the Muslim diaspora in Western Europe.[15] As a result, anti-immigrant sentiment is growing, and controls against asylum seekers are being tightened throughout Western Europe.

You might think that Western European intellectuals would be addressing these problems and other clear and present dangers. You would be wrong. Witness the self-loathing palpable in journalist Robert Fisk's condescending "understanding" when Afghan thugs beat him bloody;[16] or the "current debate in France . . . about differencing [*sic*] Islam as a religion and its prophecy through terrorist groups";[17] or the routine moral equivalence arguments that fail to differentiate between the intentional killing of civilians and civilian deaths resulting from honest mistakes, to the penchant for citing wildly erroneous and inflammatory "statistics" (like the claim that 500,000 Iraqi children have perished as a consequence of U.S. policies—no source cited or needed apparently).[18] A rather broad band of European intellectual life and political commentary seems to be gorging itself on a repast of anti-Americanism.[19]

This was evident in the German response to our statement "What We're Fighting For." Not only did the German intellectuals overlook the distinction between the intentional killing of civilians in America and the unintentional deaths of noncombatants in the Afghan theater (the "mass murder of the Afghan population," as they called it), but they made the bizarre claim that Taliban fundamentalism is equal to American fundamentalism, which respects and works through the electoral system and embraces the separation of church and state. The German writers made another equally astounding claim: that critics of the U.S. war effort in America were being "denounced as traitors." In May 2002 in Washington, D.C., I participated in a discussion with some German journalists who were rather embarrassed by much of the German reaction even as they tried to explain it. The overall effect was depressing. What is clear is that the nationalism many Europeans believe they have left behind has been displaced by often virulent anti-Americanism. Indeed, *anti-Americanism is the form that nationalism takes in many European countries.*

Most telling was the response by the German journalists when they were asked how Germany would have reacted if it had been the target of an attack equivalent to the September 11 attacks on America. The answer was unanimous: appeasement. Not pacifism, but appeasement. Appeasement may flow from desperate miscalculation. Or it may derive, as it seems to in the German case, from a kind of cultural ennui that disdains the hard work of grappling with whether, and when, the use of force is necessary or appropriate and what the limits to that force should be.[20] Instead, and from an allegedly neutral stance devoid of the belligerence said to be characteristic of "the Americans," the Germans judged us and found us wanting.[21] In the German letter to the authors and signatories of "What We're Fighting For," the most withering fire is directed not at Islamist terrorism but at the United States.

There were some thoughtful responses to the defense by American intellectuals and academics of the use of force to fight terrorism within the restraints of just war. Some of these responses recognized the pains taken by the United States and its leaders to insist repeatedly that the war against terrorism is not a war against a religion, and that many governments, including the Philippines and Sri Lanka, are seeking U.S. assistance in their fight against indigenous terrorist organizations.[22] But many other critics claimed that, as scholars and intellectuals, we are betraying our calling in supporting the actions of the American government.

It appears to be the season of anti-Americanism, some of it bizarre. The cultural analyst Alexander Stille sketched the highly popular views of the famous French intellectual and philosopher Jean Baudrillard, who expressed "'vast jubilation' over the September 11 attacks." Baudrillard delighted "at seeing the destruction of this world superpower" and claimed that because of "its unbearable potency," the United States "has roused all the world's innate violence, and thus (without knowing it) the terrorist imagination that dwells in all of us."[23]

Though *Le Monde* identified with America in the immediate aftermath of the attacks ("Nous sommes tous Americains"), Baudrillard clearly blames America's "unbearable potency" for the September 11 attacks. Nineteen extremists may have done the deed, but all of "us" wanted it, Baudrillard claims. How seriously should we take such arguments? Some would argue that there are always bizarre theories floating around. True. But these theories, including a best-seller in France arguing that the American government itself engineered the attacks, are widely read, disseminated, and even applauded.

One French social commentator, Alain Minc, suggests that Baudrillard has fallen victim to a confusion of the virtual and the real. Minc believes that Baudrillard equates the make-believe world of Disneyland (with which Baudrillard has long been obsessed) and its attempts to simulate a kind of "reality" that never existed with a real attack in which "thousands . . . were killed in cold blood. Enraptured by his own verbal prestidigitation, [Baudrillard] has turned mass murder into a 'beautiful suicide.'" Stille concludes that "only a French philosopher could turn reality on its head in such a rhetorical flourish" and find the events of September 11 breathtaking and beautiful. The majority or ordinary French citizens, lacking the pretensions of a certain intellectual class, continue to express at least residual positive feelings about the United States. Our media would do well to concentrate on the broad base of support for the American effort in the rank and file of many European countries and pay less attention to those who specialize in drawing attention to themselves.

In the final analysis, the reaction of the European intellectuals I have criticized is fueled more by resentment and envy of American power and dynamism than by a principled concern about the use of force. If the latter were the real issue, much more would be said about it. Instead, we are subjected to one attack after another on bellicose Americans, with precious little nuanced reflection on when, under what set of provocations, and within what restraints, force is ever justified. Yes, American power is an extraordinary thing, and it can be used well or it can be used badly. What is America's special burden in light of its extraordinary power?

11   STATES AND SELF-DEFENSE IN A DANGEROUS TIME

IN THIS CHAPTER, I CONSIDER two related questions: How does a democratic society defend itself? And can force be an instrument of justice? An additional feature of the just war tradition, less emphasized than self-defense, holds that the governments and citizens of one country may be called upon to protect citizens of another country, or a minority within that country, who are not in a position to defend themselves from harm. "Protecting the innocent from certain harm" may require armed force in order to interdict and punish aggressors, especially aggressors whose war aim is the death and conquest of as many noncombatants as possible. There are those who insist that no nation is obliged in this way to come to the assistance of another. They dismiss the possibility that force can be an instrument of justice. They believe that international entities should rise up to take care of the problem. Thus far, however, the track record of nonstate organizations as effective bodies to interdict violence and punish aggression is not impressive.

Given the contrast between the demonstrated ineffectiveness of international organizations to roll back violence and the track record of particular states, particularly the United States, in deflecting and muting interstate violence, let's make this question more specific. In asking, how does a democratic society defend itself, let's assume that the democratic society in question is not just any constitutional order but the United States. The role of preventing or interdicting violence in other countries is not new to the United States; it was thrust upon the United States in 1989 when it became the world's only superpower.

The shock waves that rippled around the globe in the wake of September 11 reminded us that the expectation of American power, American stability, and American continuity is a basic feature of international order. Whether people celebrate this fact or lament it, it is undeniably the case that American political, diplomatic, economic, and military power now structures and anchors the international system. Small wonder that many of us compared the plenary jolt to the world's nervous system delivered on September 11, 2001, to the sack of Rome by the Vandals in A.D. 410. As word made its way through the civilized world about Rome's vulnerability, no one could believe it, including those who were not lovers of Rome. Roman law and rule provided stability and a point of reference. Rome was the umbrella of power under which so much else stood.

The analogy is not perfect, of course. We are the world's longest-lived constitutional republic. Postrepublican Rome was governed by often brutal emperors, and transfers of power could be a bloody, not very peaceful business. But the closest modern equivalent to the city of Rome is New York City—a polyglot metropolis with an astonishingly complex mix of languages and peoples from all other cultures. New York City is an astounding achievement. Now that the dust storms of September 11 have settled, what have we learned from the attacks on Washington, our capital city, and New York, our cosmopolitan lodestar? What has been revealed through this cataclysmic event?

APPEASEMENT DOESN'T WORK

As I write these words in the summer of 2002, we have word about a cache of 251 Al Qaeda tapes captured in the Afghan operation. Several of these gruesome tapes show "what appears to be the agonizing death of three dogs exposed to a chemical agent, apparently before September 11." The tape archive also includes detailed instructions on making bombs and shooting surface-to-air missiles (SAMs) and a variety of violent tapes contributed by "affiliated groups in Bosnia, Chechnya, Somalia, Sudan and elsewhere."[1]

Experts who watched many hours of these tapes suggested that Western intelligence agencies might even now be underestimating Al Qaeda. One such expert, Magnus Ranstorp, director-designate of the Center for the Study of Terrorism and Political Violence at the University of St. Andrews in Scotland, stated: "In conjunction with the *Encyclopedia of Jihad* and other written manuals, the tapes show meticulous planning, preparation, and attention to the tradecraft of terror."[2]

Let's remind ourselves: These tapes are not about classic strategies of war and warmaking and the training of soldiers. Their theme, instead, is terror. We have defined terror as violence that targets noncombatants, is random and unpredictable, and aims to sow overwhelming fear in a population. This goal contrasts to the targeting strategies of traditional warmaking, whose goal is disabling the opponent's ability to fight back. Soldiers fight combatants. Terrorists kill civilians intentionally hoping that the terrorized survivors will eventually surrender or demand peace at any price—the definition of conquest in the terrorist lexicon.

These reflections mesh with classic Augustinian thinking, whether in its just war or Christian realist incarnations. Augustinians are painfully aware of the temptation to smash, destroy, damage, and humiliate. Such temptations may be struggled against, capitulated to, or even extolled as a form of strength and the path to victory. Violence unleashed when what Augustine called the *libido dominandi,* or lust to dominate, is unchecked is violence that recognizes no limits. It is violence that kills politics. *Whereas classic warfare is the continuation of politics by other means, terrorism is the destruction of politics by all possible means.*

Because the terrorist goal is so brutal, human beings whose capacity for compassion is intact find it difficult to believe that there are other human beings with whom we cannot calmly reason or negotiate. And indeed, paranoid persons of a terrorist mentality who have surrounded themselves with a protective cordon sanitaire and want only to be left alone may not be a huge concern (unless, of course, a group of such persons is systematically destroying a minority within its own population or otherwise abusing people in significant and harmful ways). But when the clearly stated terrorist aim is to kill Americans wherever and whenever possible, we are confronting an implacable foe with whom it is impossible to have a diplomatic "sit-down."

A distinguished Johns Hopkins University psychiatrist, Paul R. McHugh, in exploring the mentality of the fanatic, rejects the psychological thinking that claims Americans were driven to extreme anxiety by the destruction of the twin towers because the towers were such obvious "phallic symbols." McHugh is having none of this silliness as he writes:

> Americans felt anxiety not because the towers of the World Trade Center were longer than they were wide, but because witnessing the cruel deaths of so many of our fellow citizens—horribly killed as they went about their daily lives, unsuspecting and unprotected—naturally provokes grief, anger, and fear. The brutal indiscriminate slaughter of thousands of people in an instant, along with the sight of their bodies dropping like debris from dizzying heights, should produce pity [and] grief . . . in anyone with an ounce of fellow feeling.[3]

It is important to take the measure of people who not only are capable of planning and executing such deeds but are gleeful about the lives lost and exult in the terrible devastation to so many families. McHugh reminds us that we are talking about a form of behavior, not just a way of thinking or fantasizing. What we ordinarily speak of as "fanaticism" the psychiatrist is likely to call an "overvalued idea." An overvalued idea drives those who hold it to take action of a certain sort—action that examines no alternative. The fanatic surrounds himself with others of like mind, brooking no dissent. He (or she) becomes cold, paranoid, and aggressive.

The imagination of the fanatic runs wild. One horror, like September 11, must be followed by others. What can we bring down next? Terrorist behavior, once undertaken, feeds on itself, as do other forms of violent criminality. This is a point made by the great psychoanalyst and cultural historian Erik Erikson years ago in a discussion of Hitler's youth. Hitler's awareness of certain dynamics of the human mind and of human behavior led him to implicate recruits to National Socialism early on in deeds of violence from which there was no turning back. Once these recruits had assaulted, bloodied, and perhaps killed their first Jew, the second became easier, and the third easier yet. As McHugh notes, the behavior of terrorists "is maintained by its consequences, especially the publicity that draws attention to the terrorist and his ideas." The only way to stop this escalation is interdiction: "The American government should devote its energies to interrupting the terrorists' behavior in all its aspects." Governments have a responsibility to maintain civic peace. Because there are as many reasons for terrorism as there are terrorists, says McHugh, the priority *must* be to "stop the behavior first." Then, "once peace is restored," McHugh concludes, "we can deal with underlying issues. We will very likely find that many of the justifications now offered for terrorism were only rationalizations intended to excuse it. But we need not waste our energies trying to change the opinions of terrorists about us and our aims. These people . . . have overvalued ideas that are inaccessible to argument and persuasion."[4]

In a speech before the United Nations on October 1, 2001, New York City Mayor Rudy Giuliani made essentially the same point. "This is not a time for further study or vague directives," he insisted, for the "evidence of terrorism's brutality and inhumanity, of its contempt for life and the concept of peace, is lying beneath the rubble of the World Trade Center less than two miles from where we meet today."[5]

Hannah Arendt, who was always suspicious of psychological categories, would have had little difficulty signing on with McHugh's and Giuliani's conclusions. According to Arendt, the fanatic is a person whose mind is on auto-pilot. Like the war criminal Adolf Eichmann, fanatics have lost the capacity for argument that entertains multiple possibilities. It is impossible to sit down at a table and hammer out some sort of "peace agreement" or "nonaggression pact" with terrorists. Because the goals of the fanatic cannot be achieved by compromise and negotiation, any such agreement would not be worth the paper it was written on.

The only defense against terrorism in the short run is interdiction and self-defense. The best defense against terrorism in the long run is building up secure civic infrastructures in many nations. That is why a number of policymakers have spoken about a contemporary version of the great Marshall Plan that rebuilt Europe after the catastrophe of World War II. The West's generous financial commitment is required, as is the continuing presence of foreign troops and peacekeepers in Afghanistan and, as the war against terrorism goes forward, in other sites as well. As an example of what is both expected and required, Afghan President Hamid Karzai has spoken repeatedly of the need for *more* troops to be sent to Afghanistan, "for as long as we need . . . to fight terrorism, to fight warlordism, to fight anarchy . . . until we have our own institutions—a national army, a national intelligence, national police and so on."[6] He has consistently pled with the United States and its allies to remain engaged even after Al Qaeda has been rendered incapable of using Afghanistan as a base to mount attacks.

Those who condemn a continuing U.S. presence in Afghanistan as yet another intrusion by the "cowboy" Americans are compelled by their logic to ignore the pleadings of those on the ground, including the president of the country. The implication of calls for American withdrawal is that it is preferable to pull up stakes and leave a people beleaguered and vulnerable to terrorist exploitation. This strategy of abandonment, often justified as a way to respect a culture's "difference," is actually a counsel of indifference. To abandon beleaguered peoples is to give them less regard than they deserve as human beings. At the conclusion of World War II, with all its attendant horrors, Hannah Arendt insisted that human dignity needed a new guarantee. Providing that guarantee puts an enormous burden on those with power.

THE PRICE OF "PEACE" WITHOUT JUSTICE

When we look back on moments of inaction, we are ashamed. The United Nations has apologized officially for its desultory response to the crisis in Rwanda when the Hutu government systematically exterminated the Tutsis. As Samantha Power points out in her book *A Problem from Hell*, the events leading up to genocide in Rwanda in 1994 were no mystery. It was preceded by publication of a Hutu document that Power compares to both Hitler's Nuremberg laws and the 1992 edicts of the Bosnian Serbs. This document commanded, for instance, that marrying a Tutsi woman or even employing her made a Hutu "a traitor." In unequivocal language the document stated: "The Hutu should stop having mercy on the Tutsi." Power insists that the U.S. government (in the first Clinton administration) "steadfastly leveled" criticisms "at 'both sides,' although the Hutu government and militia forces were usually responsible. . . . Even after the Hutu government began exterminating the country's Tutsi in April 1994, U.S. diplomats focused most of their efforts on 're-establishing a cease-fire.'"[7]

Why such a timid response from the United States? Several reasons present themselves. Rwanda was low on the list of U.S. priorities, since essential "national interests" were said not to be involved. A bias toward governments in power also blinded American officials to the full horrors unfolding in Rwanda, for difficulties multiply exponentially if states must deal with nonstate entities. So the U.S. government accepted a stunning level of violence as just "another flare-up," argues Power. U.S. officials were instructed *not* to use the word *genocide*—"The Clinton administration opposed use of the term"—so the "g-word" was shunned.[8]

To be sure, hindsight is twenty-twenty. But even as terror is not just any violence but violence of a particular kind, so genocide is not a flare-up of mob violence but the systematic extermination of a people for being what they are, not for anything they have done. If we use false language, our politics and reactions will be hollow. Minimally, we are obliged to acknowledge what is going on even if responsible officials decide that the United States cannot act, or cannot act effectively, in a particular situation. To look the other way and avoid using the correct term or terms to describe what is going on is a strategy of evasion and timidity unbefitting a great power.

The inadequacy of our reaction to the Bosnian war mess presents yet another example of the fruits of inaction, or of problematic action. Power argues:

> Between 1992 and 1995, along with their European allies, the Bush and Clinton administrations maintained an arms embargo against the Bosnia Muslims even after it was clear that the arms ban prevented the Muslims from defending themselves. Reluctant to "Americanize" the war or to "take sides," they froze in place a gross arms disparity that benefited the aggressor. . . . To the people of Bosnia and Rwanda, the United States and its allies on the UN Security Council held out

the promise of protection—a promise that they were not prepared to keep.[9]

U.S. officials preferred not to know about the systematic detention and execution of Muslim men and the rape of Muslim women. Washington "dithered," writes one commentator, as the killing continued.[10] Talk of a kind of equivalency between the sides—both were committing atrocities, the official rhetoric held—helped to justify U.S. inaction. Moreover, many officials added, people in the Balkans have always wanted to kill one another and this was just the latest round. Once again, avoidance of the word *genocide* became a policy priority, because use of that term to characterize what was going on would trigger obligations. Instead, safe havens were declared and the people who fled to them for safety were often shot to pieces as the UN stood by and the United States kept promising action and doing nothing. President Clinton's "strong words" coupled with inaction have been criticized subsequently for giving the Bosnian Muslims false hope, "which [they] paid for with blood."[11]

The United States did intervene in Kosovo, with great fanfare and condemnation of the crimes against humanity committed there. But the United States declared from the beginning of military action under the NATO rubric that it would not introduce ground troops into the conflict. Because President Clinton wanted a zero-casualty war, he was loath to pay a political price for U.S. casualties or to educate the American people on why intervention was required and American lives might be lost. The Kosovo intervention fell dramatically short as a result. As Paul W. Kahn argues in a hard-hitting piece, "War and Sacrifice in Kosovo": "Riskless warfare in pursuit of human rights is, therefore, actually a moral contradiction. If the decision to intervene is morally compelling, it cannot be conditioned on political considerations that assume an asymmetrical valuing of human life."[12]

Our various inactions and reactions throughout the 1990s offered a murky picture to friend and foe alike, especially where the possible use of U.S. force was concerned. Too often our government promised action and did nothing, or took action but in ways that raised a host of troubling questions. If the Serbs had discovered a way to inflict real costs on the United States during the Kosovo conflict, would we simply have pulled out?

The coming to power of the second Bush administration saw the beginning of a full-fledged rethinking of the conceptual framework for U.S. foreign policy. In that systematic reassessment, multiple perspectives were represented as the new administration asked: What role was the United States to play in the world with the Cold War over? Themes of great power and great responsibility were put in play. Talk of a new paradigm or conceptual framework to guide U.S. action reverberated not only in the corridors of power in Washington but on Main Street USA. We had begun to ask: Do we stop at punishing those responsible for brutal assaults against civilians? Or are we obliged to go further, in full awareness that states that are too weak to prevent the parasitical outcroppings of terrorists within their borders pose a threat to their own people as well as to their neighbors? Should we put our hope, or at least more hope, in international organizations? Or must we rely on ourselves above all, and on other nation-states, before turning to international bodies?

Then came September 11. What had been deemed desirable became exigent. The time had come to put warmaking, peacekeeping, and justice together.

WHY WE NEED THE STATE

Faced with an unprecedented crisis that threatened to divide the American republic permanently, Abraham Lincoln called upon his countrymen and women to "disenthrall themselves." The times demanded a way of thinking not tethered dogmatically to past crises or to problems that were different from the conflict splitting the country. The United States now faces the same challenge: We must disenthrall ourselves. Our foreign policy was shaped for a half-century by the Cold War and the implacability of the Soviet Union. When I was in undergraduate school in the 1960s, my professor, a World War II veteran (as were most of my instructors), in full confidence, told the class: Bipolarity (the United States versus the Soviet Union) was the shape of both the present and the future; Germany would *never* be reunited; and the satellite states of Central Eastern Europe, which were under pressure to succumb to "Sovietism" and languished from the absence of civic freedom, would remain in this lamentable condition for the foreseeable future.

To say that the events of 1989 took foreign policy analysts and social scientists by surprise is an understatement. Analysts had failed utterly to foresee the collapse of the Soviet Union, and they were ill equipped to deal with two central phenomena that showed surprising, renewed strength: nationalism and religion.

Timothy Garton Ash summarizes why Western analysts had such difficulty coming to grips with Solidarity in Poland. Its mix of religious and national aspirations and its ability to forge "a quite original mixture of ideas drawn from diverse traditions"—including liberal democracy, local self-government, cultural conservatism, free-market entrepreneurialism, aspects of social democracy and belief in a national identity without resorting to aggressive nationalism—eluded Western analysts entirely.[13] They were especially caught off guard by the religious part, religion being epiphenomenal in left-wing ideologies and treated as such pretty much across the board in social science.

Now scholars are scrambling to catch up where Islamist fundamentalism is concerned. This fundamentalism is not ancient. It is a twentieth-century phenomenon, and one that rejects a more capacious understanding of Islam in favor of a violent, aggressive ideology. What is required for an understanding of contemporary Islamist fundamentalism is recognition of the fact that Islam is *always* a politics. The question is: What politics?

As I indicated earlier, Muhammad was his own Constantine. He established a political order, fusing religious and political power and authority. By contrast, Jesus of Nazareth insisted on a distinction between what is owed to God and what is owed to Caesar. These fundamental differences between two great religions must be recognized. If the Christian distinction has, at times, invited quietism, and a withdrawal from the world, the Islamic tradition has incited engagements with the world that have earned it a reputation as "the religion of the sword." Not that Christianity has no knowledge of the sword. But within Christianity the sword always has to justify itself. The arguments within Islam begin in another place, asking perhaps what is honorable in fighting rather than whether fighting in itself is forbidden (it is not).

A salutary first step that contemporary analysts could take toward disenthrallment would be to relinquish their long-favored secularization hypothesis, which assumes that the world is moving away from religion and nationalism. Western Europe is anomalous in this regard and should not be considered the wave of the future. We do not know which wave will carry into the future, but Brussels-style Eurocracies surrounding the globe seems unlikely. The fading away of both religion and national patriotism is not the pattern we witness in the overwhelming majority of the world's countries, nor among the world's diverse and pluralistic peoples. The Christian ethicist Bryan Hehir argues that scholars must recognize the contribution that religion can, and will, make to a new global order: "The Christian Church has the capacity to make a special contribution to the globalization debate. But for a long time people have thought it unnecessary to understand religion in order to understand world affairs."[14]

A second hypothesis, although not embraced as firmly as the secularization hypothesis, also held sway before 1989 and enthralls many still. That is that international organizations will slowly but surely take over many of the functions of nation-states. Even before the "globalization" craze of recent years—whether this globalization is extolled or excoriated—the certainty of a new and growing internationalism has held sway. Nationalism and patriotism, according to this hypothesis, will give way to internationalism and universalism. These trends are often presented as if they undeniably herald a better day. The blurring and melting away of national boundaries, we are told, will make way for a more enlightened and less aggressive international order, or so the confident promise holds.

But for the time being nation-states are surely here to stay. One reason is the spread of democratic ideals. If, as Hannah Arendt insisted, no one can be a citizen of something as vague as "the world" in the same way as he and she can be a citizen of a specific polity, then it makes enormous good sense to build up polities in which people can be citizens.

12   AMERICAN POWER AND RESPONSIBILITY

THIS CHAPTER TRIES TO ANSWER two questions: Why are states so durable and so central to democracy? And can democratic societies successfully defend themselves against wanton aggression in ways that are ethically justifiable?

With citizenship comes accountability for individuals. With statehood comes a measure of accountability for polities. There are many ways in which the international order can call states to account and restrain and discipline those states that are out of bounds. There is a dynamic *raison de system* as there is the more famous *raison d'état,* and states are the basis for what the international relations theorist Hedley Bull called international society. The internal infrastructures of particular civil societies are connected to their counterparts in other societies in many ways. Civil society of this international sort is not possible without the domestic civic peace provided by states. If states do not afford ordinary civic peace, there is no civil society, hence nothing to connect to externally. It is that simple. States in which there is a democratic deficit, so to speak, are states denuded of a flourishing civil society.

If the international system is going anywhere, it seems to be in the direction of more democratic and human rights–based polities and cultures. This is not a sure thing—nothing ever is—but it is a steady and discernible movement.

One of the major stories since the end of World War II has been the universalization of human rights. These rights are robust *only* if they become part of the statutory armamentarium of states. The international law scholar Anne-Marie Slaughter makes a similar point when she argues that the state is not disappearing but "disaggregating into its separate, functionally distinct parts."[1] To put it less academically, a variety of means are available that link together the domestic and the transgovernmental or international. But each network presupposes a domestic infrastructure of settled laws, functions, and government. We cannot look forward to Somalia's participation, say, when it lacks a state and is victimized by marauding, drug-addled, armed bands in the service of tinpot mini-dictators. First comes the state. Then comes transgovernmental and international connections.

One problem with the vast proliferation of NGOs (nongovernmental organizations) that intervene in the internal affairs of states around the globe is the thorny matter of accountability. To whom do these organizations answer? To whom are such entities beholden? I exempt here religious institutions and organizations that have been border-crossers for centuries. Instead, I refer to professional bodies that often have deep pockets and the ability to move in and through the international system. Are they "above" states? Or "below" them? What role do they play in creating a more just international system? Many of these organizations lament the use of state force. They make little distinction between the defensive use of force and offensive arms. They show little indication that they are prepared to explore the complexities of preemption in certain troubling situations—like preventing a horrible catastrophe before it happens.

THE AMBIGUOUS ROLE OF NGOS

What role do NGOs play in calling to account violent marauders who use states for their own ends but are not states themselves? The record is decidedly mixed. In the 1990s the rapid movement of globalizing economic forces unleashed a veritable tidal wave of NGOs into the internal affairs of nearly every society. International monetary agencies like the International Monetary Fund and the World Bank have long been facilitators of this economic movement. Giddy utopianism infused discussions of globalization in the 1990s: We were promised that world peace was just around the corner, given the transnational identities being forged through deep identity with recognizable consumer brands—or so I was informed in a debate.

There is no doubt a grain of truth in claims that unleashing pent-up entrepreneurial spirits can have beneficial effects. But enthusiasts of this version of a new world order are prepared to rationalize any and all dislocations and distresses to societies if these societies appear to be moving toward free-market capitalism. There are a few key regulators and players among these enthusiasts—from America's Federal Reserve to the global entities noted earlier. They urge states to regulate minimally. But too often they see the emergence of free markets as both a necessary and a sufficient means toward democracy. This is a non-Marxist version of economic determinism. Politics either disappears from many of these discussion or is treated as epiphenomenal, since economic forces drive all else.

Like all utopian projects, this one too, in its most grandiose forms, is destined to falter. Utopian versions of any vision falter. At least some of the current market floundering revolves around the issue of accountability: To whom and before whom are international financial entities and corporations responsible? Will the movement of capital and deregulated "free labor" really help to bring about both a just and a peaceful world? To the skeptic, like myself, this smacks of economic romance.

What about international juridical bodies—courts that can actually try state agents and officials, perhaps even haul states (in a manner of speaking) into the docket and charge them with various crimes? What role do these bodies play in the new world order? In the wake of September 11, some insisted that the United States turn everything over to international bodies—criminal courts, war crimes tribunals, and the like—and let them deal with issues of justice. Rather than seeing the attacks of 9/11 as an act of war, these advocates declared them to be crimes of mass murder that should be treated juridically rather than responded to politically (the use of force being an extension of politics).

Various UN agencies capable of international intervention in the name of humane values are often mentioned in this light as well. This course of action sounds enlightened and eminently reasonable to many. But there are problems with it.

A major problem with the International Criminal Court (ICC) is accountability. How can it advance the role of law when it is not accountable to anyone? Why should states vest in a court the power of judicial review unchecked by other bodies? Furthermore, the chief prosecutor of the ICC, elected by ratifying nations for a nine-year term, also has prosecutorial power of a self-initiating kind. It is the states of the European Union and their former colonies that seem most enthusiastic about the prospect of such a court; the rest of the world, for a variety of reasons, has greeted it with various degrees of skepticism.

Skepticism if not opposition is warranted. For one thing, international law lacks a dense body of precedent and sedimented law of uncontroversial status. The closest thing to such precedent is the centuries-old laws of war. So what is to be applied when? Is the court to make up law as it goes along? Even the definition of a "war crime" is often not so clear. As mentioned earlier, following September 11, many were inclined to treat those attacks not as war crimes but as mass murder—like the work of a particularly heinous serial killer. But Americans on that dreadful day had the experience of being attacked simply because they were Americans and for no other reason. As Power writes: "To earn a death sentence, it was enough in the twentieth century to be an Armenian, a Jew, or a Tutsi. On September 11, it was enough to be an American."[2] That's enough to make a war crime in most people's book. But are courts of law with a vague imprimatur and legitimacy the way to go here?

George Will correctly notes that:

> The ICC is a facet of the European elites' agenda of disparaging and diluting the sovereignty of nations. It is especially ill suited to this moment, when the primacy of the nation-state needs to be reaffirmed. Terrorism is the leakage of violence out from the control of nations. And it cannot be controlled without enforcing the principle that a nation is accountable for terrorism that emanates from its territory.[3]

If a specific concern is the lack of a settled legal system or governance to which the ICC refers in making its determinations, a specific virtue of the transgovernmental model advanced by Anne-Marie Slaughter is that it embodies real accountability, or the likelihood of such. National citizens can "hold their governments as accountable for their transnational activities as for their domestic duties."[4] Independent of the enforcing powers of individual states, however, does anyone seriously believe that the ICC will hold terrorists accountable for their deeds? And if it somehow manages to do so, would states thus become exempt from accountability for their collaboration in sustaining and supporting terrorism—as did the Taliban with Al Qaeda? No court can haul an entire state into the docket, even though it may be ultimately responsible for the "crimes" committed. In sum, relying on international courts to make a just response to attacks like those of September 11 lets those who are responsible off the hook almost by definition.

The ICC is a concrete example of liberal internationalism of the sort that yields dozens of pacts and agreements and treaties and other quasi-judicial exercises embodied at the moment in the trial of Slobodan Milosevic before the International War Crimes Tribunal in The Hague. The journalist Simon Jenkins, writing in *The Times* of London, notes that "The Hague trial is hailed as a triumph for the new world order." In his own mind, however, serious doubts have begun to emerge. Here, no doubt, is a rogue and an international criminal. But will his trial, Jenkins asks, bring the Balkans closer to achieving "democracy, stability, and predictability"? Jenkins doubts it. Why? Because international justice, "like its domestic counterpart, must be rooted in general legitimacy and consent. This is not because otherwise it is no justice, but because otherwise it will not work. It will carry no conviction and serve as no deterrent."[5] Jenkins has unkind things to say about almost everybody, including the United States, but he makes a credible point about the very idea of an international criminal court. Those who need to be held accountable and to build up a domestic culture of the rule of law based, in part, on human rights—the states in the Balkans, including Serbia—are let off the hook. It makes the new, quasi-constitutional government of Serbia look weak and untrustworthy. And his trial before an international criminal court has had the effect of once again making Milosevic a popular figure where once he was thoroughly discredited.

Moving in the direction of international criminal justice, international justice of a noncriminal nature, and the like and diminishing the power, responsibility, and legitimacy of states not only will prove ineffective, even disastrous in some cases, in the short run but will undermine the minimal or even major (depending on the states involved and the situation) pressure that the system of states can put on rogue actors among their own ranks over the long run.

DEFENDING HUMAN DIGNITY

Sometimes the most effective new frameworks are old ones resituated in a new reality. That is why some have called for a return of imperialism— not the bad old imperialism that colonized and took all power for governance out of the hands of indigenous peoples, carved up continents with no sense of tribal and naturally occurring borders and boundaries, and left a legacy of bitterness. Rather, the sort of imperialism that commentators like Sebastian Mallaby and Michael Ignatieff are groping toward is an image of the world's great superpower taking on an enormous burden and doing so with a relatively, though not entirely, selfless intent. The imperialism they suggest is not one of colonial states dominated by provincial governors, but rather a form of nation-building that is primarily concerned with a new version of deterrence. What is being deterred or forestalled are failed states, within which hapless citizens are victimized by the ruthless and terrorists are given carte blanche to operate. When states fail, we approach something like the nightmare of Thomas Hobbes's war of all against all.

The nation-state model is retained intact in this new vision, in recognition that the development of the nation-states has historically been a great achievement. The political theorist Joshua Mitchell writes:

> For all of its problems, the nation-state remains our best guarantee against the alternatives of individual anarchy, tribalism, or a global universalism without content—all of which are being entertained today, in one form or another. . . . A nation-state is a responsible world actor, whose rights of sovereignty are coterminous with their obligation to play

by the rules that emerge in times of relative peace. To consent, even tacitly, to harboring rogues whose intention it is to destroy other nation-states is to renounce, entirely, the right to sovereign integrity; it is to declare war.[6]

The alternatives, Mitchell rightly insists, are far worse. Eschewing chaos in order that problems and perplexities will take the form of interstate conflict rather than intrastate (or other entity) violence is a great step forward and one much to be desired—again, by contrast to the alternative. The international relations experts Mustapha Damal Pasha and David Blaney concur: "In the absence of an effective and democratic state, citizens of the Third World have little capacity to control their own destiny. . . . The central problem is not the state or formal political authority per se, but particular forms the state and global governance may assume."[7] The role of interdictor is to make possible the kind of stability that alone permits the building of a civil society infrastructure.

The threat presented by international terrorists who are by definition no respecters of borders is that they have an apparently "bottomless supply of recruits and allies," as Ignatieff points out. It requires power of global reach to counter this particular threat. International organizations and entities are not prepared to meet this challenge, even were they willing. They are ill equipped and lack political will. In the past they have been almost painfully ineffective. As I have already pointed out, international law lacks, for the most part, legitimate enforcing agencies. Not only is there no "standing international force to undertake urgent military action when governments are reluctant to involve their own soldiers," but the UN response "in the future is uncertain."[8]

If human dignity needs a "new guarantee," who will be the guarantor? There is no state except the United States with the power and (we hope) the will to play this role. Looking back on the recent past, we rightly fault ourselves for too little intervention in situations of genocide. Moral responsibility and enlightened self-interest combine here. The most exigent matter before the international community is bringing about the minimal civic peace in all polities necessary to attain and secure fundamental human goods, beginning with basic justice. These fundamental goods are articulated in the Universal Declaration of Human Rights and have been the basis for the international order for nearly sixty years. But without political stability, every attempt to prop up impoverished states in order that more basic human goods might be achieved is doomed to fail. Justice demands accountability, and there is no political accountability where there is no legitimate structure of power, authority, and law. A paradigmatic example of the ills attendant upon political instability is the disaster of failed states in which human beings are prey to the ruthless and the irresponsible. I would argue that true international justice is defined as the equal claim of all persons, whatever their political location or condition, to having coercive force deployed in their behalf if they are victims of one of the many horrors attendant upon radical political instability.

The principle I call "equal regard" underlies the Universal Declaration of Human Rights, just as it lies at the heart of our Declaration of Independence and Lincoln's matchless Gettysburg Address. But equal regard, as the American founders knew, as Lincoln understood, and as we are coming to understand, must sometimes be backed up by coercive force. This is an ideal of international justice whose time has come. Equal regard is a mixture of old norms given new urgency and new possibilities.

Some will understandably query: If the claim to justice as equal regard applies to all persons without distinction, shouldn't an international body be its guarantor and enforcer? Perhaps. But in our less-than-ideal world, the one candidate to guarantee this principle is the United States, for two reasons: Equal regard is the foundation of our own polity, and we are the only superpower. As we have learned to our dismay, all too often international "peacekeepers"—they are never called soldiers—are obliged by their rules of engagement to stand by as people are cornered and slaughtered. International bodies have defaulted on the use of coercive force on behalf of justice as an equal regard for all, hence a basic defense of human dignity. Failing to make a serious effort to stop genocide and "ethnic cleansing" is the most obvious case of dereliction in this respect. In such cases, force is justified in order to defend those who cannot defend themselves, to fight those engaged in unjust acts of harming, and to punish those who have engaged in unjust harm. Force that observes limits and is premised on a concern with human dignity is frequently called upon to fight force that operates without limits and makes a mockery of human dignity.

The heavy burden being imposed on the United States does not require that the United States remain on hair-trigger alert at every moment. But it does oblige the United States to evaluate all claims and to make a determination as to whether it can intervene effectively and in a way that does more good than harm—with the primary objective of interdiction so that democratic civil society can be built or rebuilt. This approach is better by far than those strategies of evasion and denial of the sort visible in Rwanda, in Bosnia, or in the sort of "advice" given to Americans by some of our European critics.

At this point in time the possibility of international peace and stability premised on equal regard for all rests largely, though not exclusively, on American power. Many persons and powers do not like this fact, but it is inescapable. As Michael Ignatieff puts it, the "most carefree and confident empire in history now grimly confronts the question of whether it can escape Rome's ultimate fate."[9] Furthermore, America's fate is tied inextricably to the fates of states and societies around the world. If large pockets of the globe start to go bad—here, there, everywhere (the infamous "failed state" syndrome)—the drain on American power and treasure will reach a point where it can no longer be borne. As Samantha Power concludes:

> People victimized by genocide or abandoned by the international community do not make good neighbors, as their thirst for vengeance, their irredentism, and their acceptance of violence as a means of generating change can turn them into future threats. In Bosnia, where the United States and Europe maintained an arms embargo against the Muslims, extremist Islamic fighters and proselytizers eventually turned up to offer support. . . . The failed state of Bosnia became a haven for Islamic terrorists shunned elsewhere in the world.[10]

It is difficult to underestimate the shock to the world's nervous system on September 11 and how much was at stake that day and in our response. We were reminded in the most cruel way that American stability and international stability are linked. As the world's superpower, America bears the responsibility to help guarantee that international stability, whether much of the world wants it or not. This does not mean that we can or should rush around imposing "solutions" everywhere. It does mean that we are obliged to evaluate all cries for justice and relief from people who are being preyed upon, whether by nonstate marauders (like terrorists) or by state-sponsored enforcers. We, the powerful, must respond to attacks against persons who cannot defend themselves because they, like us, are human beings, hence equal in regard to us, and because they, like us, are members of states, or would-be states, whose primary obligation is to protect the lives of those citizens who inhabit their polities. Thus, all nations have a stake in building up an international civic culture in which fewer horrors such as Rwanda or Kosovo or September 11 take place.

The moral imperatives at work here are not pious nostrums that we can ignore when we choose in favor of narrow evocations of national interest. Instead, these ethical considerations are themselves central to our national interest, correctly understood. It is in our long-term national interest to foster and sustain an international society of equal regard. Strategic necessity and moral requirements here meet. The giddiness of 1990s economic "growth" (much of it, we now know, not really growth at all) obscured the undeniable signs of disintegration in those relatively new states that had achieved independence only after struggling against colonialism in the aftermath of World War II. Many of these states collapsed from within, becoming easy prey for lawless warlords or, in recent years, radicalized Islamist parties. Ignatieff comments: "In states like Pakistan, where the state no longer provides basic services to the poorest people, Islamic parties, funded from Saudi Arabia, step into the breach, providing clinics, schools, and orphanages where the poor receive protection at the price of indoctrination in hatred."[11]

As these and other warning signs proliferated, the United States "paid too little heed." American officials thought that we could have empire "on the cheap, ruling the world without putting in place any new imperial structure—new military alliances, new legal institutions, new international development organizations."[12] Instead, a version of "liberal internationalism" held sway. This form of hubris—seeking power but without the expense and the responsibility—was reinforced by a reliance on courts and lawyers and the proliferation of various agreements, mostly in the area of trade, that had no tangible effect on political disintegration throughout much of the developing world. The vicious cycle of "poverty, instability, and violence" behaves rather like a perpetual motion machine—it will not stop unless some countermovement stops it.[13] Those movements must be the creation of accountable, responsible, stable states. Simply amping up the amount of financial aid to states in need does not change the picture. Economic assistance is gobbled up by corruption and only serves to fuel the instability and violence that is also part of the cycle.

At a scholarly meeting in 2002, I listened to an economist talk about the "opportunity costs" faced by small producers in a particular African country characterized by a failed state. He noted the fact that the producer himself and his workers had to literally sit on their sacks filled with their particular agricultural product until such time as the product could be shipped. The economist described this lack of security as a major *economic* problem, an example of economic inefficiency. He seemed not to realize that the problem was not an *economic* one but a *political* one. The producers had no infrastructure of law, order, and enforcement upon which to rely, so they could not entrust shipping their produce to others. They lived in a world of radical self-help. The government had absconded and degenerated into small groups of ruthless exploiters whose one specialty was graft. This problem is endemic in postcolonial sub-Saharan Africa, and not there alone.

The World Bank, for one, seems to recognize that it can do next to nothing about poverty in sub-Saharan Africa so long as "dysfunctional governments" are in charge (or fail to be in charge). As Sebastian Mallaby notes: "In the late 1980s, development theorists began to acknowledge that the main alternative to imperialism—economic aid—could not stabilize the weakest states. A political supplement was needed, starting with transparency and other principles of decent governance."[14] The favorite anodyne of the 1990s—the liberal internationalist "solution"—has proven to be no solution at all. Liberal internationalist entities cannot respond effectively to the crises produced by failed states or "imperial neglect," in Ignatieff's words. It is too easy for liberal internationalism to descend into sentimentalism, a rhetoric of high purpose not backed up by any real muscle. The evidence by now is pretty clear that various treaties and conventions often provide a cover behind which determined states go forward with whatever they want to do. A case in point would be the Soviet Union's development, as we now know, of biological weapons after signing the 1972 Biological Weapons Convention. The shocking truth about just how full bore the Soviet effort was came to light only after the collapse of the Soviet Union in 1989.

Even if such noncompliance with various conventions could be dealt with, the underlying structural problem remains: Liberal and neoliberal internationalist entities have great difficulty reckoning with the determined and the ruthless. Moreover, the leading human rights organizations—nonstate entities in this case—seem to have a difficult time naming things correctly. Amnesty International, for example, resolutely refuses to condemn "terrorism" because it refuses to use the word *terrorism*. Amnesty will speak of "vicious acts," but not terrorism. As Adrian Karatnycky and Arch Puddington point out, even the UN-sponsored International Convention for the Suppression of Terrorist Bombing avoids euphemism and defines terrorism forthrightly "as a distinct and widely-agreed-upon category of aggression."[15] Amnesty has no problem, by contrast, in characterizing the legal death penalty in the United States—which is imposed, when it is imposed, only after years of appeals have been exhausted—as an egregious violation of human rights on a par with summary lynching. In the human rights culture in which many liberal internationalist entities are bathed, imprisonment of persons for "political advocacy" is treated as an equal offense across the board whether the prisoner is an advocate of terrorist violence or an advocate of constitutional democracy. All become "prisoners of conscience." According to this logic, many historic monsters could have claimed the status of prisoners of conscience in their time. Adolf Hitler and others of his ilk were imprisoned for political advocacy and not for anything they had personally done up to that point. In fact, of course, the world would have been much better off had the Weimar Republic kept Hitler locked up. Surely we are obliged to evaluate what a person is advocating and not simply the fact of their advocacy per se. But fundamental concerns for political stability and even the long-term fate of democracy fall by the wayside when the "purity" of a moral vision is ranked above all prudential considerations.

Democratic polities laced through and through with legal protections for the accused and for defendants cannot and must not abandon those protections as fundamental principles. At the same time these polities face extraordinary demands. States fighting terrorism may err on the side of protecting the populace and ensuring basic security. But there is a danger of tilting too far in the other direction as well. We now face a variant on a perennial dilemma: Just how much room to roam do we give to those who, were they to gain power, would eliminate immediately the very freedoms from which they have benefited? That is our internal challenge.

Externally, we face the immediate issue of Afghanistan. Will the U.S. presence in Afghanistan suffice to prevent it from sliding back into tribal warfare or a resurgence of Islamist extremism? We do not know. What we do know is that half-measures will not suffice, not in Afghanistan and not in the war against terrorism more generally. Unless America proposes to close itself up behind its borders (something impossible in any case given the porousness of those borders) and revert to isolationism, we can and we must become the leading guarantor of a structure of stability and order in a violent world. We cannot do this alone, but it will not happen at all without U.S. commitment. It is that simple.

EPILOGUE

Four Brave Women

THE DEMOCRACY AWARD, symbolized by the Goddess of Democracy erected by student protesters in Tiananmen Square in 1989, is presented annually by the National Endowment for Democracy to individuals who embody the fight for political freedom around the globe. Past winners include Václav Havel and Elena Bonner, Wei Jingsheng and the Transition Monitoring Group from Nigeria. On July 9, 2002, four remarkable women from Muslim-majority countries rose to accept this award at a reception in their honor in Washington, D.C.

One of the honorees, Nadjet Bouda, is a twenty-three-year-old veteran human rights activist from Algeria whose efforts at present are devoted to determining the fates of the thousands of Algerians who have "disappeared" during Algeria's continuing civil war. Radical Islamist guerrillas have invaded villages and slaughtered tens of thousands of men, women, and children. The Algerian government has been ferocious in its response. In her comments, Bouda argued that the fight for peace and democracy in Algeria is a fight against terror and on behalf of civil society. She and other activists, she told the audience, fight "on a daily basis to establish a culture of democracy in Algeria" and to speak out in "favor of human dignity." Military force alone, she insisted, cannot cure a society of terrorism.[1]

Violence cannot be stopped effectively over the long run unless a country creates a free civil society, establishes the rule of law and an independent judiciary, makes electoral processes and political institutions legitimate, and puts an end to corruption and "poor economic management." Bouda called upon the American people "to include in your prayers the thirty million Algerians who dream one day of fully assuming their rights as citizens in a land of peace." Her plea, consistent with that of her three colleagues in the fight for democracy, was for more, not less, American engagement in order to prevent chaos and help Algeria move beyond the stalemate in its war against terrorism. Only with American involvement in its affairs, Bouda maintained, could Algeria anticipate achieving a level of civil peace sufficient to inspire Algerians themselves to build the infrastructure of a democratic, constitutional order.

The second honoree was Muborak Tashpoulatova from Uzbekistan. A short, sprightly woman with a determined manner, Tashpoulatova spoke in punchy, clear language that grabbed her audience's attention. "When I told my eleven-year-old son that I am going to receive the Democracy Award, he said, 'Oh, is it an Oscar of Democracy?'" After the appreciative laughter died down, she went on:

> I feel that it is a great honor for me but also for all my colleagues in Uzbekistan and other countries who for the last eight years helped us to build a civil society, to create out of individuals, citizens. . . . It is very important in those countries which became independent after seventy years of Communist rule that we find our own way to become citizens. It is very difficult. We have been raised as subject peoples and not as citizens, but we want our children to be different.

Tashpoulatova then asked: "What does it mean to be a citizen? First of all, to feel free, not to be afraid. To be able to think critically. To know your rights, to be able to defend them. To want to control your own life and to change it if needed." Her country too faces a threat from Islamist fundamentalism. She continued:

Throughout the centuries Islam coexisted in Uzbekistan with other religions and traditions. You can still go today to a Christian church in Samarkand, see statues of Buddha near the border of Afghanistan, or visit famous Jewish communities in Buchara. When the fanatical fundamentalists kill people . . . they do not sound like God-loving Muslims, but like Bolsheviks, who have already once destroyed our lives, our culture, our tradition, and our families. Please remember that in democratic countries the fanatics, the fundamentalists, the terrorists, are not such a threat as in dictatorships, and that is why we want to build a democracy in Uzbekistan. Only educated citizens can oppose fanatics.

She concluded by telling the president, the Congress, and the American people "that the people of Uzbekistan love freedom, democracy and independence as much as the American people do."

The third honoree to rise and receive her award offered a maternalist framework for her politics. Mariam Hussein Mohamed of Somalia told the crowd that those living on the horn of Africa have experienced

the worst atrocities in the form of abuses, mass killings, destruction of property, and looting. Most of these atrocities were directed against women and children; in the same time, women were mostly the bread earner during the civil strife. To address the above problem, we have devised the participatory Human Rights–Empowerment Approach. This approach places fundamental importance on organizing of victim groups. Individually victims are powerless, but collectively their voices are to be reckoned with.

After thanking the National Endowment for Democracy for its support of this effort, Mohamed concluded: "We would like to make an appeal to all concerned parties. The atrocities happening now in our region is not God-sent, it is manmade, and everybody knows his or her names. They are caused by the greedy and kindless warlords, who use child soldiers to terrorize women and powerless citizens. They are those who prevent the rule of law and the emergence of good governance." What is needed first and foremost, Mohamed recognized, is an enforceable and maintainable rule of law, in order to stop random violence and allow good government to emerge.

The fourth award was given to Mehrangiz Kar of Iran, who accepted it in the name of the "Iranian students who three years ago . . . rose up to peacefully protest censorship and support freedom of speech and were ruthlessly suppressed"; "in the name of the women of Iran who endanger themselves each day as they strive for the simplest and most elementary expressions of independence"; "in the name of my husband, who remains in prison, his whereabouts unknown, his fate in the hands of vigilantes who seem to answer to no one"; and in the name of "my daughters, who have grown from ordinary adolescents into fighters for justice."

Each of these remarkable women spoke a basic language of civic security and peace and basic freedoms. Each asked the United States and the wider world community for more support and engagement, not less. Each indicated that American presence and power might well be needed in her country to prevent the worst from happening from time to time. At the same time each recognized that, once civic peace has been established, a civil society must be created by engaged citizens who have wearied of being mere subjects. These women do not want to be subjected by anyone, not even by those who share their fundamental aspirations. Each would find inexplicable the strange kind of political autism that would leave everyone inside a cocoon of his and her own culture's "difference" when children are being ripped apart by explosions, people are disappearing from their homes, and women by the thousands are being violently raped and assaulted.

The violent groups faced by these women's countries represent a threat to the existence of the idea of a stable state—hence the possibility (there are no guarantees) of a relatively stable civic environment itself.[2] It may be a potentially rotten deal for the state to have a monopoly on the means of violence within a given territorial entity, as the great German sociologist Max Weber defined the state, but it is far worse to face multiple sites of contending violence.

What is the reality that Americans must face? In Michael Ignatieff's words:

> Imperialism doesn't stop being necessary just because it becomes politically incorrect. Nations sometimes fail, and when they do, only outside help—imperial power—can get them back on their feet. Nation-building is the kind of imperialism you get in a human rights era, a time when

great powers believe simultaneously in the right of small nations to gov-
ern themselves and in their own right to rule the world.[3]

I'm not sure that *imperialism* is the best word for the sort of intervention that Ignatieff calls for, but he is surely correct that "nation-building
lite" is not going to do the job. Real commitment of resources, time,
even lives, may well be the cost of increased global stability. Homes,
schools, and hospitals cannot be built unless someone is holding the
forces of anarchy at bay. That someone may well be the casual Americans "in floppy hats," as Ignatieff characterizes the informal special
forces civic teams that move in to build once a basic minimum of civic
peace is achieved. The problem is not that these teams of doctors, archi-
tects, builders, and teachers have appeared to help rebuild recently
chaotic societies, but that it seems to take a dire emergency before we
send them. We are loathe to pay the price of preventing the failure of a
state in the first place.

If we are going to talk the talk, we had better walk the walk. Often, the
United States offers too little too late. A good friend of mine, the distinguished political philosopher Martin Palous, who was then the deputy
foreign minister of the Czech Republic (and is now the ambassador
plenipotentiary to the United States), told me at the time that U.S. inaction in Bosnia signaled to the small peoples and countries of Central
Eastern Europe that they could not count on the United States when the
chips were down. They wanted to be able to count on us. Where else
were they to turn? To the United Nations, whose peacekeepers, hand-
cuffed by the rules of disengagement in Bosnia, watched as people were
shot to pieces before their very eyes?

Endangered people around the globe will be able to count on us
when American enlightened self-interest and the universal language of
human rights and civil society come together in significant and robust
warp. The stakes could not be higher. We cannot follow lines of narrow self-interest to the detriment of global stability. At the same time
we must not lose sight of our national interest in favor of a utopian
vision of a world in which states are diminished and international institutions work their will to the exclusion of the self-interests of particular polities. It is a difficult balancing act, to say the least. But our
situation of unparalleled supremacy and dire threat is unprecedented.

The time for creative thinking and action based on perduring principles is at hand.

My favorite headline coming out of Afghanistan was "Taliban Pinned Down, Music in Kabul." Music returned to Kabul because those who banned it, who beat and imprisoned those who played it or listened to it, were neutralized. Another striking headline was "Minutes from Cries of Jihad, Town Dreams of U.S." This story was about a village tucked into the mountainside in southwestern Pakistan where young boys "fly homemade kites" and dream of going to America. Says one: "I want to go to America and be a surgeon." They worry that the borders of America will be closed because of September 11 and its aftermath. But they persist in studying English, "the most popular subject in the town's schools," where "most children know a phrase or two." Abdul Hamid Changazi, twenty-four years old, speaks English well, we are told by the *New York Times* reporter; he works as a clerk in a hospital and "saves as much as possible from pay of $50 a month so he and his wife might go to America." Actually, he whispers to the journalist, his real hope is to go "home to Afghanistan," but at that point he doubted whether that would be possible.[4] Perhaps by now he has returned, as have so many thousands; the airlines and the new Afghan government could hardly accommodate and absorb them all. People return when civic peace, guaranteed by floppy-hatted Americans or someone else, is restored—if not perfectly, then sufficiently enough that life does not resemble a fearsome Hobbesian nightmare.

REMEMBERING SEPTEMBER 11, 2001

The obituary sketches accompanied by pictures in the *New York Times* haunt us yet. They told of newborns without fathers, husbands without wives, wives without husbands, policemen and firemen who rushed into the burning towers to try to save others. The short headlines accompanying each sketch gave a kind of farewell slogan to each life: "A Death, and a New Life" was about a father who would never know his new son. "Telling Sketches of Strangers" described a young woman who filled notebooks with sketches as she rode back and forth on the train to work. In "An American Dream," we learned about a young man from a small Mexican village who moved to New York City seeking the American life. "The Maximum Mom" was a hard-driving mother who exercised at 5:00 A.M. and fed "their three little guys," ages two, five, and seven, before going off to work; she coached soccer too. "New Baby Has Dad's Eyes" is self-explanatory. "A Passion for Paddleball," "She Dances in His Heart," "An Arbor of Memories"—on and on they went, day after day after day. "Portraits of Grief" the *Times* called them. This was a vital and important tribute, reminding us that the overwhelming number of deaths that day were particular human lives being snuffed out. These obituaries told us just how fragile we are and reminded us of what we need government for at the most rudimentary level.

It seems as if we have awakened from a self-indulgent dream. "As the clever hopes expire/Of a low dishonest decade," W. H. Auden wrote in a poem called "September 1, 1939." The poem was occasioned by the German blitzkrieg against Poland. But it spoke directly to many of us in 2001. In the 1990s we permitted the institutions and activities of civil society to lapse, even the governmental institutions that, had they been maintained at a certain level of robustness and efficiency, might have given us a bit of advance warning about September 11. Nothing seemed serious somehow. We lost our bearings for a time.

In his poem, Auden expresses the hope that "Accurate scholarship can/Unearth the whole offence/From Luther until now/That has driven a culture mad." That seems unlikely, then and now. The calumny against Luther aside, there is a terrible truth about evil that is very difficult to penetrate. You can add up all the economic, social, historical, political, and psychological factors, and it is still impossible to get a total that equals a Hitler or a Stalin or a bin Laden. In our quest for answers, we should not take comfort in banalities and nostrums.

The implacable hatred that animates the man who orchestrated the attacks on the World Trade Center and the Pentagon mystifies us. This depth of hatred does not derive from any specific action, or lack of action, on the part of those who are its target. As St. Augustine taught, evil is a turning of one's back on the good. It is a depletion. It cannot generate. It can only destroy. It spreads like a fungus over the living surface of things, said Hannah Arendt, herself a Jewish refugee from Nazi Germany, but it lacks true depth. We try to give evil depth with our explanations. But it just keeps spreading. That is why we must stop it: So that the good might be revealed before us.

None of the goods that human beings cherish can flourish without a measure of civic peace and security. Those who plot in darkness and secrecy, who operate stealthily and refuse to take responsibility for their wrongdoing, perpetrate harm beyond the immediate violent event. They would drive us behind closed doors and obstruct the simple but profound goods that we all cherish and that people in a free society can realize: parents raising their children, men and women going to work, citizens of a great city making their way on streets and subways, people traveling to visit family members, the faithful attending their churches, synagogues, and mosques without fear. This quotidian ideal is a great good, as we have learned so shockingly. September 11 reminded us that we have but one brief life to live. How are we to live it now that we know how fragile it is? As we struggle individually to answer this basic, existential question, governments must strive to sustain the civil space that permits us to do so.

Auden writes of "blind skyscrapers" that "use Their full height to proclaim/The strength of Collective Man." I have a contrary thought. Skyscrapers are about power, no doubt. But they are also about freedom, and ingenuity, and beauty. They are not about the strength of an indistinguishable collective, but about the combined power of many men and women. There is something exhilarating about reaching for the stars, so long as we do not become presumptuous about achieving godlikeness. Totalitarian regimes do not aim high. They build squat prisons and block houses. They build execution walls.

"We must love one another or die," Auden tells us, finally. We cannot love one another—not in the sense in which Auden meant it—if we are locked indoors and afraid to venture forth. We must "Show an affirming flame." It is called hope. It is one of the great theological virtues. But it is also a democratic virtue linked to coming to grips with the reality of what we face and responding appropriately—whether through forceful interdiction or peaceful assembly. We must stop those who would harm us and go about our business, meeting and greeting one another, for "we must love one another or die." September 11 showed us that we are bound by civic affection. All else about that terrible day must pale with the passage of time. But that remains.

APPENDIX: WHAT WE'RE FIGHTING FOR

A LETTER FROM AMERICA

      AT TIMES it becomes necessary for a nation to defend itself through force of arms. Because war is a grave matter, involving the sacrifice and taking of precious human life, conscience demands that those who would wage the war state clearly the moral reasoning behind their actions, in order to make plain to one another, and to the world community, the principles they are defending.

We affirm five fundamental truths that pertain to all people without distinction:

1. *All human beings are born free and equal in dignity and rights.*
2. *The basic subject of society is the human person, and the legitimate role of government is to protect and help to foster the conditions for human flourishing.*
3. *Human beings naturally desire to seek the truth about life's purpose and ultimate ends.*
4. *Freedom of conscience and religious freedom are inviolable rights of the human person.*

5. *Killing in the name of God is contrary to faith in God and is the greatest betrayal of the universality of religious faith.*

We fight to defend ourselves and to defend these universal principles.

WHAT ARE AMERICAN VALUES?

Since September 11, millions of Americans have asked themselves and one another, why? Why are we the targets of these hateful attacks? Why do those who would kill us, want to kill us?

We recognize that at times our nation has acted with arrogance and ignorance toward other societies. At times our nation has pursued misguided and unjust policies. Too often we as a nation have failed to live up to our ideals. We cannot urge other societies to abide by moral principles without simultaneously admitting our own society's failure at times to abide by those same principles. We are united in our conviction—and are confident that all people of good will in the world will agree—that no appeal to the merits or demerits of specific foreign policies can ever justify, or even purport to make sense of, the mass slaughter of innocent persons.

Moreover, in a democracy such as ours, in which government derives its power from the consent of the governed, policy stems at least partly from culture, from the values and priorities of the society as a whole. Though we do not claim to possess full knowledge of the motivations of our attackers and their sympathizers, what we do know suggests that their grievances extend far beyond any one policy, or set of policies. After all, the killers of September 11 issued no particular demands; in this sense, at least, the killing was done for its own sake. The leader of Al Qaeda described the "blessed strikes" of September 11 as blows against America, "the head of world infidelity." Clearly, then, our attackers despise not just our government, but our overall society, our entire way of living. Fundamentally, their grievance concerns not only what our leaders do, but also *who we are.*

So who are we? What do we value? For many people, including many Americans and a number of signatories to this letter, some values sometimes seen in America are unattractive and harmful. Consumerism as a way of life. The notion of freedom as no rules. The notion of the individual as self-made and utterly sovereign, owing little to others or to society. The weakening of marriage and family life. Plus an enormous entertainment and communications apparatus that relentlessly glorifies such ideas and beams them, whether they are welcome or not, into nearly every corner of the globe.

One major task facing us as Americans, important prior to September 11, is facing honestly these unattractive aspects of our society and doing all we can to change them for the better. We pledge ourselves to this effort.

At the same time, other American values—what we view as our founding ideals, and those that most define our way of life—are quite different from these, and they are much more attractive, not only to Americans, but to people everywhere in the world. Let us briefly mention four of them.

The first is the conviction that all persons possess innate human dignity as a birthright, and that consequently each person must always be treated as an end rather than used as a means. The founders of the United States, drawing upon the natural law tradition as well as upon the fundamental religious claim that all persons are created in the image of God, affirmed as "self-evident" the idea that all persons possess equal dignity. The clearest political expression of a belief in transcendent human dignity is democracy. In the United States in recent generations, among the clearest cultural expressions of this idea has been the affirmation of the equal dignity of men and women, and of all persons regardless of race or color.

Second, and following closely from the first, is the conviction that universal moral truths (what our nation's founders called "laws of Nature and of Nature's God") exist and are accessible to all people. Some of the most eloquent expressions of our reliance upon these truths are found in our *Declaration of Independence,* George Washington's *Farewell Address*, Abraham Lincoln's *Gettysburg Address* and *Second Inaugural Address*, and Dr. Martin Luther King, Jr.'s *Letter from the Birmingham Jail.*

The third is the conviction that, because our individual and collective access to truth is imperfect, most disagreements about values call for civility, openness to other views, and reasonable argument in pursuit of truth.

The fourth is freedom of conscience and freedom of religion. These intrinsically connected freedoms are widely recognized, in our own country and elsewhere, as a reflection of basic human dignity and as a precondition for other individual freedoms.

To us, what is most striking about these values is that they apply to all persons without distinction, and cannot be used to exclude anyone from recognition and respect based on the particularities of race, language, memory, or religion. That's why anyone, in principle, can become an American. And in fact, anyone does. People from everywhere in the world come to our country with what a statue in New York's harbor calls a yearning to breathe free, and soon enough, they are Americans. Historically, no other nation has forged its core identity—its constitution and other founding documents, as well as its basic self-understanding—so directly and explicitly on the basis of universal human values. To us, no other fact about this country is more important.

Some people assert that these values are not universal at all, but instead derive particularly from Western, largely Christian civilization. They argue that to conceive of these values as universal is to deny the distinctiveness of other cultures. We disagree. We recognize our own civilization's achievements, but we believe that all people are created equal. We believe in the universal possibility and desirability of human freedom. We believe that certain basic moral truths are recognizable everywhere in the world. We agree with the international group of distinguished philosophers who in the late 1940s helped to shape the United Nations Universal Declaration of Human Rights, and who concluded that a few fundamental moral ideas are so widespread that they "may be viewed as implicit in man's nature as a member of society." In hope, and on the evidence, we agree with Dr. Martin Luther King, Jr., that the arc of the moral universe is long, but it bends toward justice, not just for the few, or the lucky, but for all people.

Looking at our own society, we acknowledge again the all too frequent gaps between our ideals and our conduct. But as Americans in a time of war and global crisis, we are also suggesting that the *best* of what we too casually call "American values" do not belong only to America, but are in fact the shared inheritance of humankind, and therefore a possible basis of hope for a world community based on peace and justice.

WHAT ABOUT GOD?

Since September 11, millions of Americans have asked themselves and one another, what about God? Crises of this magnitude force us to think anew about first principles. When we contemplate the horror of what has occurred, and the danger of what is likely to come, many of us ask: Is religious faith part of the solution or part of the problem?

The signatories to this letter come from diverse religious and moral traditions, including secular traditions. We are united in our belief that invoking God's authority to kill or maim human beings is immoral and is contrary to faith in God. Many of us believe that we are under God's judgment. None of us believe that God ever instructs some of us to kill or conquer others of us. Indeed, such an attitude, whether it is called "holy war" or "crusade," not only violates basic principles of justice, but is in fact a negation of religious faith, since it turns God into an idol to be used for man's own purposes. Our own nation was once engaged in a great civil war, in which each side presumed God's aid against the other. In his *Second Inaugural Address* in 1865, the sixteenth president of the United States, Abraham Lincoln, put it simply: "The Almighty has his own purposes."

Those who attacked us on September 11 openly proclaim that they are engaged in holy war. Many who support or sympathize with the attackers also invoke God's name and seem to embrace the rationale of holy war. But to recognize the disaster of this way of thinking, we as Americans need only to remember our own, and Western, history. Christian religious wars and Christian sectarian violence tore apart Europe for the better part of a century. In the United States, we are no strangers to those who would murder at least in part in the name of their religious faith. When it comes to this particular evil, no civilization is spotless and no religious tradition is spotless.

The human person has a basic drive to question in order to know. Evaluating, choosing, and having reasons for what we value and love are characteristically human activities. Part of this intrinsic desire to know concerns why we are born and what will happen when we die, which leads us to seek the truth about ultimate ends, including, for many people, the question of God. Some of the signatories to this letter believe that human beings are by nature "religious" in the sense that everyone, including those who do not believe in God and do not participate in organized religion, makes choices about what is important and reflects on ultimate values. All of the signatories to this letter recognize that, across the world, religious faith and religious institutions are important bases of civil society, often producing results for society that are beneficial and healing, at times producing results that are divisive and violent.

So how can governments and societal leaders best respond to these fundamental human and social realities? One response is to outlaw or repress religion. Another possible response is to embrace an ideological secularism: a strong societal skepticism or hostility regarding religion, based on the premise that religion itself, and especially any *public* expression of religious conviction, is inherently problematic. A third possible response is to embrace theocracy: the belief that one religion, presumably the one *true* religion, should be effectively mandatory for all members of society and therefore should receive complete or significant state sponsorship and support.

We disagree with each of these responses. Legal repression radically violates civil and religious freedom and is incompatible with democratic civil society. Although ideological secularism may have increased in our society in recent generations, we disagree with it because it would deny the public legitimacy of an important part of civil society as well as seek to suppress or deny the existence of what is at least arguably an important dimension of personhood itself. Although theocracy has been present in Western (though not U.S.) history, we disagree with it for both social and theological reasons. Socially, governmental establishment of a particular religion can conflict with the principle of religious freedom, a fundamental human right. In addition, government control of religion can cause or exacerbate religious conflicts and, perhaps even more importantly, can threaten the vitality and authenticity of religious institutions. Theologically, even for those who are firmly convinced of the truth of their faith, the coercion of others in matters of religious conscience is ultimately a violation of religion itself, since it robs those other persons of the right to respond freely and in dignity to the Creator's invitation.

At its best, the United States seeks to be a society in which faith and freedom can go together, each elevating the other. We have a secular state—our government officials are not simultaneously religious officials—but we are by far the Western world's most religious society. We are a nation that deeply respects religious freedom and diversity, including the rights of nonbelievers, but one whose citizens recite a Pledge of Allegiance to "one nation, under God," and one that proclaims in many of its courtrooms and inscribes on each of its coins the motto, "In God We Trust." Politically, our separation of church and state seeks to keep politics within its proper sphere, in part by limiting the state's power to control religion, and in part by causing government itself to draw legitimacy from, and operate under, a larger moral canopy that is not of its own making. Spiritually, our separation of church and state permits religion to *be* religion, by detaching it from the coercive power of government. In short, we seek to separate church and state for the protection and proper vitality of both.

For Americans of religious faith, the challenge of embracing religious truth *and* religious freedom has often been difficult. The matter, moreover, is never settled. Ours is a social and constitutional arrangement that almost by definition requires constant deliberation, debate, adjustment, and compromise. It is also helped by, and helps to produce, a certain character or temperament, such that religious believers who strongly embrace the truth of their faith also, not as a compromise with that truth but as an aspect of it, respect those who take a different path.

What will help to reduce religiously based mistrust, hatred, and violence in the 21st century? There are many important answers to this question, of course, but here, we hope, is one: Deepening and renewing our appreciation of religion by recognizing religious freedom as a fundamental right of all people in every nation.

A JUST WAR?

We recognize that all war is terrible, representative finally of human political failure. We also know that the line separating good and evil does not run between one society and another, much less between one religion and another; ultimately, that line runs through the middle of every human heart. Finally, those of us—Jews, Christians, Muslims, and others—who are people of faith recognize our responsibility, stated in our holy scriptures, to love mercy and to do all in our power to prevent war and live in peace.

Yet reason and careful moral reflection also teach us that there are times when the first and most important reply to evil is to stop it. There are times when waging war is not only morally permitted, but morally necessary, as a response to calamitous acts of violence, hatred, and injustice. This is one of those times.

The idea of a "just war" is broadly based, with roots in many of the world's diverse religious and secular moral traditions. Jewish, Christian, and Muslim teachings, for example, all contain serious reflections on the definition of a just war. To be sure, some people, often in the name of realism, insist that war is essentially a realm of self-interest and necessity, making most attempts at moral analysis irrelevant. We disagree. Moral inarticulacy in the face of war is itself a moral stance—one that rejects the possibility of reason, accepts normlessness in international affairs, and capitulates to cynicism. To seek to apply objective moral reasoning to war is to defend the possibility of civil society and a world community based on justice.

The principles of just war teach us that wars of aggression and aggrandizement are never acceptable. Wars may not legitimately be fought for national glory, to avenge past wrongs, for territorial gain, or for any other nondefensive purpose.

The primary moral justification for war is to protect the innocent from certain harm. Augustine, whose early 5th century book, *The City of God,* is a seminal contribution to just war thinking, argues (echoing Socrates) that it is better for the Christian as an individual to suffer harm rather than to commit it. But is the morally responsible person also required, or even permitted, to make for *other* innocent persons a commitment to non-self-defense? For Augustine, and for the broader just war tradition, the answer is no. If one has compelling evidence that innocent people who are in no position to protect themselves will be grievously harmed unless coercive force is used to stop an aggressor, then the moral principle of love of neighbor calls us to the use of force.

Wars may not legitimately be fought against dangers that are small, questionable, or of uncertain consequence, or against dangers that might plausibly be mitigated solely through negotiation, appeals to reason, persuasion from third parties, or other nonviolent means. But if the danger to innocent life is real and certain, and especially if the aggressor is motivated by implacable hostility—if the end he seeks is not your willingness to negotiate or comply, but rather your destruction—then a resort to proportionate force is morally justified.

A just war can only be fought by a legitimate authority with responsibility for public order. Violence that is free-lance, opportunistic, or individualistic is never morally acceptable.

A just war can only be waged against persons who are combatants. Just war authorities from across history and around the world—whether they be Muslim, Jewish, Christian, from other faith traditions, or secular—consistently teach us that noncombatants are immune from deliberate attack. Thus, killing civilians for revenge, or even as a means of deterring aggression from people who sympathize with them, is morally wrong. Although in some circumstances, and within strict limits, it can be morally justifiable to undertake military actions that may result in the unintended but foreseeable death or injury of some noncombatants, it is not morally acceptable to make the killing of noncombatants the operational objective of a military action.

These and other just war principles teach us that, whenever human beings contemplate or wage war, it is both possible and necessary to affirm the sanctity of human life and embrace the principle of equal human dignity. These principles strive to preserve and reflect, even in the tragic activity of war, the fundamental moral truth that "others"—those who are strangers to us, those who differ from us in race or language, those whose religions we may believe to be untrue—have the same right to life that we do, and the same human dignity and human rights that we do.

On September 11, 2001, a group of individuals deliberately attacked the United States, using highjacked airplanes as weapons with which to kill in less than two hours over 3,000 of our citizens in New York City, southwestern Pennsylvania, and Washington, D.C. Overwhelmingly, those who died on September 11 were civilians, not combatants, and were not known at all, except as Americans, by those who killed them. Those who died on the morning of September 11 were killed unlawfully, wantonly, and with premeditated malice—a kind of killing that, in the name of precision, can only be described as murder. Those murdered included people from all races, many ethnicities, most major religions. They included dishwashers and corporate executives.

The individuals who committed these acts of war did not act alone, or without support, or for unknown reasons. They were members of an international Islamicist network, active in as many as 40 countries, now known to the world as Al Qaeda. This group, in turn, constitutes but one arm of a larger radical Islamicist movement, growing for decades and in some instances tolerated and even supported by governments, that openly professes its desire and increasingly demonstrates its ability to use murder to advance its objectives.

We use the terms "Islam" and "Islamic" to refer to one of the world's great religions, with about 1.2 billion adherents, including several million U.S. citizens, some of whom were murdered on September 11. It ought to go without saying—but we say it here once, clearly—that the great majority of the world's Muslims, guided in large measure by the teachings of the Qur'an, are decent, faithful, and peaceful. We use the terms "Islamicism" and "radical Islamicist" to refer to the violent, extremist, and radically intolerant religious-political movement that now threatens the world, including the Muslim world.

This radical, violent movement opposes not only certain U.S. and Western policies—some signatories to this letter also oppose some of those policies—but also a foundational principle of the modern world, religious tolerance, as well as those fundamental human rights, in particular freedom of conscience and religion, that are enshrined in the United Nations Universal Declaration of Human Rights, and that must be the basis of any civilization oriented to human flourishing, justice, and peace.

This extremist movement claims to speak for Islam, but betrays fundamental Islamic principles. Islam sets its face *against* moral atrocities. For example, reflecting the teaching of the Qur'an and the example of the Prophet, Muslim scholars through the centuries have taught that struggle in the path of God (i.e., *jihad*) forbids the deliberate killing of noncombatants, and requires that military action be undertaken only at the behest of legitimate public authorities. They remind us forcefully that Islam, no less than Christianity, Judaism, and other religions, is threatened and potentially degraded by these profaners who invoke God's name to kill indiscriminately.

We recognize that movements claiming the mantle of religion also have complex political, social, and demographic dimensions, to which due attention must be paid. At the same time, philosophy matters, and the animating philosophy of this radical Islamicist movement, in its contempt for human life, and by viewing the world as a life-and-death struggle between believers and unbelievers (whether nonradical Muslims, Jews, Christians, Hindus, or others), clearly denies the equal dignity of all persons and, in doing so, betrays religion and rejects the very foundation of civilized life and the possibility of peace among nations.

Most seriously of all, the mass murders of September 11 demonstrated, arguably for the first time, that this movement now possesses not only the openly stated desire, but also the capacity and expertise—including possible access to, and willingness to use, chemical, biological, and nuclear weapons—to wreak massive, horrific devastation on its intended targets.

Those who slaughtered more than 3,000 persons on September 11 and who, by their own admission, want nothing more than to do it again, constitute a clear and present danger to all people of good will everywhere in the world, not just the United States. Such acts are a pure example of naked aggression against innocent human life, a world-threatening evil that clearly requires the use of force to remove it.

Organized killers with global reach now threaten all of us. In the name of universal human morality, and fully conscious of the restrictions and requirements of a just war, we support our government's, and our society's, decision to use force of arms against them.

CONCLUSION

We pledge to do all we can to guard against the harmful temptations—especially those of arrogance and jingoism—to which nations at war so often seem to yield. At the same time, with one voice we say solemnly that it is crucial for our nation and its allies to win this war. We fight to defend ourselves, but we also believe that we fight to defend those universal principles of human rights and human dignity that are the best hope for humankind.

One day, this war will end. When it does—and in some respects even before it ends—the great task of conciliation awaits us. We hope that this war, by stopping an unmitigated global evil, can increase the possibility of a world community based on justice. But we know that only the peacemakers among us in every society can ensure that this war will not have been in vain.

We wish especially to reach out to our brothers and sisters in Muslim societies. We say to you forthrightly: We are not enemies, but friends. We must not be enemies. We have so much in common. There is so much that we must do together. Your human dignity, no less than ours—your rights and opportunities for a good life, no less than ours—are what we believe we're fighting for. We know that, for some of you, mistrust of us is high, and we know that we Americans are partly responsible for that mistrust. But we must not be enemies. In hope, we wish to join with you and all people of good will to build a just and lasting peace.

SIGNATORIES

Enola Aird
Director, The Motherhood Project; Council on Civil Society

John Atlas
President, National Housing Institute; Executive Director, Passaic County Legal Aid Society

Jay Belsky
Professor and Director, Institute for the Study of Children, Families and Social Issues, Birkbeck University of London

David Blankenhorn
President, Institute for American Values

David Bosworth
University of Washington

R. Maurice Boyd
Minister, The City Church, New York

Gerard V. Bradley
Professor of Law, University of Notre Dame

Margaret F. Brinig
Edward A. Howry Distinguished Professor, University of Iowa College of Law

Allan Carlson
President, The Howard Center for Family, Religion, and Society

Khalid Durán
Editor, TransIslam Magazine

Paul Ekman
Professor of Psychology, University of California, San Francisco

Jean Bethke Elshtain
Laura Spelman Rockefeller Professor of Social and Political Ethics, University of Chicago Divinity School

Amitai Etzioni
University Professor, The George Washington University

Hillel Fradkin
President, Ethics and Public Policy Center

Samuel G. Freedman
Professor at the Columbia University Graduate School of Journalism

Francis Fukuyama
Bernard Schwartz Professor of International Political Economy, Johns Hopkins University

William A. Galston
Professor at the School of Public Affairs, University of Maryland; Director, Institute for Philosophy and Public Policy

Claire Gaudiani
Senior Research Scholar, Yale Law School and Former President, Connecticut College

Robert P. George
  McCormick Professor of Jurisprudence and Professor of Politics, Princeton University

Neil Gilbert
  Professor at the School of Social Welfare, University of California, Berkeley

Mary Ann Glendon
  Learned Hand Professor of Law, Harvard University Law School

Norval D. Glenn
  Ashbel Smith Professor of Sociology and Stiles Professor of American Studies, University of Texas at Austin

Os Guinness
  Senior Fellow, Trinity Forum

David Gutmann
  Professor Emeritus of Psychiatry and Education, Northwestern University

Kevin J. "Seamus" Hasson
  President, Becket Fund for Religious Liberty

Sylvia Ann Hewlett
  Chair, National Parenting Association

James Davison Hunter
  William R. Kenan, Jr., Professor of Sociology and Religious Studies and Executive Director, Center on Religion and Democracy, University of Virginia

Samuel Huntington
  Albert J. Weatherhead, III, University Professor, Harvard University

Byron Johnson
  Director and Distinguished Senior Fellow, Center for Research on Religion and Urban Civil Society, University of Pennsylvania

James Turner Johnson
  Professor, Department of Religion, Rutgers University

John Kelsay
  Richard L. Rubenstein Professor of Religion, Florida State University

Diane Knippers
  President, Institute on Religion and Democracy

Thomas C. Kohler
  Professor of Law, Boston College Law School

Glenn C. Loury
  Professor of Economics and Director, Institute on Race and Social Division, Boston University

Harvey C. Mansfield
  William R. Kenan, Jr., Professor of Government, Harvard University

Will Marshall
  President, Progressive Policy Institute

Richard J. Mouw
  President, Fuller Theological Seminary

Daniel Patrick Moynihan
  University Professor, Maxwell School of Citizenship and Public Affairs, Syracuse University

John E. Murray, Jr.
  Chancellor and Professor of Law, Duquesne University

Michael Novak
  George Frederick Jewett Chair in Religion and Public Policy, American Enterprise Institute

Rev. Val J. Peter
Executive Director, Boys and Girls Town

David Popenoe
Professor of Sociology and Co-Director of the National Marriage Project, Rutgers University

Robert D. Putnam
Peter and Isabel Malkin Professor of Public Policy at the Kennedy School of Government, Harvard University

Gloria G. Rodriguez
Founder and President, AVANCE, Inc.

Robert Royal
President, Faith & Reason Institute

Nina Shea
Director, Freedom's House's Center for Religious Freedom

Fred Siegel
Professor of History, The Cooper Union

Theda Skocpol
Victor S. Thomas Professor of Government and Sociology, Harvard University

Katherine Shaw Spaht
Jules and Frances Landry Professor of Law, Louisiana State University Law Center

Max L. Stackhouse
Professor of Christian Ethics and Director, Project on Public Theology, Princeton Theological Seminary

William Tell, Jr.
The William and Karen Tell Foundation

Maris A. Vinovskis
Bentley Professor of History and Professor of Public Policy, University of Michigan

Paul C. Vitz
Professor of Psychology, New York University

Michael Walzer
Professor at the School of Social Science, Institute for Advanced Study

George Weigel
Senior Fellow, Ethics and Public Policy Center

Charles Wilson
Director, Center for the Study of Southern Culture, University of Mississippi

James Q. Wilson
Collins Professor of Management and Public Policy Emeritus, UCLA

John Witte, Jr.
Jonas Robitscher Professor of Law and Ethics and Director, Law and Religion Program, Emory University Law School

Christopher Wolfe
Professor of Political Science, Marquette University

Daniel Yankelovich
President, Public Agenda

ENDNOTES

Preamble
human beings are born free: From the United Nations Universal Declaration of Human Rights, Article 1.

basic subject of society: A Call to Civil Society (New York: Institute for American Values, 1998), 16; Aristotle, *Politics* VII, 1–2.

Human beings naturally desire to seek the truth: Aristotle, *Metaphysics*, 1–1; John Paul II, *Fides et Ratio*, 25 (Vatican City, 1998).

Religious freedom: United Nations Universal Declaration of Human Rights, Articles 18–19.

Killing in the name of God: Bosphorus Declaration (Istanbul, Turkey, February 9, 1994); Berne Declaration (Wolfsberg/Zurich, Switzerland, November 26, 1992); and John Paul II, Papal Message for World Day of Peace, Articles 6–7 (Vatican City, January 1, 2002).

What Are American Values?

"the head of world infidelity": "Excerpt: Bin Laden Tape," *Washington Post*, December 27, 2001.

briefly mention four of them: See *A Call to Civil Society* (New York: Institute for American Values, 1998).

widely recognized . . . as a precondition for other individual freedoms: See John Witte, Jr. and M. Christian Green, "The American Constitutional Experiment in Religious Human Rights: The Perennial Search for Principles," in Johan D. van der Vyver and John Witte, Jr. (eds.), *Religious Human Rights in Global Perspective,* vol. 2 (The Hague: Martinus Nijhoff Publishers, 1996). See also Harold J. Berman, *Law and Revolution: The Formation of the Western Legal Tradition* (Cambridge, MA: Harvard University Press, 1983); and Michael J. Perry, *The Idea of Human Rights: Four Inquiries* (New York: Oxford University Press, 1998).

deny the distinctiveness of other cultures: Some people make this point as a way of condemning those "other" cultures that are presumably too inferior, or too enthralled by false beliefs, to appreciate what we in this letter are calling universal human values; others make this point as a way of endorsing (usually *one* of) those cultures that are presumably indifferent to these values. We disagree with both versions of this point.

"implicit in man's nature as a member of society": Richard McKeon, "The Philosophic Bases and Material Circumstances of the Rights of Man," in *Human Rights: Comments and Interpretations* (London: Wingate, 1949), 45.

arch of the moral universe is long, but it bends toward justice: Martin Luther King, Jr., "Where Do We Go From Here?" in James M. Washington (ed.), *The Essential Writings and Speeches of Martin Luther King, Jr.* (New York: HarperCollins, 1986), 245.

What About God?

an idol to be used for man's own purposes: John Paul II, Papal Message for World Day of Peace, Article 6 (Vatican City, January 1, 2002).

no religious tradition is spotless: Intra-Christian examples of holy war or crusade emerged with particular force in Europe during the 17th century. According to some scholars, the principle characteristics of holy war are: that the cause for which the war is fought has a clear connection to religion (i.e., that the cause is "holy"); that the war is fought under the banner and with the presumption of divine authority and assistance (the Latin term used by 11th century Christian crusaders was *"Deus Volt,"* or "God wills it"); that the warriors understand themselves to be godly, or "warrior saints"; that the war is prosecuted zealously and unsparingly, since the enemy is presumed to be ungodly and therefore fundamentally "other," lacking the human dignity and rights of the godly; and finally, that warriors who die in battle are favored by God as martyrs. Eventually, in Christianity, the development of just war doctrine, with its emphasis on moral universalism, largely called for the elimination of religion as a just cause for war. As early as the 16th century, some natural law theorists such as Franciscus de Victoria and Francisco Suarez were explicitly condemning the use of war to spread religion. "Difference in religion," Victoria wrote, "is not a cause of just war." See James Turner Johnson, *Ideology, Reason, and the Limitation of War: Religious and Secular Concepts 1200 –1740* (Princeton: Princeton University Press, 1975), 112–123, 154. See also Roland H. Bainton, *Christian Attitudes Toward War and Peace: A Historical Survey and Critical Re-evaluation* (Nashville: Abingdon, 1960), 148.

characteristically human activities: A Call to Civil Society (New York: Institute for American Values, 1998), 16. This theme is developed in Aristotle, *Metaphysics*, 1–1; Bernard J. Lonergan, *Insight: A Study of Human Understanding* (New York: Longmans, 1958); and others.

embrace an ideological secularism: We wish here to distinguish "secular" from "secularism." Secular, derived from the Latin term meaning "world" and suggesting "in the world," refers merely to functions that are separate from the church. Secularism, by contrast, is a philosophy, an "ism," a way of seeing the world based on rejection of religion or hostility to religion.

an important dimension of personhood itself: For this reason, advocates of secularism may underestimate the degree to which human societies, even in theory, can simply dispense with "religion." Moreover, they almost certainly miscalculate, even accepting many of their own premises, the social consequences of suppressing traditional religion. For if we understand religion to be values of ultimate concern, the 20th century saw two world-threatening examples—Nazism in Germany, and communism in the Soviet Union—of the emergence of secular religions, or what might be called replacement religions, each violently intent on eliminating its society's traditional religious faiths (in effect, its competitor faiths), and each, when in power, ruthlessly indifferent to human dignity and basic human rights.

moral canopy that is not of its own making: A Call to Civil Society (New York: Institute for American Values, 1998), 13.

separate church and state for the protection and proper vitality of both: As the leaders and scholars who produced *The Williamsburg Charter* put it in 1988, "the government acts as a safeguard, but not the source, of freedom for faiths, whereas the churches and synagogues act as a source, but not the safeguard, of faiths for freedom. . . . The result is neither a naked public square where all religion is excluded, nor a sacred public square with any religion established or semi-established. The result, rather, is a civil public square in which citizens of all religious faiths, or none, engage one another in the continuing democratic discourse."

See James Davison Hunter and Os Guinness (eds.), *Articles of Faith, Articles of Peace: The Religious Liberty Clauses and the American Public Philosophy* (Washington, DC: The Brookings Institution, 1990), 140.

A Just War?

middle of every human heart: see Alexander Solzhenitzyn, *The Gulag Archipelago*, vol. I (New York: Harper and Row, 1974), 168.

diverse religious and secular moral traditions: See Jean Bethke Elshtain (ed.), *Just War Theory* (Oxford: Blackwell, 1992); Elshtain, Stanley Hauerwas, and James Turner Johnson, Pew Forum on Religion and Public Life Conference on "Just War Tradition and the New War on Terrorism" (*http://pewforum.org/events/1005/*); James Turner Johnson, *Ideology, Reason, and the Limitation of War: Religious and Secular Concepts 1200–1740* (Princeton: Princeton University Press, 1975); Johnson, *Just War Tradition and the Restraint of War: A Moral and Historical Inquiry* (Princeton: Princeton University Press, 1981); Johnson, *The Quest for Peace: Three Moral Traditions in Western Cultural History* (Princeton: Princeton University Press, 1987); Johnson, *Morality and Contemporary Warfare* (New Haven: Yale University Press, 1999); Johnson and John Kelsay (eds.), *Cross, Crescent, and Sword: The Justification and Limitation of War in Western and Islamic Tradition* (New York: Greenwood Press, 1990); Majid Khadduri, *War and Peace in the Law of Islam* (Baltimore: Johns Hopkins University Press, 1955); John Kelsay and James Turner Johnson (eds.), *Just War and Jihad: Historical and Theoretical Perspectives on War and Peace in Western and Islamic Tradition* (New York: Greenwood Press, 1991); Terry Nardin (ed.), *The Ethics of War and Peace: Religious and Secular Perspectives* (Princeton: Princeton University Press, 1996); William V. O'Brien, *The Conduct of War and Limited War* (New York: Praeger, 1981); Rudolf Peters, *Jihad in Classical and Modern Islam* (Princeton: Markus Wiener, 1996); Paul Ramsey, *Speak Up for Just War or Pacifism* (University Park, PA: Pennsylvania State University Press, 1988); Michael Walzer, *Just and Unjust Wars* (New York: Basic Books, 1977); and Richard Wasserstrom (ed.), *War and Morality* (Belmont, CA: Wadsworth, 1970).

attempts at moral analysis irrelevant: The Latin axiom is: *Inter arma silent leges* (In times of war the law is silent). Classical exemplars of this perspective include Thucydides, Niccolo Machiavelli, and Thomas Hobbes; for a more recent treatment, see Kenneth Waltz, *Man, the State and War* (Princeton: Princeton University Press, 1978). For a sensitive but critical survey of the contribution of this school of thought to international theory, see Jack Donnelly, *Realism and International Relations* (Cambridge: Cambridge University Press, 2000).

We disagree: Intellectual and moral approaches to war as a human phenomenon can generally be divided into four schools of thought. The first can be called realism: the belief that war is basically a matter of power, self-interest, necessity, and survival, thereby rendering abstract moral analysis largely beside the point. The second can be called holy war: the belief that God can authorize the coercion and killing of nonbelievers, or that a particular secular ideology of ultimate concern can authorize the coercion and killing of nonbelievers. The third can be called pacifism: the belief that all war is intrinsically immoral. And the fourth is typically called just war: the belief that universal moral reasoning, or what some would call natural moral law, can and should be applied to the activity of war. The signatories to this letter largely disagree with the first school of thought. We unequivocally reject the second school of thought, regardless of the form it takes, or whether it springs from and purports to support our own society ("our side") or the side of those who wish us ill. Some of the signatories have much respect for the third school of thought (particularly its insistence that nonviolence does not mean retreat or passivity or declining to stand for justice; quite the opposite), even as we respectfully, and with some degree of fear and trembling, differ from it. As a group we seek largely to embrace and build upon the fourth school of thought.

(echoing Socrates): Socrates's judgment that it is better to suffer evil rather than to do it is conveyed to us by Plato in the *Apology* (32-c to 32-e) and constitutes a key moment in moral philosophy.

might plausibly be mitigated solely through . . . non-violent means: Some people suggest that the "last resort" requirement of just war theory—in essence, the requirement to explore all other reasonable and plausible alternatives to the use of force—is not satisfied until the resort to arms has been approved by a recognized international body, such as the United Nations. This proposition is problematic. First, it is novel; historically, approval by an international body has not been viewed by just war theorists as a just cause requirement. Second, it is quite debatable whether an international body such as the U.N. is in a position to be the best final judge of when, and under what conditions, a particular resort to arms is justified; or whether the attempt by that body to make and enforce such judgments would inevitably compromise its primary mission of humanitarian work. According to one observer, a former U.N. Assistant Secretary-General, transforming the U.N. into "a pale imitation of a state" in order to "manage the use of force" internationally "may well be a suicidal embrace." See Giandomenico Picco, "The U.N. and the Use of Force," *Foreign Affairs* 73 (1994): 15. See also Thomas G. Weis, David P. Forsythe, and Roger A. Coate, *United Nations and Changing World Politics* (Boulder, CO: Westview Press, 2001), 104–106; and John Gerard Ruggie, *The United Nations and the Collective Use of Force: Whither? Or Whether?* (New York: United Nations Association of the USA, 1996).

Violence that is free-lance . . . is never morally acceptable: In just war theory, the main goal of the legitimate authority requirement is to prevent the anarchy of private warfare and warlords—an anarchy that exists today in some parts of the world, and of which the attackers of September 11 are representative embodiments. The legitimate authority requirement does not, on the other hand, for several reasons, apply clearly or directly to wars of national independence or succession. First, these latter types of conflict occur within a state, not internationally. Moreover, in many such conflicts, the question of public legitimacy is exactly what is being contested. For example, in the war for independence that resulted in the founding of the United States, just war analysts frequently point out that the rebelling colonies themselves constituted a legitimate public authority, and further that the colonies had reasonably concluded that the British government had, in the words of our Declaration of Independence, become "destructive of these ends" of legitimate government, and therefore itself had ceased to function as a competent public authority. Indeed, even in cases in which those waging war do not in any plain sense constitute a currently functioning public authority—for example, the "Warsaw Ghetto Uprising" of Polish Jews in 1943 against the Nazi occupation—the legitimate authority requirement of just war theory does not morally invalidate the resort to arms by those resisting oppression by seeking to overthrow illegitimate authority.

other just war principles: For example, just war principles often insist that legitimate warfare must be motivated by the intention of enhancing the likelihood of peace and reducing the likelihood of violence and destruction; that it must be proportionate, such that the social goods that would result from victory in war discernably outweigh the evils that will attend the war; that it must contain the probability of success, such that lives are not taken and sacrificed in futile causes; and that it must pass the test of comparative justice, such that the human goods being defended are important enough, and gravely enough in danger, to outweigh what many just war theorists view as the standing moral presumption against war. This letter focuses largely on principles of justice in declaring war (in the terminology employed by many Christian just war thinkers, *jus ad bellum*) and in waging war (*jus in bello*). Other principles focus on justice in settling the war and restoring conditions of peace (*jus post bellum*). See Jean Bethke Elshtain (ed.), *Just War Theory* (Oxford: Blackwell, 1992); U.S. Conference of Catholic Bishops, *The Challenge of Peace: God's Promise and Our Response* (Washington, DC: United States Catholic Conference, 1983); and other sources cited above.

over 3,000 of our citizens: As of January 4, 2002, official estimates were that 3,119 persons had been killed by the September 11 attackers, including 2,895 in New York, 184 in Washington, and 40 in Pennsylvania. Although this letter refers to "our citizens," included among those murdered on September 11 were many citizens of other countries who were living in the U.S. at the time of the attack. "Dead and Missing," *New York Times,* January 8, 2002.

use murder to advance its objectives: In addition to the murders of September 11, members of radical Islamicist organizations are apparently responsible for: the April 18, 1983, bombing of the U.S. Embassy in Beirut, killing 63 persons and injuring 120; the October 23, 1983, bombings of U.S. Marine and French paratroop barracks in Beirut, killing 300 persons; the December 21, 1988, bombing of U.S. Pan Am Flight 103, killing 259 persons; the February 26, 1993, bombing of the World Trade Center in New York City, killing 6 persons and injuring 1,000; the June 25, 1996, bombing outside the Khobar Towers U.S. military barracks in Dhahran, Saudi Arabia, killing 19 U.S. soldiers and wounding 515; the August 7, 1998, bombing of U.S. embassies in Nairobi, Kenya, and Dar es Salaam, Tanzania, killing 224 persons and injuring more than 5,000; and the October 12, 2000, bombing of the USS *Cole* in Aden, Yemen, killing 17 U.S. sailors and wounding 39. This list is incomplete. (See *Significant Terrorist Incidents, 1961–2001* (Washington, DC: U.S. Department of State, Bureau of Public Affairs, October 31, 2001). In addition, members of organizations comprising this movement are also responsible for numerous failed attempts at mass murder, both in the U.S. and in other countries, including the attempt to bomb the United Nations and the Lincoln and Holland Tunnels in New York in 1993 and the attempt to bomb the Los Angeles International Airport on New Year's Eve 2000.

struggle in the path of God (i.e., jihad) *forbids:* The relationship between the *jihad* and just war traditions is complex. Premodern *jihad* and just war perspectives overlapped in important ways. Both could legitimate wars aimed at advancing religion, and both sought clearly to disassociate such wars from wars involving indiscriminate or disproportionate tactics. In the modern era, *jihad* has largely retained its confessional component—that is, its aim of protecting and propagating Islam as a religion. The confessional dimension of *jihad* thinking in turn seems to

be closely linked to the view of the state widely held by Muslim authorities—a view that envisions little or no separation of religion from the
state. By contrast, modern Christian thinking on just war has tended to
downplay its confessional elements (few Christian theologians today
emphasize the value of "crusade"), replacing them with more religiously neutral arguments about human rights and shared moral norms,
or what some Christian and other thinkers term "natural moral law."
Some Muslim scholars today seek, in the case of *jihad*, more fully to recover the sense of the term as "exertion" or "striving for good" in the
service of God, thereby similarly downplaying its confessional elements
and emphasizing, for our increasingly plural and interdependent world,
the term's more universal dimensions and applications. For example,
see Sohail M. Hashmi, "Interpreting the Islamic Ethics of War and
Peace," in Terry Nardin (ed.), *The Ethics of War and Peace: Religious and
Secular Perspectives* (Princeton, NJ: Princeton University Press, 1996),
146–166; and Hilmi Zawati, *Is Jihad a Just War? War, Peace, and Human
Rights under Islamic and Public International Law* (Lewiston, NY: Edwin
Mellen, 2001).

Muslim scholars . . . remind us forcefully: For example, Muslim scholars affiliated with the Muslim World League, meeting in Mecca, recently reaffirmed that *jihad* strictly prohibits "the killing of noncombatants" and
attacks against "installations, sites and buildings not related to the fighting." See "Muslim scholars define 'terrorism' as opposed to legitimate jihad," *Middle East News Online* [*www.middleeastwire.com*], posted January 14,
2002. See also Bassam Tibi, "War and Peace in Islam," in Terry Nardin
(ed.), *The Ethics of War and Peace: Religious and Secular Perspectives* (Princeton, NJ: Princeton University Press, 1996), 128–145.

devastation on its intended targets: The historian Eric Hobsbawm, in his
study of the 20th century, published in 1995, warns us in particular, as
we confront the new millennium, of the emerging crisis of "non-state
terrorism," made possible by the growing "privatization of the means of
destruction," such that organized groups, operating at least to some degree independently of public authorities, are increasingly willing and
able to perpetrate "violence and wreckage *anywhere* on the globe." Eric
Hobsbawm, *Age of Extremes: The Short Twentieth Century 1914–1991*
(London: Abacus, 1995), 560.

Conclusion

but friends. We must not be enemies: From Abraham Lincoln, *First Inaugural Address*, March 1861.

© February 2002, Institute for American Values, 1841 Broadway, Suite 211, New York, NY 10023, Tel: (212) 246-3942, Email: info@americanvalues.org, Website: www.americanvalues.org (ISBN:_1–931764–02–6).

The signatories wish to thank Dan Cere of McGill University in Montreal for research and editorial assistance.

NOTES

INTRODUCTION

1. "Jihad Against Jews and Crusaders," World Islamic Front statement, available at: www.fas.org/irp/world/para/docs/980223-fatwa.htm.

2. Ibid.

3. Elisabeth Bumiller, "Bin Laden, on Tape, Boasts of Trade Center Attacks; U.S. Says It Proves His Guilt," *New York Times,* December 14, 2001, pp. 1, B4.

4. Paul McCartney, "Freedom," lyrics available at: www.songlyrics.co.naz/lyrics/p/paulmccartney/freedom.htm. McCartney speaks of freedom as "a right given by God."

5. "Jihad Against Jews and Crusaders," p. 2.

6. The title of the letter was "How Can We Coexist?" and it was released in Riyadh. The two letters can be read in their entirety at www.americanvalues.org. As well, the text of "What We're Fighting For" appears as an appendix to this text.

CHAPTER 1

1. Amir Taheri, "Semantics of Murder," *Wall Street Journal,* May 8, 2002, p. A188.

2. Albert Camus, "The Human Crisis" (lecture delivered in America in the spring of 1946), *Twice a Year* 1 (1946–47): 21.

3. Richard Rorty, "Robustness: A Reply to Jean Bethke Elshtain," in Daniel Conway and John Seery, eds., *The Politics of Irony* (New York: St. Martin's Press, 1992), pp. 219–23.

Rorty was responding to an essay of mine in this edited volume that was critical of his work and entitled "Don't Be Cruel: Reflections on Rortyian Liberalism" (pp. 199–217).

4. Quoted in *The New Republic,* November 5, 2001, p. 12, from Fish's appearance on Fox News Channel, *The O'Reilly Factor,* October 17, 2001.

5. Stephen L. Carter, *Reflections of an Affirmative Action Baby* (New York: Basic Books, 1991), pp. 144–45.

6. Robert Fisk, "My Beating by Refugees Is a Symbol of the Hatred and Fury of This Filthy War," *The Independent,* December 10, 2001.

7. Fisk's article is quoted at length and commented on by Andrew Sullivan in his "Daily Dish," available at: www.andrewsullivan.com (December 10, 2001).

8. Robin Lovin, *Reinhold Niebuhr and Christian Realism* (Cambridge: Cambridge University Press, 1995), pp. 106–7.

9. Václav Havel, *Open Letters* (New York: Alfred A. Knopf, 1991), p. 292.

10. Ibid.

11. Jean Bethke Elshtain, "Politics Without Cliché," *Social Research* 60, no. 3 (Fall 1993): 433–44.

12. That terrorism, past and present, has always had its apologists says nothing about how one accurately defines the phenomenon.

13. To be sure, it would only be fair to point out that the Vietnam War was a terrible one in part because it was often difficult to distinguish combatants from noncombatants (although one is obliged to try), and because noncombatants often harbored combatants who lay in wait to ambush American soldiers. The soldiers at My Lai were inflamed, having just lost comrades. But none of that exculpates or justifies what happened. Massacre it was. Anyone who claimed a glorious victory over these villagers and belittled their suffering would rightly be regarded as morally reprehensible.

14. Michael Walzer, *Just and Unjust Wars* (New York: Basic Books, 1977), p. 197.

15. On some international debates about terrorism, see Todd S. Purdum, "What Do You Mean 'Terrorist'?" *New York Times,* April 7, 2002, sect. 4, pp. 1, 5.

16. Jason Burke, "'You Have to Kill in the Name of Allah Until You Are Killed,'" *The Observer,* January 27, 2002, pp. 6–7.

17. Ibid.

18. Francis Fukayama, "Their Target: The Modern World," *Newsweek,* December 17, 2001.

19. Ibid.

20. "The Need to Speak Up," *The Economist,* October 13, 2001, p. 14. It is also important to note that "the laws of jihad categorically preclude wanton and indiscriminate slaughter. . . . What the classical jurists of Islam never remotely considered is the kind of unprovoked, mass slaughter of uninvolved civil populations that we saw in New York. . . . For this there is no precedent and no authority in Islam." Bernard Lewis, "Jihad vs. Crusade," *Wall Street Journal,* September 27, 2001, p. A18.

21. President George W. Bush, "Address to a Joint Session of Congress, September 20, 2001," in *Our Mission and Our Moment: Speeches Since the Attacks of September 11* (Washington, D.C.: White House Printing Office, 2002), pp. 11, 12.

22. Dietrich Bonhoeffer, *Letters and Papers from Prison* (New York: Collier Books, 1971), p. 5.

23. Ibid., p. 4.

CHAPTER 2

1. This proclamation is displayed at the Roosevelt Museum as a tribute to both Franklin and Eleanor Roosevelt and the principles for which they stood.

2. Thus, the woman suffragists of the nineteenth century who argued for civic equality for women issued a "Declaration of Sentiments" in 1848 modeled explicitly on the Declaration of Independence. They too claimed inclusion based on the great document, not in opposition to it.

3. *Dred Scott v. John F. A. Sandford,* March 6, 1857, preceded by *Scott v. Sandford,* U.S. 393 (1856) (USSC+).

4. Bernard Lewis, *What Went Wrong?: Western Impact and Middle Eastern Response* (Oxford: Oxford University Press, 2002), p. 96.

5. Peter Brown, *The Rise of Western Christendom* (London: Basil Blackwell, 1997), pp. 26, 32.

6. The early centuries that mark the beginning of the Middle Ages were so complex, and filled with such a bewildering mix of authorities and movements of peoples into the territory that had once centrally defined the Roman Empire, that I am embarrassed by my summary account. To all scholars of late antiquity, I apologize. My aim is not to offer a complete history but to show the emergence of certain distinctions and their centrality to Western religious and political history.

7. Robert A. Markus, *Saeculum: History and Society in the Theology of St. Augustine* (Cambridge: Cambridge University Press, 1970), p. 42.

8. "The Constitutions of Clarendon, 1164," in Norton Downs, ed., *Basic Documents in Medieval History* (Princeton, N.J.: Van Nostrand, 1959), pp. 90–91.

9. John of Salisbury, "The Nature of a True Prince," from *Policraticus,* in *The Portable Medieval Reader* (New York: Viking, 1959), pp. 256, 258.

10. St. Augustine, *The Confessions* (London: Penguin Books, 1961), book 12, p. 296.

11. Ibid., book 13, p. 335.

12. Portions of this section are derived from my essay "Faith of Our Fathers and Mothers," in Azizah Y. al-Hibri, Jean Bethke Elshtain, and Charles C. Haynes, *Religion in American Public Life,* with an introduction by Martin E. Marty (New York: W. W. Norton, 2001), pp. 39–61.

13. St. Augustine, *The City of God,* (New York: Penguin Classics, 1972), book 3, ch. 21, p. 122.

14. Lewis, *What Went Wrong?* p. 73.

15. Peter L. Bergen, *Holy War, Inc.* (New York: Free Press, 2001), p. 144.

16. Ibid., p. 155.

17. Ibid.

18. Ian Fisher, "Seeing No Justice, a Rape Victim Chooses Death," *New York Times,* July 28, 2002, p. 3.

19. "'Alarming' Illiteracy Among Arabs," *New York Times,* January 10, 2002, p. A6.

20. "A Real Thirst for Knowledge," *USA Today,* January 22, 2002, p. 6D.

21. Tim McGirk and Shomali Plain, "Lifting the Veil on Sex Slavery," *Time,* February 18, 2002, p. 8.

22. "Blair Sees 'No Moral Ambiguity' in War on Terrorism," *Washington Times,* October 8–14, 2001, p. 25.

23. Ahmed Rashid, *Taliban* (New Haven, Conn.: Yale University Press, 2001), appendix 1, "A Sample of Taliban Decrees Relating to Women and Other Cultural Issues, After the Capture of Kabul, 1996," pp. 217–19.

24. Julia Duin, "Wine and Women: Muslims See Afterlife Filled with Pleasure," *Washington Times,* October 22–28, 2001, p. 27. The Qur'an does teach that martyrs find a reward in paradise, but it also declares suicide wrong. Sura 52 depicts paradise as a lush place in which virtuous men recline on thrones or cushions and are waited upon by companions. Here is a sample: "Reclining upon couches ranged in rows; and We shall espouse them to wide-eyed houris [female companions]. And those who believed, and their seed followed them in belief, We shall join their seed with them, and We shall not defraud them of aught of their work; every man shall be pledged for what he earned." Sura 56 also depicts reclining on "close-wrought couches," "immortal youths," and "wide-eyed houris as the likeness of hidden pearls, a recompense for that they labored." See A. J. Arberry, trans., *The Koran* (New York: Simon & Schuster/Touchstone, 1955); sura 52, pp. 241–43; sura 56, pp. 254–57.

25. Cited in Paul Marshall, Roberta Green, and Lela Gilbert, *Islam at the Crossroads* (Grand Rapids, Mich.: Baker Books, 2002), p. 29.

26. Lewis, *What Went Wrong?* pp. 53, 73.

CHAPTER 3

1. I know I read this somewhere in Luther—I'm probably paraphrasing—but the closest I can come to the quote is volume 45 of *Luther's Works* (pp. 90–96). If any Luther buff out there knows a more precise location for this cite, please e-mail me. For an edition of Luther's works readily available to English-language readers, see Jaroslav Pelikan and Helmut T. Lehrmann, eds., *Luther's Collected Works* (St. Louis, Concordia, and Philadelphia: Fortress, 1955–86).

2. Thomas Hobbes, *Leviathan* (New York: Penguin Books, 1983), pp. 183, 186.

3. George Weigel, *Tranquillitas Ordinis: The Present Failure and Future Promise of American Catholic Thought on War and Peace* (Oxford: Oxford University Press, 1987), p. 31, note.

4. Quoted in Herbert Deane, *The Political and Social Ideas of St. Augustine* (New York: Columbia University Press, 1963), cited in ibid., pp. 28–29.

5. Excerpts from key documents of the early Church and information on its history are from Louis J. Swift, *The Earthly Fathers on War and Military Service* (Wilmington, Del.: Michael Glazier Publishers, 1983).

6. Romans 13 continues, as it has for centuries, to generate heated debates on interpretation, implication, and Christian obligation.

7. See Protocol Additional to the Geneva Conditions of August 12, 1949, and relating to the Protection of Victims of International Armed Conflicts, Protocol 1 of June 8, 1977.

8. Mark Bowden's book *Black Hawk Down* (New York: Penguin, 1999) was made into a film (2001) that depicts in horrifying detail the loss of eighteen U.S. Rangers in Mogadishu in 1993. What happened in Somalia illustrates a problem with so-called humanitarian intervention. (I discuss this in detail in chapters 9–12.) Humanitarian intervention in Somalia began in 1992; U.S. troops were pulled out in 1994.

9. The Quakers did have a try at earthly governance in William Penn's "Holy Experiment" in Pennsylvania, where Quaker control lasted for seventy-four years (1682–1756). But well before the end the high hopes that had inaugurated the experiment—based on the certainty that a peaceable kingdom would be established—had disintegrated. Forbidden to use violence themselves, Quaker legislators had voted for war credits and hired others to fight "the Indians."

10. John Howard Yoder, *When War Is Unjust: Being Honest in Just-War Thinking* (Maryknoll, N.Y.: Orbis Books, 1996), p. 119.

11. Michael Walzer, *Just and Unjust Wars* (New York: Basic Books, 1977), p. 15.

12. See St. Augustine, *The City of God,* book 19, p. 12.

13. Joseph E. Capizzi, "On Behalf of the Neighbor," *Studies in Christian Ethics* 14, no. 2 (2002): 81–108. See also Richard B. Miller, "Aquinas and the Presumption Against Killing and War," *Journal of Religion* 82, no. 2 (April 2002): 173–204. Miller agrees that the presumption against violence frames just war thinking and must always be brought to bear when considering the resort to force. This, he insists, is the only way of parsing accurately Aquinas's complex arguments on war and peace.

CHAPTER 4

1. See the British "Bill of Particulars," entitled "Responsibility for the Terrorist Atrocities in the United States, September 11, 2001," reprinted in the *New York Times,* October 5, 2001, p. B4.

2. Dexter Filkins, "The Legacy of the Taliban Is a Sad and Broken Land," *New York Times,* December 31, 2001, pp. l, B4.

3. Nicholas D. Kristof, "A Merciful War," *New York Times,* February 1, 2002, p. A31.

4. James Dao, "GIs Fight Afghan Devastation with Plaster and Nails," *New York Times,* June 24, 2002, p. A5.

5. Michael Quinlan, "The Just War Litmus Test," *The Tablet,* October 13, 2001, p. 1451.

6. See Jean Bethke Elshtain, *Women and War* (New York: Basic Books, 1987).

7. President George W. Bush, "Address to a Joint Session of Congress, September 20, 2001," in *Our Mission and Our Moment: Speeches Since the Attacks of September 11* (Washington, D.C.: White House Printing Office, 2002), pp. 9–15.

8. "Baghdad Republic of Iraq Television in Arabic 1705 GMT 12 Sep 01," pp. 1–2. The transcript of this broadcast was forwarded to me from a scholar who monitors Arab-language telecasts out of Iraq.

9. Quoted in Andrew Sullivan, "Protocols" ("Washington Diarist" column), *The New Republic*, November 5, 2001, p. 46.

10. Jonathan Rosen, "The Uncomfortable Question of Anti-Semitism," *New York Times Magazine*, November 4, 2001, pp. 48–51.

11. Under the Taliban, various internal Afghani groups were declared infidels because they were labeled non-Muslim by fiat, being the wrong sort of Muslim. Evidently Taliban soldiers searched for people with certain physical features they perceived as "Asiatic" and forced such persons to convert on the spot to the rigid Sunni form of Islam embodied by the Taliban. "Those who did not were killed immediately or taken to the city jail from which many were transported to the countryside and then executed." The dead bodies were left to rot on the streets for a week as further punishment. At least six thousand people, it is estimated, lost their lives in this way. This is the sort of indiscriminate horror that just war precludes absolutely. See Peter Beinart, "Life Support," *The New Republic*, November 19, 2001, p. 6.

12. Caleb Carr, *The Lessons of Terror* (New York: Random House, 2002), pp. 13–14.

13. Eric Schmitt, "Improved U.S. Accuracy Claimed in Afghan Air War," *New York Times*, April 9, 2002, p. A14.

14. Opponents of the war in the academy and in religious communities knowingly exaggerate the number of civilian casualties in order to discredit the war effort. This is routine fare for op-ed pages. For just one example, see Juergen Todenhofer, "It's a Lot Easier to Declare a Victory Than to Earn It," *Chicago Tribune*, June 30, 2002, pp. 1, 7. Todenhofer claims six-thousand Afghani civilian casualties without offering any support for this figure from any source, as if it were an uncontroverted fact of the matter. He is described as a "judge who presided over a terrorism trial" as well as an eighteen-year member of the German Bundestag. We are not told which trial he presided over, or the party he represented. Clearly, he has a very casual—shall we say—approach to data.

15. Quoted from a printout forwarded to me by a colleague. The byline is David Zucchino, "The Untold War," published in the *Los Angeles Times*, June 1–2, 2002.

16. Ibid.

17. Carlotta Gall, "In Kabul, Rumsfeld Aide Regrets Toll in Raid," *New York Times*, July 16, 2002, p. A6.

18. Dexter Filkins, "Flaws in U.S. Air War Left Hundreds of Civilians Dead," *New York Times*, July 21, 2002, pp. 1, 12.

19. Clifford Longley, "When Just War Theory Fails," *The Tablet*, September 29, 2001, p. 1358.

CHAPTER 5

1. "Academic Pseudo-Radicalism," ch. 10 in Christopher Lasch, *The Revolt of the Elites and the Betrayal of Democracy* (New York: W. W. Norton, 1995), pp. 176–93.

2. An example of just how narcissistic this attitude can get is illustrated by Joan Baez's reaction to September 11. She told the *New York Times* (April 9, 2002, p. B8) that

she exploded in tears and cried out to her adult son—toward whom she feels guilty about having ignored when he was young and she was trying to save the world, as she herself more or less put it—"I did everything to try to make the world better. And now, I wish I had stayed here with you." In the interview, Baez condemned the American military and, instead of looking at the injury the United States sustained and our response in light of that, she proclaimed that "we've . . . gone in, guns blazing." Of course, we did not go in "guns blazing." We stepped back, waited, assessed the situation, built up a coalition, and reported to the United Nations before acting. But the actual American response does not seem to interest Baez much. What is telling and typical in her reaction is the immediate reduction of what is going on to *herself:* She tried to make the world better, but the world has betrayed her. On this conflation of the personal and the political, see Jean Bethke Elshtain, *Democracy on Trial* (New York: Basic Books, 1995).

3. The statement appears in its entirety in the appendix. The test and the debate it engendered can be found at: www.americanvalues.org.

4. The full text can be accessed at: www.americanvalues.org/html/us_letter_to_europeans.html. No authors are credited; some of the signatories are well known (like Gore Vidal); nearly all are academics. The "letter" is three pages long. The rhetoric is inflamed throughout.

5. For a fascinating account of how bad information about U.S. action—or purposeful misinformation—circulates and takes on the status of hard data, see Joshua Muravchik, "The Prof Who Can't Count Straight," *Weekly Standard,* August 26–September 2, 2002, pp. 12–15.

6. Yet the "Letter from the United States" signed by over one hundred U.S. academics *denies* that U.S. power is *ever* used in defense of the values we articulate in "What We're Fighting For," including fundamental human rights and human dignity. This means, of course, that we must assume that *everyone* who has spoken on Taliban violations as a reason for U.S. opposition is a cynic and a liar, including successive presidents, secretaries of State, etc. Indeed, nearly everyone, save the authors and signatories of the "Letter from the United States," falls under the pall of being traduced and corrupted by the spectacle of American power. Why can the far left and its allies *never* credit those who disagree with either intelligence or goodwill?

7. Quoted in Caleb Carr, *The Lessons of Terror* (New York: Random House, 2002), p. 63.

8. Hannah Arendt, *The Origins of Totalitarianism* (New York: Harcourt Brace Jovanovich, 1973), p. 474.

9. Hannah Arendt, "Truth and Politics," cited in Jean Bethke Elshtain, "Arendt's Truth and Politics," in Jean Bethke Elshtain, *Real Politics: At the Center of Everyday Life* (Baltimore: Johns Hopkins University Press, 1997), pp. 36–43.

10. Michael Walzer, "Can There Be a Decent Left?" *Dissent* (Spring 2002): 19–23.

11. Peter L. Bergen, *Holy War: Inside the Secret World of Osama Bin Laden* (New York: Free Press, 2001), p. 63.

12. Bergen quotes this charge, which is a commonplace in academic discussions, from the generally anti-American British newspaper *The Guardian.* Similarly, one routinely heard the assertion in April 2002, as if it were a fact of the matter, that hundreds, perhaps even thousands, died in the fighting in the Jenin camp between Israeli soldiers

and the Palestinians defending the camp—this during the Israeli reoccupation of territories in response to the horrific killings of Israeli citizens by Palestinian suicide bombers. See, for example, Justin Huggler, "The Camp That Became a Slaughterhouse," *The Independent,* April 14, 2002, p. 5. As horrible as civilian deaths in Jenin may have been, they came nowhere near a massacre of hundreds or thousands.

13. Bergen, *Holy War,* pp. 64, 66.

14. Barbara Crossette, "Feverish Protests Against the West Trace to Grievances Ancient and Modern," *New York Times,* October 22, 2001, p. B4.

15. I discuss Havel's essay on evasive language in "Politics Without Cliché," *Social Research* 60, no. 3 (Fall 1993): 433–44.

16. Walzer, "Can There be a Decent Left?" p. 21.

17. Anti-American diatribe along these lines is perennially provided by Noam Chomsky. In a 125-page paperback entitled *9–11,* Chomsky pieces together fragments of an argument based on interviews, e-mails, and so on. He sanitizes bin Laden's call to kill Americans, men, women, and children, wherever they may be found, as a call to the overthrow of "corrupt and brutal regimes of gangsters and torturers." I have not put Chomsky's outrageous and wholly irresponsible tirade in the body of this text because analyzing it is like shooting fish in a barrel—it just isn't very interesting.

18. Louis Menand, "Faith, Hope, and Charity," *The New Yorker,* September 16, 2002, pp. 98–104.

19. Mark Taylor, "The Way of the Cross as Theatric of Counter-Terror," paper presented at a conference on justice and mercy, University of Chicago (Spring 2002), p. 2. This essay is part of the widely published Professor Taylor's future book.

20. Ibid., p. 10.

21. Walzer, "Can There Be a Decent Left?" p. 21. See also Michael H. Shuman, "My Fellow Lefties . . . Stop It with the America Bashing," *Weekly Standard,* February 18, 2002, pp. 13–14; and Franklin Foer, "Disoriented," *The New Republic,* December 3, 2001, pp. 15–17. In presenting his account of the post–September 11 shock to the Middle East Studies Association, Foer suggests that something as dramatic and traumatic as September 11 might have invited a rethinking of certain basic presuppositions, but "one would have been wrong."

CHAPTER 6

1. Donald Kagan, "Terrorism and the Intellectuals," *Intercollegiate Review* 37, no. 2 (Spring 2002): 3–8.

2. Edward Said, "Thoughts About America," *Al-Ahram Weekly Online,* February 28–March 6, 2002, issue 565, pp. 1–4.

3. The poll on attitudes toward Muslims pre- and post–9/11 can be found at www.pewforum.org, in the section on surveys. In March 2001, the "favorable" attitude toward Muslim Americans was 45 percent, and "unfavorable" was 24 percent. Remarkably, in November 2001, when the study was repeated, those expressing *favorable* views had risen to 59 percent, and *unfavorables* were down to 17 percent. Those who claim on

the basis of their *own* prejudice—against ordinary Americans—a precipitous rise in anti-Muslim prejudice are just wrong. They rely on a few anecdotes—or none at all. The prejudices of their ideology tell them all they need to know.

4. Said launched a conspiratorial innuendo by describing the Institute for American Values as "financially well-endowed." In fact, this small think tank, with a staff of five, is always financially strapped. He also launched ad hominem attacks against Michael Walzer, portraying him as a tool of the "pro-Israel lobby" and charging him with hypocrisy and inconsistency. He described me as a "conservative feminist," a label pinned on me over twenty years ago by a Marxist feminist who could not be bothered with reading what I had actually written but knew that I deserved condemnation for insisting that motherhood is not the source of all political evil. One can see how ideological labels, once pinned, stay pinned in the minds of ideologues.

5. Said, "Thoughts About America," p. 4.

6. Lawrence Freedman, "Blaming America," *Prospect* (December 2001): 34–37.

7. Ibid., p. 36.

8. Said, "Thoughts About America," p. 4.

9. Franklin Foer, "Disoriented," *The New Republic,* December 3, 2001, p. 16. Evidently, you also do not get to remain a member of the board of a respected academic journal if you are an Israeli. In a report in the *New York Times* (July 11, 2002, p. A12) by Diana Jean Schemo, we learn that two Israeli scholars were fired from the board of two academic journals by one Mona Baker, a professor at the University of Manchester, England. Baker is an Egyptian-born scholar. One of the Israelis she fired was Professor Miriam Shlesinger, "who teaches at Bar Ilan University in Tel Aviv" and "has fought for Palestinian rights but believes in her country's right to exist." This belief, evidently, is unacceptable. Professor Baker stated that she "deplores the Israeli state" and that, because Professor Shlesinger and another professor, Gideon Toury, also described as a "highly regarded scholar," are Israelis, they had to be fired.

10. Clancy Sigal, "John Ashcroft's Palmer Raids," *New York Times,* March 13, 2002, p. A27.

11. A *Chicago Tribune* columnist also warns that our war on terrorism may "kill democracy" and calls the legislation passed in the aftermath of the attacks the "Ashcroft Police State Act." See Salim Muwakkil, "Doing Battle in the Twenty-first Century: The Road Less Traveled May Yield Success for America," *Chicago Tribune,* November 5, 2001, p. 17. In a tone of mock horror, this same commentator poses the fake rhetorical question: "Why are we bombing Afghanistan? None of the terrorists who commandeered the four aircraft that flew into history on September 11 were Afghani." This is balderdash. Surely Muwakkil knows that the Taliban regime hosted Al Qaeda in Afghanistan, and that the terrorists made regular trips back and forth to Afghanistan.

12. Sam Tanenhaus, "Bush's Great Accomplishment: Outside In," *The New Republic,* October 8, 2001, pp. 22–23.

13. Adam Liptak, Neil A. Lewis, and Benjamin Weiser, "After September 11, a Legal Battle on the Limits of Civil Liberty," *New York Times,* August 4, 2002, pp. 1, 16.

14. The rules and regulations applying to aliens are complex and convoluted. Besides *Zadvydas v. Davis,* 459 U.S. 21 (2001), other relevant cases include *Aleida-Sanchez v. United*

States, 413 U.S. 266 (1973), *United States v. Lopez-Mendoza,* 468 U.S. 1032 (1984), and *United States v. Plasencia,* 459 U.S. 21 (1982), which held that due process rights are not extended to aliens seeking admission to the United States.

15. Michael Walzer, "Can There Be a Decent Left?" *Dissent* (Spring 2002): 22.

16. The law can be downloaded from Lexis-Nexis at: web.lexis-nexis.com/cong-comp/docu. Early on, the United States went to war under presidential authority alone, for example: the First Barbary War, 1801–1805; and the Second Barbary War, 1815. Congress did authorize the War of 1812, but the first Senate report on foreign relations, in 1816, spoke of the need to "centralize foreign relations in the presidency." In Lincoln's deft hands, the commander-in-chief clause was merged with Article II, Section 3, of the Constitution to justify enormous presidential powers. Lincoln, a careful student of constitutional law, provided a reasoned defense of his power: "If I be wrong on this question of constitutional power, my error lies in believing that certain proceedings are constitutional when, in cases of rebellion or invasion, the public safety requires them, would not be constitutional when, in the absence of rebellion or invasion, the public safety does not require them; in other words, that the Constitution is not in its application in all respects the same in cases of rebellion or invasion involving the public safety, as it is in times of profound peace and public security." When President Theodore Roosevelt defended the 1904 Santo Domingo incident, in which U.S. forces were involved, it was on the basis that, although the Constitution did not explicitly give him power to act as he did, it nevertheless "did not forbid my doing what I did." From Jean Bethke Elshtain, "The Power to Make War: The President v. Congress and the Supreme Court," an unpublished paper.

17. Edward Steers, Jr., "Precedents for Military Tribunals Date Back to 1846," *Washington Times,* January 7 13, 2002, p. 28. See also "Is the President a 'Dictator'?" *Weekly Standard,* December 3, 2001, pp. 9–11.

18. "Rules Set on Afghan War Prosecutions," *New York Times,* March 21, 2002, pp. 1, A15.

19. *Coalition of Clergy v. President George W. Bush,* U.S. Dist. LEXIS 2748 (February 21, 2002). The court found that the case of *Johnson v. Eigenstager,* 339 U.S. 763 (1950) was controlling. My thanks to Kevin Lee for looking up these and other cases and summarizing their findings and the implications of these findings.

20. Ruth Wedgwood, "The Case for Military Tribunals," *Wall Street Journal,* December 3, 2001, p. A18; Ronald Dworkin, "The Threat to Patriotism," *New York Review of Books,* February 28, 2002, pp. 44–49.

21. Andrew Sullivan, "The Agony of the Left," available at: andrewsullivan.com; Beard quoted in Tony Judt, "America and the War," *New York Review of Books,* November 15, 2001, pp. 4–6.

22. Hannah Arendt, *On Violence* (New York: Harcourt Brace Jovanovich, 1970), p. 8.

23. Quoted in Judt, "America and the War," p. 4.

24. Kagan, "Terrorism and the Intellectuals," p. 3.

25. Ibid., pp. 3–4.

26. Judt, "America and the War," p. 5.

27. Salman Rushdie, "Fighting the Forces of Invisibility," *Washington Post,* October 2, 2001, p. A25.

28. Thomas L. Friedman, "Yes, But What?" *New York Times,* October 5, 2001, p. A23.

29. Patricia Leigh Brown, "Heavy Lifting Required: The Return of Manly Men," *New York Times,* October 28, 2001, p. 5.

30. Naomi Wax, "Not to Worry: Real Men Can Cry," *New York Times,* October 28, 2001, p. 5.

31. "The Problem of the Law-Abiding Terrorist," *Weekly Standard,* June 24, 2002, p. 2.

32. Freedman, "Blaming America," p. 37.

CHAPTER 7

1. H. Richard Niebuhr, *Christ and Culture* (New York: Harper Torchbook, 1951), p. 9.

2. Ibid., pp. 128–29, 130.

3. Martin Luther, quoted in ibid., p. 178.

4. No more. All nuance falls out of the pleas of those who seem to know *precisely* what Jesus would do in certain circumstances—forgetting that Jesus, for Christians, is God Incarnate and it is rather presumptuous to claim a direct pipeline to Him. For example, in a full-page ad in the *New York Times,* a group called "Religious Leaders for Sensible Priorities" argues that it is "inconceivable that Jesus Christ, our Lord and Savior and the Prince of Peace, would support this attack." They describe a possible war with Iraq as "*your* war"—addressing Mr. Bush—as if the nature of the international order and the Iraqi regime is more or less incidental to the issue, and they tell the president flat out that he would violate his faith to go to war. Most of us do not feel authorized to drag Jesus to our own side in a political dispute with such dogmatic certainty. As Abraham Lincoln put it in the great Second Inaugural, "The Almighty has His own purposes."

5. Niebuhr, *Christ and Culture,* p. 234.

6. The most famous passages along these lines are in book 19 of *The City of God* (New York: Penguin Classics, 1972), pp. 860ff. I am indebted to a discussion of this theme in William Schweiker's unpublished manuscript "Criminal Justice and Responsible Mercy."

7. Michael Ignatieff, "Nation-Building Lite," *New York Times Magazine,* July 28, 2002.

8. Ronald H. Stone and Matthew Lon Weaver, eds., introduction to *Against the Third Reich: Paul Tillich's Wartime Radio Broadcasts into Nazi Germany* (Louisville, Ky.: Westminster John Knox Press, 1998), p. 1.

9. Ibid., p. 18. This is eerily similar to bin Laden's paeans to Islamist youth.

10. Gerhard Rempel, *Hitler's Children: The Hitler Youth and the SS* (Chapel Hill: University of North Carolina Press, 1989), pp. 233, 241. See also Jay W. Baird, *To Die for Germany* (Bloomington: Indiana University Press, 1990).

11. Stone and Weaver, *Against the Third Reich,* pp. 21–22, 27.

12. Ibid., pp. 54, 64.

13. Ibid., pp. 96–98.

14. Ibid., p. 218.

15. I am not indicting committed pacifists—who believe they have a responsibility to stand up against evil forthrightly, even unto martyrdom—but rather those who take a position I call "pseudo-pacifist": the apparent belief that, by definition, inaction is better than action if force or compulsion is involved. This belief has very little to do with authentic Christian pacifism, but a great deal to do with certain ideological tendencies and dogma.

16. Reinhold Niebuhr, *Discerning the Signs of the Times: Sermons for Today and Tomorrow* (London: SCM Press, 1946), p. 10.

17. Ibid., p. 91.

18. Ibid., pp. 157, 160.

19. Robin Lovin, *Reinhold Niebuhr and Christian Realism* (Cambridge: Cambridge University Press, 1995), p. 161.

20. Ibid., p. 165.

21. Gilbert Meilaender, "After September 11," *Christian Century* (September 26–October 3, 2001): 7–8.

22. Ibid.

23. D. B. Robertson, ed., *Love and Justice: Selections from the Shorter Writings of Reinhold Niebuhr* (Louisville, Ky.: Westminster John Knox Press, 1957), pp. 28–29, 41.

24. Ibid., p. 41.

25. Lovin, *Niebuhr and Christian Realism,* p. 190.

26. Robertson, *Love and Justice,* p. 218. "Love Your Enemies" was first published in *Christianity and Society* (Autumn 1942).

27. Ibid., pp. 218, 222.

28. "To Prevent the Triumph of an Intolerable Tyranny" was reprinted in Robertson, *Love and Justice* (pp. 272–77); all quotations from the essay are drawn from these pages.

29. James Turner Johnson, *Just War Tradition and the Restraint of War* (Princeton, N.J.: Princeton University Press, 1981), p. 336.

CHAPTER 8

1. By pseudo- or crypto-pacifism I mean that the position does not embrace a pacifism we associate with the historic "peace" churches (Quakers, Anabaptists) but rather, *tends* to denounce any resort to force by the United States—so much so that exculpatory language kicks in where those who have attacked—or are attacking—the United States are concerned. As well, the language of "peace" is not critically scrutinized, so many horrible situations go by the name "peace"—for example, we are not yet in a war with Iraq as of Christmas 2002, so we are at "peace" and that is always better than war. Is it? This must be addressed rather than avoided.

2. Reverend John Dear, S.J., "An Open Letter to George W. Bush," *Promotio Iustitiae* (Rome: C.P. 6139), p. 25.

3. Pax Christi USA Statement on the Devastation of September 11, available at: www.paxchristiusa.org//new_events_more.asp?id=100.

4. Ibid. A similar argument appears in Father Dennis Lyle's "Catholic Response to September 11 from Moral Theology." Father Lyle demands that the suspects (of course, those who perpetrated the deeds of September 11 are all dead) be turned over to an "international court (as with the planners of the Pan Am bombing)" because this is the "easiest and most acceptable" solution "for the world community." Since when are the key criteria for responding to terror ease and acceptability to that vague entity, "the world community"? Where is the theology in this?

5. The Reverend Canon John L. Peterson, sermon at Trinity Anglican Church, Aurora, Ontario, Canada, available at: www.anglicancommunion.org/secretariat/speeches/20011216.html.

6. Dr. Tony Compolo, chapel address at North Park University, October 9, 2001, available at: www.northpark.edu/media/campolotxt.html.

7. David S. Yeager, "Just War: Reflections from the Lutheran Tradition in a Time of Crisis," *Pro Ecclesia* 10, no. 4 (Fall 2001): 401–27.

8. Ibid., p. 4.

9. Paul Marshall, Roberta Green, and Lela Gilbert, *Islam at the Crossroads: Understandings Its Beliefs, History, and Conflicts* (Grand Rapids, Mich.: Baker Books, 2002), pp. 104–5.

10. Alan B. Krueger and Jitka Maleckova, "Does Poverty Cause Terrorism?" *The New Republic,* June 24, 2002, pp. 27–33.

11. Alan F. H. Wisdom, "Religious Left Still Off Balance After September 11," *Faith and Freedom* (Winter-Spring 2002): 4–6. Wisdom provides excerpts from over a dozen sermons or statements that largely wind up "blaming the victim," to use some of the religious left's own favorite language.

12. Alan F. H. Wisdom, "9–11 Responses Expose Cracks in Churches," *Faith and Freedom* (Fall 2001): 4–7.

13. Pope John Paul II, *Evangelium Vitae,* in Michael Miller, C.S.B., ed., *The Encyclicals of Pope John Paul II* (Huntington, Ind.: Our Sunday Visitor, 1996), pp. 772–894, sections 55.1 and 55.2.

14. Pope John Paul II, "No Peace Without Justice: No Justice Without Forgiveness," New Year's Day Peace Message, 2002, *The Tablet* (December 22–29, 2001): 1858–60.

15. Ibid., pp. 1858, 1859.

16. United States Conference of Catholic Bishops, "Living with Faith and Hope After September 11," *Origins* 31, no. 25 (November 29, 2001): 413–20. See also Archbishop John Myers, "Faith and Terrorism: Reflections on the Questions People Ask," *Origins* 31, no. 24 (November 22, 2001): 408–11; and William Joseph Wagner, "As Justice and Prudence Dictate: The Morality of America's War Against Terrorism—A Response to James V. Schall, S.J.," *Catholic University Law Review* 51, no. 1 (Fall 2001): 35–54.

17. Billy Graham, message delivered on the National Day of Prayer and Remembrance, National Cathedral, Washington, D.C., September 14, 2001, available at: www.billygraham.org/newsevents/ndprbmessage.asp.

18. Albert Camus, "The Unbeliever and Christians," in *Resistance, Rebellion, and Death* (New York: Alfred A. Knopf, 1961), pp. 69–74.

19. Albert Camus, *The Rebel* (New York: Alfred A. Knopf/Vintage, 1956), p. 304.

CHAPTER 9

1. Michael Howard, *War and the Liberal Conscience* (New York: Alfred A. Knopf, 1961).

2. Joseph Schumpeter, *Imperialism and Social Classes,* translated by Heinz Norden (New York: Meridian, 1955).

3. Bassam Tibi, "War and Peace in Islam," in Terry Nardin, ed., *The Ethics of War and Peace* (Princeton, N.J.: Princeton University Press, 1996), pp. 128–45. If Tibi is right—and I am inclined to trust the words of an internationally respected scholar of Islam who is himself from the Muslim tradition—the many commentaries on Islamic teachings on war and peace that assimilate jihad to just war are misconstrued. All agree, however, that extending the boundaries of the territory of Islam is by definition a just cause in the Islam tradition. Extending the boundaries of Christianity through war, and as an occasion to go to war, would *not* pass muster as justifiable within the just war tradition.

4. Michael Ignàtieff, *The Warrior's Honor* (New York: Metropolitan Books, 1997), p. 147. See also Tibi, "War and Peace in Islam," p. 133.

5. Tibi, "War and Peace in Islam," p. 133.

6. Bassam Tibi, "War and Peace in Islam," in Sohail H. Hashmi, ed., *Islamic Political Ethics: Civil Society, Pluralism, and Ethics* (Princeton, N.J.: Princeton University Press, 2002), pp. 175–93.

7. John Kelsay, *Islam and War: A Study in Comparative Ethics* (Louisville, Ky.: Westminster John Knox Press, 1993), p. 35.

8. Tibi, "War and Peace in Islam" (Hashmi), p. 129.

9. Ibid., p. 133.

10. Kelsay, *Islam and War,* p. 45.

11. Ibid., p. 47.

12. Bernard Lewis, *What Went Wrong?: Western Impact and Middle Eastern Response* (Oxford: Oxford University Press, 2002), pp. 98–99.

13. Bernard Lewis, "The Roots of Muslim Rage," *Atlantic Monthly* (September 1990), quoted in Kelsay, *Islam and War,* p. 44.

14. Sohail H. Hashmi, "Interpreting the Islamic Ethics of War and Peace," in Nardin, *The Ethics of War and Peace,* p. 156.

15. The American Academy of Religion announced that it has a "content-rich site about the Muslim responses to September 11" at: groups.colgate.edu-aarislam/response.htm.

16. Richard W. Bulliet, "The Crisis Within Islam," *Wilson Quarterly* (Winter 2002): 11–19.

17. Alan Cooperman, "Scholars Plan to Show How Attacks Violated Islamic Law," *Washington Post,* January 20, 2002 (online version).

18. Gilbert Meilaender, "After September 11," *Christian Century* (September 26–October 3, 2001): 7–8.

19. See, for example, the statements from Muslim students at Villanova University, which can be found at: www.villanova.edu/mission/muslim.htm. Muslim Peace Fellowship documents are available at: www.mpfweb.org/9w1101_response.html. The U.S. Department of State International Information Programs offers a bibliography of

American Muslim responses at: usinfo.state.gov/usa./islam/musresp.htm. Shaykh Hamza Yusuf, writing in *Q-news,* a Muslim magazine (www.q-news.com), condemned the rejoicing of Muslims in "some parts of the world," calling this "something explicitly prohibited in Islam"; see 66.34.131.5/ISLAM/misc/shhamza_sep11.htm. The documents of Muslims Against Terrorism can be accessed at: www.matusa.org/aboutus.asp. IslamOnline.net remains more concerned with a "conscious and deliberate effort by the established global order [whatever that is] to discredit a universal belief system which has been presenting itself as a civilizational alternative to western secularism"; see www.muslims.net/English/contemporary/media–1/media2.shtml. This site also offers "Live Fatwa Sessions."

20. Charles Krauthammer, "The Silent Imams," *Washington Post,* November 23, 2001, p. A43.

21. Jack Tapper, "Islam's Flawed Spokesmen," *Salon Magazine,* available at: salon.com (n.d.).

22. Salman Rushdie, "Yes, This Is About Islam," *New York Times,* November 2, 2001, p. A21.

23. Ibid.

24. Lewis, *What Went Wrong?* p. 152.

25. From a review by Thomas M. Disch of Ibn Warraq, *What the Koran Really Says,* in *Weekly Standard,* February 11, 2002, pp. 37–39. Ibn Warraq is a nom de guerre. The author writes under this pseudonym because he fears for his life.

CHAPTER 10

1. Hugh Kennedy, review of Michael Cook, *Commanding Right and Forbidding Wrong in Islamic Thought, Times Literary Supplement,* April 12, 2002, pp. 5–6.

2. See M. E. Yapp, review of Gilles Kepel, *Jihad: The Trail of Political Islam, Times Literary Supplement,* June 28, 2002, 3–4. Some Islamists have gone so far as to declare Europe "dar Al-Islam"—the abode of Islam—in part to justify the fact that they live there rather than in an official Muslim state and society, and in part because they aim to take over European societies, using freedom of association and religion, press, and speech to that end.

3. Andrew Sullivan, "This *Is* a Religious War," *New York Times Magazine,* October 7, 2001, pp. 44–57.

4. Sayyed Nadeem Kazmi, "What Muslim Leaders Can Do for the World," *The Tablet,* November 24, 2001, 1660–61. Along with this self-critique, the essay includes the almost requisite attack on U.S. Middle Eastern policy and "Israeli terrorism against Palestinians."

5. Laurie Goodstein, "Muslim Leader Who Was Once Labeled an Alarmist Is Suddenly a Sage," *New York Times,* October 28, 2001, p. B5.

6. Neil MacFarquhar, "A Few Saudis Defy a Rigid Islam to Debate Their Own Intolerance," *New York Times,* July 12, 2002, pp. 1, A10.

7. Douglas Frantz and Desmond Butler, "Imam at German Mosque Preached Hate to 9/11 Pilots," *New York Times,* July 16, 2002, p. A3. See also the review by Rory McCarthy of two new books on Islam, "Forces of Militant Islam Arrayed Against the West," *The Tablet,* August 31, 2002, pp. 14–15; and Stephen Schwartz, "All the Hate That's Fit to Print," *The Weekly Standard,* July 22, 2002, pp. 16–17.

8. Thomas Friedman, "Fighting bin Ladenism," *New York Times,* November 6, 2001, p. A23. See also Thomas L. Friedman, "The Hidden Victims," *New York Times,* May 3, 2002, p. A23, on the silencing of Arab liberals; David Pinault, "Humanistic Islam: An Opportunity Not to Be Squandered," *Commonweal,* January 8, 2002, pp. 8–9; and Elaine Sciolino, "Radicalism: Is the Devil in the Demographics?" *New York Times,* December 9, 2001, pp. 1, 5.

9. In "Making Nice with Muslims" (*Commonweal,* December 7, 2001, pp. 6–7), John Garvey discusses his attempt to embark on a Christian-Muslim dialogue. His Muslim counterparts gave him a book entitled *Quranic Psychiatry,* which claims that "no practicing Muslim has ever suffered from mental illness." Garvey finds this "merely silly." But other passages are more sinister, including the association of science—and the claim that most scientists are Jews—with antireligious materialism. The book also claims that Freud had perverted Jewish habits, that Christians profess blind faith in "irrational dogmas," and that priests have murdered "millions of innocent patients suffering from hysteria, seizures, and other mental maladies" over the last fifteen centuries.

10. Thomas Friedman, "Arabs at the Crossroads," *New York Times,* July 3, 2002, p. A19.

11. Joseph Capizzi, "On Behalf of the Neighbor," *Studies in Christian Ethics* 14, no. 2 (2002): 107.

12. Pope John Paul II, "No Peace Without Justice, No Justice Without Forgiveness," message for New Year's Day 2002, reprinted in *The Tablet,* December 22–29, 2001, pp. 1858–60.

13. Susan Sachs, "Anti-Semitism Is Deepening," *New York Times,* April 27, 2002, pp. A19, B21.

14. Suzanne Daley, "Surge in Anti-Semitic Crime Worries French Jews," *New York Times,* February 26, 2002, p. A3. See also Christopher Caldwell, "Liberte, Egalite, Judeophobie," *Weekly Standard,* May 6, 2002, pp. 20–26.

15. See Neil MacFarquhar, "Anti-Western and Extremist Views Pervade Saudi Schools," *New York Times,* October 19, 2001, pp. B1, B3.

16. See chapter 1. See also Mark Steyn, "Hate-Me Crimes," *Wall Street Journal,* December 14, 2001, p. A14.

17. "September 11—Transatlantic Response," *Politalk,* moderated by Tim Erickson, available at: www.politalk.com/topics/terrorism/day07.html (downloaded April 4, 2002).

18. Ibid.

19. Anti-American protesters in Paris and Rome compare the leader of a constitutional democracy who has, since September 11, 2001, preached welcoming tolerance toward faithful Muslims to Adolph Hitler. A protester carries a banner, "U.S.A. and Israel,

the True Terrorists." Given the often violent and irrational nature of anti-American protest, many observers worry that much, much worse is to come. See Christopher Caldwell, "How Do I Hate Thee?" *The Weekly Standard,* November 25, 2002, pp. 25–29.

20. The German statement and our response, together with the original document "What We're Fighting For," can be found at iav@worldnet.att.net.

21. Michael Walzer, in "Can There Be a Decent Left?" *Dissent* (Spring 2002), finds the European response puzzling as well as troubling.

22. Barbara Crossette, "Sri Lankan Says U.S. Drive on Terror Helps Peace Effort," *New York Times,* July 22, 2002, p. A6.

23. Alexander Stille, "Nous sommes tous Americans?" in "The World Responds to September 11," *Correspondence: An International Review of Culture and Society* (published by the Council on Foreign Relations), no. 9 (Spring 2002): 7. Baudrillard finds the actions of the terrorists breathtaking; he cannot get over their audacity, especially the way they fell into the "banality" of daily American life and hid among us. He extols their "faultless mastery." His essay, "L'Esprit du Terrorisme," is reprinted in Stanley Hauerwas and Frank Lentriechia, eds., *Dissent from the Homeland* (Durham, N.C.: Duke University Press, 2002), pp. 405–17.

CHAPTER 11

1. Judith Miller, "Qaeda Videos Seem to Show Chemical Texts," *New York Times,* August 19, 2002, pp. A1, A8. An Al Qaeda–affiliated group just narrowly missed bringing down a commercial Israeli jetliner with a surface-to-air missile in attacks in Kenya in November 2002.

2. Ibid., p. A8.

3. Paul R. McHugh, "A Psychiatrist Looks at Terrorism," *Weekly Standard,* December 10, 2001, pp. 21–24.

4. Ibid., p. 23.

5. Rudolph Giuliani, "Words to a Hurt World: Action, Not Deliberation," speech before the United Nations, October 1, 2001, reprinted in the *New York Times,* October 2, 2001, p. B5.

6. Steven Komarow, "Karzai: Foreign Troops Needed Indefinitely," *USA Today,* June 28, 2002, p. 17A. See also Walter Shapiro, "Bush Mentions Marshall, but Media Miss the Plan," *USA Today,* April 19, 2002, p. 2A.

7. Samantha Power, *A Problem from Hell: America and the Age of Genocide* (New York: Basic Books, 2002), pp. 338–39, 346–47.

8. Ibid., p. 359.

9. Samantha Power, "Genocide and America," *New York Review of Books,* March 14, 2002, pp. 15–18.

10. Jane Perlez, review of David Halberstam, *War in a Time of Peace, New York Times Book Review,* September 30, 2001, p. 8.

11. Mark Danner, "Clinton, the UN, and the Bosnian Disaster," *New York Review of Books,* December 18, 1997, pp. 65–81.

12. Paul W. Kahn, "War and Sacrifice in Kosovo," *Philosophy and Public Policy* 19, nos. 2–3 (Spring-Summer 1999): 1–6.

13. Timothy Garton Ash, *The Polish Revolution: Solidarity* (New York: Scribner's, 1983), p. 338.

14. Bryan Hehir, "Wanted: A New Global Order," *The Tablet,* December 1, 2001, pp. 1700–1702.

CHAPTER 12

1. Anne-Marie Slaughter, "The Real New World Order," *Foreign Affairs* 76 (September-October 1997): 183–97.

2. Samantha Power, *A Problem from Hell: America and the Age of Genocide* (New York: Basic Books, 2002), pp. 511–12.

3. George Will, "'Up From' Accountability," *Washington Post,* July 11, 2001, p. A21. Tony Judt, in an essay in the *New York Review of Books* ("Its Own Worst Enemy," August 15, 2002, pp. 12–17), almost entirely misses the boat when he argues that Washington's opposition to the ICC "suggests that the U.S. does not trust the rest of the world to treat Americans fairly. But if America displays a lack of trust in others, the time may come when they will return the compliment." This is beside the point. The central point is that there are no settled standards of what counts as fair or unfair treatment, and for what violations, in the realm of international criminal law.

4. Slaughter, "The Real New World Order," p. 184.

5. Simon Jenkins, "New World Order Beset by Old World's Flaws," *The [London] Times,* July 4, 2001, p. 12.

6. Joshua Mitchell, "Confessions of a Former Arabist," in John Carlson and Erik Owens, eds., *The Sovereign and the Sacred,* with a foreword by Jean Bethke Elshtain (Washington, D.C.: Georgetown University Press, in press).

7. Mustapha Damal Pasha and David L. Blaney, "Elusive Paradise: The Promise and Peril of Global Civil Society," *Alternatives* 23 (1998): 418.

8. Brian Urquhart, "Shameful Neglect," *New York Review of Books,* April 25, 2002, pp. 12–14. For a rather acerbic look at American power, see James Dao, "One Nation Plays the Great Game Alone," *New York Times,* July 7, 2002, pp. 1, 5.

9. Michael Ignatieff, "Barbarians at the Gate?" *New York Review of Books,* February 28, 2002, pp. 4–6.

10. Samantha Power, "Genocide and America," *New York Review of Books,* March 14, 2002, pp. 15–18. See also *A Problem from Hell,* p. 513.

11. Ignatieff, "Barbarians at the Gate?" p. 4.

12. Ibid.

13. Sebastian Mallaby, "The Reluctant Imperialist," *Foreign Affairs* (March-April 2002): 2–7.

14. Ibid., p. 4.

15. Adrian Karatnycky and Arch Puddington, "The Human-Rights Lobby Meets Terrorism," *Commentary* (January 2002): 28–31.

EPILOGUE

1. National Endowment for Democracy (NED), typescript of comments on the occasion of the presentation of the Democracy Awards, July 9, 2002. I was present at this event. First Lady Laura Bush distributed the trophies. National Endowment for Democracy President Carl Gershman spoke. In the interest of full disclosure, I should add that I am a member of the board of directors of the NED.

2. See Michael Ignatieff, "Nation-Building Lite," *New York Times Magazine,* July 28, 2002, pp. 26–31, 54–59.

3. Ibid., p. 59.

4. Douglas Frantz, "Minutes from Cries of Jihad, Town Dreams of U.S.," *New York Times,* October 24, 2001, p. A4.

INDEX